Memoirs Of The Private Life, Return, And Reign Of Napoleon In 1815 Vol.2

by
baron Pierre Alexandre Édouard
Fleury de Chaboulon

Memoirs Of The Private Life, Return, And Reign Of Napoleon In 1815
Vol.2
by baron Pierre Alexandre Édouard Fleury de Chaboulon

Copyright © 2023

All Rights reserved.

No part of this publication may be reproduced, stored in a retrieval system, or transmitted in any form or by any means, electronic, mechanical, photocopying or Otherwise, without the written permission of the publisher.
The author/editor asserts the moral right to be identified as the author/editor of this work.

ISBN: 978-93-59957-18-0

Published by

DOUBLE 9 BOOKS

2/13-B, Ansari Road
Daryaganj, New Delhi – 110002
info@double9books.com
www.double9books.com
Tel. 011-40042856

This book is under public domain

ABOUT THE AUTHOR

Baron Pierre Alexandre Édouard Fleury de Chaboulon (April 14, 1779 - September 28, 1835) become a French baby-kisser who served as the private secretary to Napoleon Bonaparte. At the young age of 16, he offered himself as a battalion leader in the National Guard and participated inside the uprising towards the National Convention in Paris on October 5, 1795. After being taken into captivity, given his adolescents, he turned into pardoned. Minister Fermont then took him underneath his wing, presenting him with in-intensity information of monetary management. This allowed him to be employed as an auditor inside the Council of State, specializing in financial topics. Later, he has become the sub-prefect of Château-Salins (Meurthe), wherein he distinguished himself now not simplest for his talent but also for his kindness. Napoleon entrusted him with diverse missions. He became eventually appointed sub-prefect of Reims in 1814, and throughout the invasion, he valiantly and determinedly fought in opposition to the Allies throughout the campaign of France.

CONTENTS

MEMOIRS, &c. &c. 7

MEMOIRS, &c. &c.

At the same period (May the 1st) the Emperor received a fresh proof of the little confidence, that men deserve, and of the horrible facility, with which they sacrifice their duties and their sentiments, to the suggestions of their covetousness or their ambition.

Of all the ministers of Napoleon there was not one, who, at the time of his return, lavished on him so many protestations of fidelity and devotion to his service, as the Duke of Otranto. "And this fidelity, if he could have doubted it, would have been guarantied by the mandate, under which he (M. Fouché) groaned, at the moment when the return of Napoleon restored him to liberty, and perhaps to life[1]."

Yet what was the astonishment of the Emperor, when the Duke of Vicenza came to inform him, that a secret agent of M. de Metternich had arrived at Paris from Vienna, and appeared to have had a mysterious interview with M. Fouché! The Emperor immediately ordered M. Réal, prefect of the police, to make search after this emissary. He was arrested, and declared:

That, being employed by a banking-house at Vienna, to settle accounts of interest with several bankers at Paris, he had been sent for by M. de Metternich; and that this prince had entrusted him with a letter for the French minister of police:

That he was ignorant of the contents of this letter; but knew it was interlined with sympathetic ink: and the prince had delivered to him a powder for making the hidden characters appear:

That Baron de Werner, diplomatic agent, was to be at Bâle on the 1st of May, to receive the answer of the Duke of Otranto:

That a fictitious statement of an account had been given him, which was to serve as a sign, to make known to M. Werner the agent sent by the French minister:

In fine, that he had delivered the letter and the account to the Duke of Otranto, who had told him, to attend quickly to his business, and return to Vienna as soon as possible.

The Emperor immediately sent for M. Fouché, under pretence of conversing with him on affairs of state.

M. Fouché preserved the most profound silence on what had passed with the envoy of M. de Metternich, and displayed no marks of embarrassment or uneasiness.

The first thought of Napoleon was, to seize the papers of his treacherous minister: but persuaded, that he was too adroit, and too prudent, to retain any traces of his treason, he deemed it preferable, in order to come at the truth, to send some one to Bâle, who should introduce himself to M. Werner as from the Duke. Napoleon attached great importance to this mission. He condescended to cast his eyes on me to execute it; and, after having disclosed to me *"the perfidy of that infamous Fouché,"* he said to me: "You will go immediately to the Duke of Vicenza: he will give you passports both in the King's name and in mine: you will learn at the frontier, which will avail you most. Here is an order under my own hand, to all the generals, prefects, and lieutenants of police, who may be on the Rhine, to furnish you with the means of leaving and returning to France, and with all the assistance you may require, within the kingdom and even without. I command them, strictly to conform to every thing you may judge proper to direct. I think you will pass. I have never heard of this M. Werner, but M. de Metternich is a man of honour: he would not be concerned in a plot against my life. I do not believe the business is to renew the attempts of Georges, or the snares of the 3d of Nivose. However, you will sound M. Werner on this head. I believe, they are desirous of fomenting disturbances, and forming a conspiracy, rather against my throne, than against my life. This point it is essential to ascertain. I give you no farther instructions: you will act as your own master: I rely entirely on you. If the safety of the state be threatened, or if you discover any thing of importance, apprise me of it by the telegraph, and send off a courier with all speed. If you find there is nothing in it but the commencement of an intrigue, nothing but a trial; waste no time in useless parleying, but frankly avail yourself of the opportunity, to make M. de Metternich acquainted with my situation, and my pacific intentions; and endeavour to establish a reconciliation between me and Austria. I should also like to know, what the allies think of Eugene; and whether they would be disposed to call him to the head of affairs in a regency, if I should lose my life on the field of battle. Go and see the Duke of Vicenza, talk with him, and return in half an hour. I will see if I have any thing more to say to you." Half an hour after, I returned. The Emperor was in his saloon, surrounded by Marshal Ney and several persons of consequence. Making a motion with his hand, he said to me: "I rely upon you: fly."

It was by such expressions, that he knew how to flatter self-love, and animate zeal. I flew to Bâle. Had it been necessary for me, in order to justify the expectations of Napoleon, to cross the Rhine under the mouths of the enemy's cannon, I should have done it.

I began to employ the unlimited powers given me by the Emperor, by directing provisionally, that no person coming from Paris should be allowed to quit France. I was not willing to be preceded by the real agent of the Duke of Otranto.

The communication with Bâle was not yet interrupted: but it was necessary, to have a permit to enter the city, another to go out of it, and, on the slightest suspicion, you were carried before the director of the police, who, without taking his pipe out of his mouth, gave orders, according to his own good pleasure, either to turn you out at the gate, or to throw you into prison, I had provided myself with a commission of inspector general of provision, and presented myself at Bâle under the pretence of making large purchases there. Money will always secure a good reception in Switzerland.

I repaired without meeting any obstacle to the Three Kings inn, where M. Werner had alighted. He was already arrived. I announced to him, that I had been commissioned by a person at Paris, to confer with him. He showed me the account he had as a token; and I showed him *at a distance* that I had, for I knew it was good for nothing. It had been written out from memory by our prisoner, the token having remained in the hands of M. Fouché.

M. Werner began by expressing to me with all the pomp of diplomatic politeness the pleasure, which he felt at seeing me; that he had expected me ever since the 1st of May (this was the 3d); and that he began to fear, that M. Fouché was indifferent about entering into a conference with the prince. This conjecture led me to suppose, that nothing had yet been agreed upon or proposed. I answered M. Werner, that in fact the Duke of Otranto had shown a little hesitation, because the letter of M. de Metternich left *some uncertainty*; but that, still filled with esteem and deference for this prince, he would be eager to offer him every proof of his zeal, that should be in his power; that he had chosen me for his interpreter, and that I should take a pleasure in answering with unbounded confidence the *new* overtures, which M. Werner was no doubt commissioned to make to me. I added, that the Duke of Otranto had recommended to me, to lay aside diplomatic forms, and to explain myself with that complete *absence of restraint*, which M. de Metternich must inspire. That in consequence, I intreated him, to follow my example, and to tell me without circumlocution, *what he expected of us*.

He answered me, that M. de Metternich had retained the highest opinion of M. Fouché's merit: that he imagined, a man like him could not suppose, that Napoleon would maintain himself on the throne: that he was persuaded, he had accepted the ministry of police, only to spare France the calamities of a civil and a foreign war: and that, under this persuasion, he hoped M. Fouché would not hesitate, to second the efforts the allies were about to make, to get rid of Bonaparte, and re-establish the Bourbons in France.

I replied, that M. Fouché, whose patriotism was well known, had not been able to contemplate without pain the misfortunes, with which France was threatened; but that hitherto he had not perceived the possibility of remedying them. "Frequently," I said, "people at a distance see more clearly, than those who are nigh: what are the views of M. de Metternich and the allies on this point? *what means do they conceive may be employed, to get rid of Napoleon?*"

"M. de Metternich," said he, "has not fully communicated to me his views in this respect. I have even reason to believe, that nothing has yet been determined; and that it is in order to arrive at some certain result, that he is desirous of concerting matters with M. Fouché, who must be better acquainted with the true state of affairs than he is. As to the means of getting rid of Bonaparte, there is one, the issue of which cannot be doubtful: this is force: but the allies are unwilling to have recourse to it, unless in the last extremity; and they would have wished, *that M. Fouché could have found means of delivering France from Bonaparte*, without shedding fresh torrents of blood."

This ambiguous answer giving me some uneasiness, I replied: "I know but two ways of overturning the throne of Napoleon: the first is, to assassinate him!" As I pronounced these words, I turned my eyes a little aside, that I might not embarrass M. Werner, and might observe him at my ease. "Assassinate him!" exclaimed he with indignation: "such a step never entered into the thoughts of M. de Metternich." — "So I presume; and accordingly I began with expressing to you the high veneration, which I feel for M. de Metternich. The second way," I continued, "is of secretly uniting, or, to speak plainly, of conspiring against Napoleon; and I do not see very clearly at present, *on whom we can reckon*: have M. de Metternich and the allies *any connexions yet formed?*"

"They have none," he answered: "scarcely have they had time to come to any mutual understanding at Vienna. It is for M. Fouché to prepare and arrange his plans: it is to him, that the allies are desirous of confiding the care and honour of saving France from the calamities of a new war, and from the tyranny prepared for her by the Emperor."

Convinced by the turn the conversation had taken, that there had been no previous connexion between the Duke of Otranto and M. de Metternich; convinced, that the life of the Emperor, and the safety of the state, were not threatened; I changed my style, and proceeded straight to the end, which I had principally in view; that of endeavouring to establish, if not a reconciliation, at least conferences between France and Austria.

"Do the allies then imagine," resumed I, "that it would be easy for M. Fouché to stir France against Napoleon? There was a time, it is true, when the Emperor was not liked; but the Bourbons have treated the nation so ill, that they succeeded in rendering him regretted, so that his enemies are become his partisans."

"What you tell me," answered M. Werner with astonishment, "is completely the reverse of the reports, that reach us from Paris."

"I can assure you," continued I, "that they have deceived you. The acclamations and good wishes, that accompanied Napoleon from the gulf of Juan to Paris, ought however to have informed you, that he had in his favour the unanimous suffrages of the army, and of the nation."—"Say of the army."—"No: I persist in saying of the nation, and of the army. From the moment when Napoleon re-appeared on French ground, he was received with enthusiasm, not only by his soldiers, but by the citizens also. If he had the suffrages of only a few regiments in a state of insubordination, would he have traversed France without any obstacle? Would he have received on his journey that unanimous testimony of love and devotion, which the whole population of Dauphiny, the Lyonese, and Burgundy, emulated each other in displaying?"—"It is possible, that Bonaparte may have been well received in some places; but a few solitary acclamations do not express the wishes of a whole nation; and, had it not been for the army, he would never have re-entered the Tuileries."—"It is certain, that, if Napoleon had had the army against him, he could never have dethroned Louis XVIII. with eight hundred men: but we must not conclude, that, because the army declared for him, it was the army alone, that re-established him on the throne. When he took Lyons, he had with him only two thousand men; he had but eight thousand, when he marched for Paris; and he had only eight hundred with him, when he entered the capital. Had not the nation entertained the same sentiments as the army, could he, with such a contemptible force, have given the law to two millions of individuals scattered on his road; and to the fifty thousand soldiers, national guards and volunteers, who were assembled under the walls of Paris? If indeed the nation had opposed the proceedings and wishes of the army, and the army had overcome the nation, it might have been asserted with reason, that the restoration of Napoleon was the work of the soldiers exclusively: but you know, as well as I, that not a single act of violence was committed, not a single musket was fired, and that they were every where welcomed and feasted as friends and deliverers. I ask you, now, what ought we to conclude from this union, this unanimity of sentiments and actions?" —

"We may infer, that the people, naturally weak and timid, were afraid of the army; and gave it a good reception, that they might not be exposed to its violence: but this does not prove, that in the bottom of their hearts they shared the sentiments of the army for Napoleon."

"God alone knows what passes in the bottom of the heart: we mortals can judge only by appearances, by men's words and actions. Now actions, words, and appearances combine to prove evidently, that the nation approved and shared the enthusiasm of the army. Besides, you are wrong in thinking, that in France the people can entertain sentiments different from those of the army. Under the ancient monarchy, when the army was composed of the dissolute reduced to want, of malefactors pursued by the hand of justice, there did not, and could not, exist any affinity between the army and the nation: but now that the army is a national body, composed of the sons and brothers of our best citizens; and that these sons, these brothers, though separated from their families, remain united with them in heart, mind, and interests; the nation and the army are one. If the allies have founded their hopes solely on a disagreement of opinions and wishes between the nation and the army, they have calculated erroneously: the approach of their troops, far from dividing the French, will only draw their union closer. They will not fight for Napoleon, they will fight for the honour and independence of the nation." — "From what you tell me it would seem, that France is determined to run the hazard of war; and that it is ready, if Napoleon require it, to second as heretofore his schemes of conquest." — "No, sir: the glory of Napoleon has cost us too dear; we desire no more laurels at such a price. Napoleon has the wishes of the nation on his side, less from affection to his person, than because he is a man of the revolution, and his government will secure us pledges, which we have demanded in vain from the Bourbons; but if the Emperor were to suffer himself to be led away by the thirst of conquest, France would abandon him; and then you might reckon on M. Fouché and all true patriots uniting, to get rid of Napoleon for ever." —

"You do not think, then, it appears to me, that M. Fouché is disposed at the present moment, to second the views of the allied sovereigns and M. Metternich?" — "I do not; M. Fouché is convinced, that the Bourbons cannot reign: that the nation has an antipathy to them, which nothing can remove." — "The allies are not so much bent on restoring the crown to Louis XVIII., as on taking it from Napoleon, whose remaining on the throne is incompatible with the safety and repose of Europe: I am even authorized to think, that they would leave the French free to choose whatever sovereign, and whatever government, they might think proper. The Duke of Orleans, for instance, would not he suit the nation? He served formerly in the republican armies; he has been a partisan of the revolution; his father voted for the death of Louis XVI."—"The Duke of Orleans, no doubt, would offer the nation most of the pledges it requires: but his elevation to the throne, far from annihilating our troubles, would increase them; he would have against him the partisans of Louis XVIII., of Napoleon, and of the regency; that is to say, almost the whole nation."—"Well, then, the allies might consent to give you the young prince Napoleon and the regency, or perhaps a federal government."—"At the time of the invasion in 1814, we had several times occasion to debate the question of the regency with M. Fouché. He thought, that, with a regency, France would experience the renovation of those discords, to which minorities commonly give birth. A people, that has been at war with itself, and with its neighbours, has need of being swayed by a man, who knows how to hold the reins of government with a firm hand, and to make himself respected at home and abroad."—"But you have no want of firm and able men; and a council of regency might be composed for you, that would answer the wishes both of the allies and of France."—"I know well, that we have in the archchancellor, in the Duke of Vicenza, and in several of our principal functionaries, statesmen abounding in talents, wisdom, and moderation: but the difficulty would be, to make a choice among the military men. Most of these have equal rights, and their pretensions, their jealousies, their rivalries, could not but be fatal to our tranquillity."—"We should know how to keep them in order; and I do not see one among them whose ambition could prove formidable."—"Their ambition has not displayed itself for want of opportunity. I know but one military man, who could be placed at the head of the government with safety; this is Eugene, the prince who said, in 1814, in his memorable proclamations, that 'they alone are immortal, who know how to live and die faithful to their duty, faithful to gratitude and honour:' this prince, I say, far from aspiring to the throne, would be on the contrary its glory and support: but his family ties, and the duties they impose on him, perhaps would not permit him to quit Bavaria. Perhaps too the allies would not allow the direction of affairs in France, to be entrusted to him: do you think they would?"—"I am perfectly ignorant of what might be the determination of the prince and his family."—"But cannot you guess, what would be that of the allies?"—"Not in the least."—"What men," said I to him jocularly, "you diplomatists are! why are not you as open with me, as I am with you? have I left one of your desires unsatisfied? have I avoided answering one of your questions?"—"I am not endeavouring to dissemble, I assure you: but, as the question you have put to me was not foreseen, I cannot, and ought not, to allow myself to answer it."—"Well, we will say no more of it. As to a federal government, this would too much resemble our republic, and we have paid so dear for the honour of being republicans, that we have no farther inclination for it. A federal government may suit a country with a scanty population, like Switzerland; or a new nation, like America; but it would be a calamity to our old France: we are too volatile, too impassioned; we want a ruler, a master who knows how to make himself obeyed. Hark you, M. Werner, I must continue to speak to you frankly: the only chief, that suits us, is Napoleon: no longer Napoleon the ambitious and the conqueror, but Napoleon corrected by adversity. The desire of reigning will render him docile to the will of France, and of Europe. He will give them both such pledges, as they may require: and I believe the Duke of Otranto will then esteem himself very happy, to be able to concur with M. de Metternich in pacifying Europe, re-establishing harmony between Austria and France, and so restricting the power of the Emperor, that it shall no longer be possible for him, to disturb a second time the general tranquillity. This, I believe, must be the object of the allies; it depends on themselves alone to attain it: but if they reckon upon subjugating us by means of our intestine divisions, they will be deceived; of this you may assure M. de Metternich.

"For the rest, I shall give the Duke of Otranto an account of the overtures you have made me, and particularly of those relating to a regency: but, suppose we should consent to accept either one or the other of your proposals, what is to be done with Napoleon? for, as it is neither your intention, nor ours, to kill him, he must live; and where shall he live? Have the allies come to any determination on this point?"—"I do not know: M. de Metternich did not explain himself on this point: I will submit the question to him. I will acquaint him with your opinion of the state of France, and the situation of Napoleon, and of the possibility of a general arrangement: but I foresee, that the present sentiments of M. Fouché will astonish him greatly. He thought, that he detested Bonaparte."—"Men change with circumstances: M. Fouché may have detested the Emperor, when he tyrannized over France; yet be reconciled to him, since he has been willing to render it free and happy."

We parted, after having exchanged a few supplementary questions, and agreed to return with all speed, he to Vienna, and I to Paris; and to meet again at Bâle in the course of a week.

As soon as I arrived at Paris, I presented myself before the Emperor. I had spent only four days in going and returning; and he imagined, on seeing me so quickly, that I had not been able to pass. He was surprised and delighted to learn, that I had seen and conversed with M. Werner; led me into the garden (it was at the Élysée), and there we talked together, if I may use the term, for near two hours. Our conversation was so desultory, that it almost entirely escaped my memory: I could retain only a few fragments of it. "I was fully persuaded," said Napoleon to me, "that M. de Metternich had plotted nothing against my life: he does not like me, but he is a man of honour. If Austria chose it, every thing might be arranged: but she has an expectant policy, that loses every thing: she never knew how to take a decided part at the proper moment. The Emperor is ill advised: he does not know Alexander; and is not aware, how crafty and ambitious the Russians are: if once they get the upper hand, all Germany will be subverted. Alexander will set the good-natured Francis, and all the little kings, to whom I gave crowns, playing at catch-corners. The Russians will become masters of the world when I have nothing to do in it. Europe will not be sensible of my value, till she has lost me. There was no one but myself strong enough, to tame England with one hand, and restrain Russia with the other. I will spare them the trouble of deliberating where they shall put me: if they dared, they would cram me into an iron cage, and show me to their cockneys as a wild beast: but they shall not have me; they shall find, that the lion is still alive, and will not suffer himself to be chained. They do not know my strength: *if I were to put on the red cap, it would be all over with them.* Did you inquire of M. Werner after the Empress and my son?"—"Yes, Sire: he told me, that the Empress was well, and the young prince a charming boy."—The Emperor, with fire: "Did you complain, that the law of nations, and the first rights of nature, had been violated in respect to me? Did you tell him how detestable it is, to deprive a husband of his wife, a father of his son? that such an action is unworthy a civilized people?"—"Sire, I was only the ambassador of M. Fouché."

After a few moments' silence, the Emperor continued: "Fouché, during your absence, has come and told me the whole affair[2]: he has explained the whole to my satisfaction. It is his interest not to deceive me. He has always been fond of intriguing; we must let him do it. Go and see him, tell him all that has passed with M. Werner; show confidence in him; and, if he question you about me, tell him, that I am perfectly easy, and that I have no doubt of his attachment and fidelity."

Already the Emperor had had reason to complain of M. Fouché on several important occasions; but, subjugated by I know not what charm, he had always placed more confidence in him than he wished.

Few men, it is true, possess the gift of pleasing and persuading in a higher degree than the Duke of Otranto: equally profound and witty, equally endowed with foresight and ability, his mind embraces at once the past, present, and future: he alternately seduces and astonishes by the boldness of his thoughts, the acuteness of his perception, and the solidity of his judgment.

Unhappily his mind, overstrained by the revolution, has contracted a habit and taste for strong emotions: quiet is tiresome to him: he wants agitation, danger, convulsions: hence that desire of stirring, intriguing, I had almost said of conspiring, which has driven M. Fouché into errors so deplorable, and so fatal to his reputation.

Conformably to the orders of Napoleon, I repaired immediately to the Duke of Otranto's, and told him laughing, that I was come to give him an account of the mission which he had confided to me. "A fine mission, indeed!" said he to me. "It is just like the Emperor; he is always suspicious of those who serve him best. Do you think, for example, that you are sure of him? You deceive yourself. If you should involuntarily be guilty of the slightest inconsistency, and he knew it (these words he pronounced in such a way, as to give me to understand, that it was through him the Emperor might be informed of it), nothing more would be wanting to ruin you. But let us have done with princes, and talk together." Leading me to his sofa, he said: "Do you know, that you gave me some uneasiness? if you had been betrayed, you would probably have been sent to some fortress, and kept there till a peace took place." —"Very true; I certainly ran that risk; but when an affair of such importance is at stake, a man should not think of himself."

I gave him a faithful account of what M. Werner said; but took care, not to let him know the time of our next interview; for I was afraid, that he would play me some trick with the Swiss, or would hasten to undeceive M. de Metternich.

When I had finished my tale, he resumed: "I first thought the whole of this a hum, but I find I was mistaken. Your conference with M. Werner may lead to a reconciliation between us and Austria; what you said must open the eyes of M. Metternich. To convince him completely, I will write to him; and depict with so much clearness and truth the real situation of France, as will make him sensible, that the best thing that can be done is, to abandon the Bourbons to their unlucky fate, and leave us to arrange matters with Bonaparte in our own way. When you are ready to set off, come to me, and I will give you my letter."

He then said, "I did not speak to Napoleon about the letter of M. de Metternich immediately, because his agent had not delivered to me the powder, necessary to make the writing appear; I was obliged to have recourse to chemical experiments, which required time. Here is the letter (he made me read it): you see it says nothing: however, if I could have deciphered it immediately, Napoleon should have known nothing of it; I would have served him, without saying any thing to him. In affairs of this kind secrecy is necessary; and Napoleon is incapable of it: he would have been so much agitated, and have set so many men and so many pens in motion, that the whole would have taken wind. He ought to know my sentiments and opinions; and no person, but himself, could have taken it into his head for a moment, that I could betray him for the Bourbons: I despise and detest them at least as much as he."

The indirect threats of M. Fouché, and the whole of his discourse, persuaded me, that he was not sincere. I imparted my suspicions to the Emperor, who did not agree in them: he told me, that M. Fouché's insinuation of his having it in his power to ruin me was only meant, to give himself an air of importance. That, however, I had nothing to fear from him, or from any other person. In fact, I did not fear; for, when the Emperor had conceived a liking for any one, he took him under his own protection, and no person whatever was allowed to hurt him.

The next day but one I went to the Duke of Otranto's, to receive the letters he had promised me. He appeared surprised, to see me so soon. In fact I had made him believe, that I was not to return to Bâle till the 1st of June. To give a colour to this hasty departure, I informed him, that M. Werner, whom I had requested to write to me, in case of any unforeseen occurrence, under cover to M. **** the banker, had just desired me, to repair to Bâle immediately. He let me see, that he was not the dupe of this falsehood yet nevertheless delivered me with a good grace two letters for M. de Metternich.

One of these, which has been published in the English newspapers, tended to show, that the throne of Napoleon, supported by the love and confidence of the French, had nothing to fear from the attacks of the coalition.

In the other he went over the proposals of M. Werner: he discussed with admirable sagacity the advantages and inconveniences, that might result from them to the interests of France and of Europe; and he finished, by declaring, after having successively rejected a republic, a regency, and the Duke of Orleans, that Napoleon, whom he loaded with extravagant praises, was evidently the chief best suited to the French, and to the interests of the allied monarchs rightly understood. Nevertheless, he had contrived to turn his expressions with so much art and address, that it was impossible not to perceive, that he thought in the bottom of his heart the Duke of Orleans the only prince, capable of ensuring the happiness of France, and the tranquillity of foreign nations.

I laid this letter before the Emperor, and endeavoured in vain to make him sensible of the treachery. He could see nothing but the eulogiums of his genius: the rest he overlooked.

M. Werner had been punctual to his rendezvous and I hastened to his residence. "I was afraid," said he to me obligingly, "that you had been refused admission into Bâle: I have spoken about it to the authorities, and, if you wish it, I will cause to be delivered to you the necessary passport, to enable you to enter Switzerland, depart, or reside in it, without obstacle, and without danger."

I thanked him for this offer, which convinced me, that the Swiss were as well disposed towards our enemies, as they were the reverse to us. We afterwards entered on business. "I related to M. de Metternich," said he to me, "the frank and loyal conversation, which I had the honour of holding with you. He hastened to give an account of it to the allied sovereigns: and the sovereigns have thought, that it ought to produce no alteration in the resolution they have formed, never to acknowledge Napoleon as sovereign of France, or to enter into any negotiation with him individually: *but at the same time, I am authorized formally to declare to you, that they renounce the idea of re-establishing the Bourbons on the throne, and that they consent to grant you the young Prince Napoleon.* They know, that in 1814 a regency was the wish of France; and they would think themselves happy, to be able to accomplish it now."

"This is direct," answered I: "but what is to be done with the Emperor?"—"Begin you with deposing him: the allies will afterwards come to a suitable determination, according to circumstances. They are great, generous, and humane; and you may depend on it, they will treat Napoleon with the respect due to his rank, his alliance, and his misfortunes."—"This answer does not explain, whether Napoleon will be free, to choose a place of retreat for himself; or remain a prisoner to France and the allies."—"This is all I know."—"I perceive, that the allies want Napoleon to be delivered up to them bound hand and foot: never will the French be guilty of such a cowardly act. Since our interview, the public opinion in his favour has been expressed with fresh strength; and I protest to you, that he never possessed the love of the French to so high a degree. The electors convoked for the *Champ de Mai*, and the new representatives of France[3], are arriving at Paris from all quarters. Do you think, that these electors, and these deputies, who are the choice of the nation, would have embraced the perilous cause of Napoleon, were it not the common cause of all France? Do you think, that if they were not resolved to defend it against all the world, they would be so stupid, or so imprudent, as to come forward in the face of that world, to swear fealty to the Emperor, and proscription and hatred to the Bourbons? The allies subdued us in 1814, because we were then without union, without will, without the means of resistance. But a great nation is not to be subdued two years following; and every thing indicates, that, if a contest take place, it will turn out to the advantage of the French this time." —"If you knew the force, that will be opposed to you, you would hold a different language: you will have twelve hundred thousand men to fight against, twelve hundred thousand men accustomed to conquer, and who already know the road to Paris." —"They know it, because they were taught it by treachery." — "Consider, too, that you are without artillery, without an army, without cavalry." —"The Spaniards resisted all the force of Bonaparte, though they had fewer resources than we have." —"You have no money." —"We shall procure it at the expense of the nobles and royalists, or do without it. The armies of the republic were paid with garlands of oak, yet were they the less able, to overcome the armies of the coalition?" —"You are wrong, I assure you, in viewing your situation under such fine colours. This new war will be more cruel, and more obstinate, than the others. The allies are determined, never to lay down their arms, while Napoleon remains on the throne." —"I by no means look with tranquillity on the war that is preparing. I cannot think of it without alarm. If Napoleon prove victorious, it is possible, that success may turn our brains, and inspire us anew with the desire of revisiting Vienna and Berlin. If he be unsuccessful, it is to be feared, that our defeats will animate the people with rage and despair, and that the nobles and royalists will be massacred." —"The prospect is no doubt extremely distressing; but I have already told you, and I repeat it, nothing will alter the determination of the allied monarchs: they have learned to know the Emperor, and will not leave him the means of disturbing the world. Even would the sovereigns consent, to lay down their arms, their people would oppose it: they consider Bonaparte as the scourge of the human race, and would all shed their blood to the last drop, to tear from him the sceptre, and perhaps his life." —

"I know, that the Prussians have sworn him implacable animosity: but the Russians and Austrians surely are not so exasperated as the Prussians." —

"On the contrary, the Emperor Alexander was the first, to declare against Napoleon." —

"Be it so: but the Emperor of Austria is too virtuous, and too politic, to sacrifice his son-in-law, and his natural ally, a second time to vain considerations." —

"The Emperor is not guided by vain considerations: he had to choose between his affections as a father, and his duties as a sovereign; he had to decide between the fate of a wife and child, and the fate of Europe: the choice he would make could not be doubted, and the magnanimous resolution taken by the Emperor is incontestably a noble title to the gratitude of his contemporaries, and the admiration of posterity." —

"I am fully aware, how much it must have cost him, to overturn the throne of his daughter, and of his grandson; and condemn them to lead a painful life on the face of the earth, without father, without husband, without a country. Though a Frenchman, I do justice to the strength of mind, that the Emperor has shown on this memorable occasion: but if the part he then took were proper, it appears to me, that the path he now seems inclined to pursue will be as dangerous, as it is impolitic. Austria, in the critical situation in which it is placed by the vicinity, ambition, and alliance of Prussia and Russia, has need of being protected and supported by a powerful ally; and no prince is more capable of succouring and defending it than Napoleon." —

"Austria has nothing to fear from its neighbours: such harmony reigns between them, as nothing can disturb: their sentiments and principles are the same. M. de Metternich has charged me, to declare to you positively, that he acted only in concert with the allies; and that he would enter into no negotiation without their consent." —

This word, negotiation, struck me. "Since we must not think, M. Werner," answered I, "of re-establishing that union and friendship between Austria and France separately, which their interests, and their family connexion, demand; at least let us not renounce the hope of a general accommodation. Never perhaps was humanity threatened with a war so terrible: it will be a conflict to the death, not between army and army, but between nation and nation. The idea makes me tremble. The name of M. de Metternich is already celebrated; but with what glory would it be surrounded, if M. de Metternich, in becoming the mediator of Europe, should accomplish its pacification! And we, too, M. Werner, do you think we should not obtain a share in the blessings of the people? Let us lay aside our character of negotiators, and examine the situation of the belligerent powers, not as their agents, but as disinterested persons, as friends of humanity. You say, you have twelve hundred thousand fighting men; but we had a million in 1794, and shall have still. The love of honour and independence is not extinct in France; it will fire every heart, when the business is to repel the humiliating and unjust yoke, that you would impose on us.

"If the picture I have drawn you of the state of France, and the patriotism with which she is animated, appear to you unfaithful, or exaggerated, come with me; I offer you a passport, and all the pledges you can require; we will travel together incognito; we will go wherever you please; we will hear, we will interrogate, the peasants, the townspeople, the soldiers, the rich, and the poor; and when you have seen, seen every thing with your own eyes, you may aver to M. de Metternich, that he has been deceived; and that the efforts of the allies, to impose upon us the law, can have no other result, than that of watering the ground in vain with blood."

The emotion, that I could not restrain, had transfused itself into M. Werner: "I wish," said he to me with tenderness, "it was in my power to second your wishes, and to concur with you in stopping the effusion of human blood: but I dare not indulge this hope. However, I will give M. de Metternich an account of the energy, with which you have pleaded the cause of humanity: and, if he can accept the office of a mediator, I know so well the loftiness of his soul, to pledge myself to you, that he will not refuse it."

Thus far, in order to accustom M. de Metternich to treat directly with me, I had avoided bringing forward M. Fouché. However, as he had directed me to make use of his letters, I took an opportunity of mentioning them to M. Werner. I read them to him; and took care to comment on them in such a way, as to destroy the unpleasant impression, which I foresaw the partiality of the praises lavished on Napoleon would make upon him. When we came to the passage, where M. Fouché discussed the inconveniences of a republic, M. Werner stopped me, and said, that I certainly had not conceived him rightly; that he had spoken to me merely indirectly of a republic, as it never entered into the thoughts of the allied monarchs, to give way to its re-establishment; for their endeavours would rather be exerted, to crush the seeds of a republican spirit, than to favour their dangerous germination. I reminded him of the conversation we had had on the subject; but, as it was of little importance to me, to prove myself in the right, I readily admitted myself to be in the wrong.

"At any rate," said he, taking the letters, "the language of M. Fouché will greatly surprise M. de Metternich. He repeated to me again, the evening before I set out, that the Duke of Otranto had on all occasions expressed to him an inveterate hatred of Bonaparte; and that even in 1314 he blamed him, for not having caused him to be confined in some strong fortress; predicting to him, that he would return from the island of Elba, to ravage Europe anew. M. Fouché must be totally ignorant of what passes at Vienna, to believe in the Emperor's security: what he will learn from M. de Montron and M. Bresson will no doubt lead him to adopt a different opinion; and will make him sensible, that it will be for his own interest, as well as that of France, to second the efforts of the allies."

"I know the connexions of the Duke of Otranto with those gentlemen," answered I: "he will not pay much credit to what they tell him. I regret that you were not commissioned to say so much to me on our first interview, it would unquestionably have made a very different impression on him; but what has not yet been done may be done; and, if you wish it, I will readily be your interpreter."

"M. de Metternich," replied M. Werner, "did not positively inform me what he had commissioned those gentlemen to say to the Duke of Otranto; but I presume it could only be a repetition of what he directed me to say to you."

"If this be the case," rejoined I, "you would be wrong, to flatter yourself with the least success. If the question related to Napoleon alone, we should not hesitate to sacrifice the cause of one man to that of a whole people: Napoleon, personally, is nothing to us; but his continuance on the throne is so connected with the happiness and independence of the nation, that we cannot betray him, without betraying our country at the same time; and this is a crime, of which M. Fouché and his friends will never render themselves guilty.

"In short, M. Werner, I hope you will succeed in convincing our enemies, that they would attempt in vain to dethrone Napoleon by force of arms; and that the most prudent part that can be taken is, to be contented with tying his hands in such a manner, as to prevent him from oppressing France and Europe anew.

"If M. de Metternich approve this step, he will find us disposed, secretly or openly to second his salutary views; and to join with him in rendering it morally and physically impossible for Napoleon, to recommence his tyranny. I will then return to Bâle, and I will go to Vienna, if you desire it: and in a word I will do every thing, that can be done, to arrive promptly at a secure result.

"But if M. de Metternich will not enter frankly into a conference, and his sole intention be, to instigate treachery, his endeavours will prove fruitless; and M. Fouché requests, that M. de Metternich and the allies will spare him the trouble of convincing them of it."

M. Werner assured me, that he would faithfully report to M. de Metternich all he had heard; and we parted, after promising to meet at Bâle again on the 1st of June.

I gave the Emperor an account of this new conference. He appeared, to conceive some hopes from it. "These gentlemen," said he, "begin to soften, since they offer me the regency: my attitude imposes on them. Let them allow me another month, and I shall no longer have any fear of them."

I did not forget to remark to him, that M. M. de Montron and Bresson had been charged with fresh communications for M. Fouché. "He has never opened his mouth to me on the subject," said Napoleon. "I am now persuaded, that he is betraying me. I am almost certain, that he is intriguing both at London and at Ghent: I regret, that I did not dismiss him, before he came to disclose to me the intrigues of Metternich: at present, the opportunity is gone by; and he would every where proclaim me for a suspicious tyrant, who had sacrificed him without any cause. Go to him: say nothing to him of Montron or Bresson; let him prate at his ease, and bring me a full account of all he says."

The Emperor imparted this second interview to the Duke of Vicenza; and directed him, to send for M. de Montron, and M. Bresson, and endeavour to set them talking. The Duke de Vicenza having been able to get nothing out of them, the Emperor, as I have been informed, would see them himself; and, after having questioned and sounded them for four hours, he dismissed them both, without having heard any thing but accounts of the hostile dispositions of the allies, and the conversations they had had at Vienna with M. de Talleyrand and M. de Metternich, the substance of which was the same as that of my conferences with M. Werner.

As the Emperor had rejected my first suspicions with so much indifference, I was flattered to see him sharing my distrust: but this gratification of self-love gave way to the most painful reflexions.

I had conceived the highest opinion of the character and patriotism of the Duke of Otranto; I considered him as one of the first statesmen in France; and I bitterly regretted, that such qualities, and such talents, instead of being devoted to the good of his country, should be employed in favouring the designs of our enemies, and in coolly contriving with them the means of subjugating us.

These reflexions, which ought to have inspired me with horror for M. Fouché, had on me an opposite effect: I was staggered by the enormity of the crime I ascribed to him. No, said I to myself, M. Fouché cannot be guilty of such baseness: he has received too many benefits from the Emperor, to be capable of betraying him, and has given too many proofs of attachment and affection to his country, to conspire its dishonour and ruin. His propensity to intrigue may have led him astray; but his intrigues, if reprehensible, are at least not criminal.

Thus I repaired to the Duke of Otranto's in the persuasion, that I had judged him too severely. But his air of constraint, and his captious endeavours, to penetrate what M. Werner might have said to me, convinced me, that his conscience was not at ease; and I felt my just prejudices revived and increased[4]. The time I staid with him was spent in idle questions and dissertations on the probabilities of peace or war. It would be useless and tiresome, to recite them here.

The rising of the King of Naples became afterwards the subject of our conversation. "Murat is a lost man," said M. Fouché to me: "he is not strong enough, to contend with Austria. I had advised him, and I have written again lately to the Queen, to keep himself quiet, and wait the course of events: they would not listen to me, and have done wrong: they might have had it in their power to treat; now they cannot; they will be sent about their business without pity, and without any conditions."

The Emperor, who had become uneasy, directed M. de Montron and M. Bresson to be watched. He was informed, that the latter had just been sent to England by order of the minister at war.

The Prince of Eckmuhl, being questioned, said, that an English dealer had forty thousand muskets to sell; and he had commissioned M. Bresson, to go and examine them, and treat for their purchase. This mission, which did not at first excite the Emperor's attention, afterwards recurred to his mind: he first thought it strange, and then suspicious. "If Davoust," said he, "had not had some motive for concealing this business from me, he would have mentioned it: it is not natural: he is acting in concert with Fouché."

This glimpse of light produced no effect. Napoleon contented himself with severely reprimanding the minister at war; and ordering him, never again to send any person whatever out of France, without his consent.

A new incident occurred, to strengthen the Emperor's apprehensions. He was informed by the prefect of police, that M. Bor..., formerly one of the principal agents of the police, and one of the habitual confidants of the minister, had set off for Switzerland with a passport from M. Fouché. An order for arresting M. Bor... was transmitted by telegraph to General Barbanegre, who commanded at Huninguen: but it arrived too late; M. Bor..., as quick as lightning, had already passed the frontier.

The Emperor no longer had any doubt of M. Fouché's treachery; but he was afraid the disclosure of it would occasion alarm and discouragement. In fact, people would not have failed to infer, that the imperial cause was lost; since this minister, whose perspicacity was well known, quitted it to join the Bourbons.

Napoleon foresaw too the approaching commencement of hostilities; and, convinced, that the fate of France would not be decided by the manœuvres of the Duke of Otranto, he resolved, to wait for a more favourable opportunity of getting rid of him. If the victory of Fleurus had not been followed by the disasters of Waterloo, the first decree the Emperor would have signed, on his arrival at Brussels, would probably have been for displacing the Duke of Otranto.

The time of the rendezvous given me by M. Werner being come, I asked Napoleon for orders. "Fouché," said he to me, "will no doubt have warned

Metternich; and it is probable, that his agent will return no more: it is even possible, that measures will be taken, to arrest you. I think, therefore, you may as well remain here."—"I do not think, sire, that M. de Metternich is capable of such an action. The patriotism and frankness, which I displayed in my conferences with M. Werner, appear to have pleased the prince; and M. Werner informed me, that he was particularly directed, to express to me the good opinion (permit me to repeat the terms) which he had conceived of my character and merit. Your Majesty would be wrong, I think, not to allow me to make this last attempt. As the point in question was not a conspiracy, but to set on foot a negotiation, it is possible, that M. Werner may return."—"You have my consent very willingly; but I am afraid, they will lay hold of you: be prudent."

I was afraid so too. I set off.

It happened as the Emperor foresaw. M. Werner appeared no more.

Thus ended this negotiation, which might perhaps have realized many hopes, had not M. Fouché occasioned its failure.

At the period when it took place, England, in its celebrated Memoir of the 25th of April, and Austria, in that it published the 9th of May following, had authentically declared, subsequently to my first interview at Bâle, that they had not engaged by the treaty of the 29th of March, to restore Louis XVIII. to the throne; and that their intentions in pursuing the war were not, to impose on France any particular government whatever.

These declarations gave great weight to the proposals of M. Werner. The Emperor thought them sincere; and in one of those moments of openness, which he was not always sufficiently master of himself to suppress, he said at his levee: "Well, gentlemen, they offer me the regency already: it depends only on myself, whether I shall accept it." These inconsiderate words made some impression; and they who remembered them have since asserted, that, if the Emperor had not been enamoured of the crown, he might have placed his son on the throne, and spared France the carnage of Mont St. Jean. The Emperor descending from his throne, to place on it his son, and peace, would have added, no doubt, a noble page to his history: but, ought he to have accepted the loose proposals of M. Werner, and trusted to the faith of his enemies? I think not. The first question to be decided, before treating of a regency, was this: What is to be done with Napoleon? and it has been seen, that on this point the allies held the profoundest silence.

I am far from thinking, that the Emperor would have consented in any case, to lay aside his crown, which he considered as the price of twenty years toil and victory; I only maintain, that he cannot be blamed on this occasion, for having retained it.

This confidential avowal to his courtiers is not the only indiscretion, of which they laid hold, to charge him with imaginary faults. What will appear surprising is, that, with the character for negation and dissimulation ascribed to him, he was capable of indiscretions.

Napoleon conceived in secret, and conducted to their close in mystery, schemes, that did not call his passions into play, because then he never ceased to be master of himself: but it was excessively rare for him, to preserve a continued, and complete dissimulation in affairs, that strongly agitated his soul. The object, on which he was then occupied, assailed his mind, and heated his imagination: his head, continually at work, abounded in ideas, that diffused themselves in spite of him, and displayed themselves externally by broken words, and demonstrations of joy or anger, that afforded a clew to his designs, and entirely destroyed the mystery, in which he would have enveloped them.

This narration, which I would not interrupt, has made me lose sight of Napoleon. I left him meditating the constitution he had promised the French, and now return to him.

Napoleon had at first announced his intention of amalgamating the ancient constitutions with the charter, and composing from the whole a new constitution, which should be subjected to the free discussion of the delegates of the nation. But he thought, that present circumstances, and the agitation of men's minds, would not permit subjects of such high importance, to be debated publicly without danger; and he resolved to confine himself for the moment, to sanction by a particular act, supplementary to the constitutions of the empire, the new guarantees, that he had promised the nation.

Napoleon was swayed also by another consideration. He considered the constitutions of the empire as the title-deeds of his crown; and he was afraid, if he annulled them, that he should effect a sort of novation, that would give him the appearance of beginning a new reign. For Napoleon, such is human weakness, after having devoted to ridicule the pretensions of "*the King of Hartwell*," was inclined to persuade himself, that his own reign had not been interrupted by his residence in the island of Elba.

The Emperor had entrusted to M. Benjamin Constant, and to a committee composed of ministers of state, the double task of preparing the bases of a new constitution. After having seen and amalgamated their labours, he subjected the result to the examination of the council of state, and of the council of ministers. Toward the end of the discussion, Napoleon suggested the idea of not submitting this constitution to public debate, but presenting it only as an additional act to the preceding constitutions. This idea was combated unanimously. M. Benjamin Constant, the Duke Decrès, the Duke of Otranto, the Duke of Vicenza, &c. &c., remonstrated with the Emperor, that this was not what he had promised France; that a new constitution was expected from him, purged from the despotic acts of the senate; and that he must fulfil the expectations of the nation, or prepare to lose its confidence for ever.

The Emperor promised to reflect on it: but, after having weighed in his sagacity the observations, that had been submitted to him, he persisted in his scheme; and the next day the additional act appeared in the Moniteur in the following form:

ADDITIONAL ACT.

Paris, April the 24th.

Napoleon, by the grace of God and the constitutions, Emperor of the French, to all present and to come, health.

Since we were called, fifteen years ago, by the wishes of France, to the government of the empire, we have sought to bring to perfection, at different periods, the forms of the constitution, according to the wants and desires of the nation, and profiting by the lessons of experience.

Thus the constitution of the empire has been formed by a series of acts, which have been invested with the acceptance of the people. We had then for our object, to organize a grand European federal system, which we had adopted as conformable to the spirit of the age, and favourable to the progress of civilization. To effect its completion, and give it all the extension and stability, of which it is susceptible, we had adjourned the establishment of several domestic institutions, more particularly designed to protect the liberty of the citizens. Our object is nothing more henceforward, than to increase the prosperity of France by the confirmation of public liberty; whence results the necessity of several important modifications of the constitution, the decrees of the senate, and other acts, by which this empire is governed.

For these reasons, willing, on the one hand, to retain whatever is good and salutary of the past, and on the other to render the constitution of our empire conformable in every respect to the wishes and wants of the nation, as well as to that state of peace, which we are desirous of maintaining with Europe, we have resolved, to propose to the people a series of arrangements, tending to modify and improve its acts, to surround the rights of citizens with all their guarantees, to give to the representative system its full extent, to invest the intermediate bodies with the respectability and powers that are desirable; in a word, to combine the highest degree of political liberty, and personal security, with the strength and concentration necessary, to render the independence of the French people, and the dignity of our crown, respected by foreigners: in consequence, the following articles, forming an act supplementary to the constitution of the empire, will be submitted to the free and solemn acceptance of all the citizens, throughout the whole extent of France[5].

HEAD I.

General provisions.

Art. 1. The constitution of the empire, consisting of the constitutional act of the 22d of Frimaire, year 8; of the decrees of the senate of the 14th and 16th of Thermidor, year 10; and of that of the 28th of Floreal, year 12; will be modified by the provisions following: all the rest of their provisions are maintained and confirmed.

Art. 2. The legislative power is exercised by the Emperor and by two chambers.

Art. 3. The first chamber, styled the chamber of peers, is hereditary.

Art. 4. The Emperor names its members, who are irremovable, they and their male descendants, from eldest to eldest, in direct descent. The number of peers is unlimited. Adoption does not transmit the dignity of the peerage to the person adopted. The peers take their seats at the age of twenty-one; but have no deliberative voice before the age of twenty-five.

Art. 5. The chamber of peers has for its president the archchancellor of the empire, or, in the case provided for by article 5 of the decree of the senate of the 28th of Floreal, year 12, by one of the members of the chamber appointed by the Emperor.

Art. 6. The members of the imperial family, in hereditary succession, are peers by right. They are seated next to the president. They take their seats at the age of eighteen, but have no deliberative voice before the age of twenty-one.

Art. 7. The second chamber, styled the chamber of representatives, is elected by the people.

Art. 8. The members of this chamber are to the number of six hundred and twenty-nine: they must be twenty-five years of age at least.

Art. 9. The president of the chamber of representatives is appointed by the chamber at the opening of the session. He remains in office, till the chamber is renewed. His appointment is submitted to the approbation of the Emperor.

Art. 10. The chamber of representatives verifies the powers of its members, and decides on the validity of contested elections.

Art. 11. The members of the chamber of representatives receive for travelling expenses, and during the session, the indemnity decreed by the constituent assembly.

Art. 12. They are re-eligible without limit.

Art. 13. The chamber of representatives is entirely renewed, of right, every five years.

Art. 14. No member of either chamber can be arrested, except in case of being taken in the fact of committing a crime; or prosecuted for a criminal or correctional cause, during the sessions, except in consequence of a resolution of the chamber to which he belongs.

Art. 15. No one can be arrested or detained for debt, from the time of convening the meeting till forty days after the session.

Art. 16. The peers are to be tried by their own chamber in criminal or correctional cases, according to the forms prescribed by the law.

Art. 17. The quality of peer and of representative is compatible with all public functions, except those that are responsible (*comptables*).

All prefects and subprefects are not eligible by the electoral college of the department or circle (*arrondissement*), for which they are serving.

Art. 18. The Emperor sends to the chambers the ministers of state, and counsellors of state, who sit, and take a part in the discussions, but have no deliberative voice, unless they are members of the chamber, either as peers or being elected by the people.

Art. 19. The ministers, who are members of the chamber of peers, or of that of representatives, or who sit in consequence of being sent by the government, will give the chambers the information deemed necessary, when making it public does not compromise the interests of the state.

Art. 20. The sittings of both chambers are public. Nevertheless, they may resolve themselves into secret committees; the chamber of peers on the demand of ten members, that of deputies on the demand of twenty-five. The government also may demand secret committees for any communications it may have to make. In all cases deliberations and votes can take place only in a public sitting.

Art. 21. The Emperor may prorogue, adjourn, or dissolve, the chamber of representatives. The proclamation, that pronounces the dissolution, convokes the electoral colleges for a new election, and indicates the re-assembling of representatives in six months at the latest.

Art. 22. During the interval between the sessions of the chamber of representatives, or in case of the dissolution of this chamber, the chamber of peers cannot assemble.

Art. 23. The government has the proposal of the law: the chambers may propose amendments: if these amendments be not adopted by the government, the chambers are bound to vote for or against the law, in the form in which it was proposed.

Art. 24. The chambers have the power of inviting the government to propose a law on a given subject, and to draw up what appears to them proper to be inserted in the law. This demand may be made by either of the two chambers.

Art. 25. When a draught of a law is adopted by one of the two chambers, it is carried to the other; and, if it be approved there, it is carried to the Emperor.

Art. 26. No written discourse, except the reports of committees, the reports of ministers on the laws that are presented, and the accounts that are delivered, can be read in either of the chambers.

HEAD II.

Of the electoral colleges, and the mode of election.

Art. 27. The electoral colleges of the departments and circles are retained, conformably to the decree of the senate of the 16th of Thermidor, year 10, excepting the following modifications.

Art. 28. The district assemblies (*les assemblées de canton*) will fill up every year, by annual elections, all the vacancies in the electoral colleges.

Art. 29. From the year 1816, a member of the chamber of peers, appointed by the Emperor, will be president of the electoral college of each department for life, and not removable.

Art. 30. Dating from the same period, the electoral college of each department will appoint, from among the members of the college of each circle, the president and two vice-presidents: for this purpose the assembling of the electoral college of the department will precede that of the college of the circle fifteen days.

Art. 31. The colleges of departments and circles will appoint the number of representatives established for each by the annexed table and act, No. 1.[6]

Art. 32. The representatives may be chosen throughout the whole extent of France indifferently.

Every college of a department or circle, that shall choose a member not belonging to the department or circle, shall appoint a substitute (*suppléant*), who must necessarily be taken from the department or circle.

Art. 33. Manufacturing and commercial labour and property shall have a particular representation.

The election of commercial and manufacturing representatives shall be made by the electoral college of the department from a list of eligible persons, drawn up by the chambers of commerce and consulting chambers in conjunction, according to the annexed table and act, No. 2.

HEAD III.
Of the law of taxation.

Art. 34. Direct general taxes, whether on land or personal property, are voted only for one year: indirect taxes may be voted for several years. In case of a dissolution of the chamber of representatives, the taxes voted in the preceding session are continued, till the chamber meets anew.

Art. 35. No tax, direct or indirect, in money or in kind, can be levied; no loan can take place; no entry of credit in the great book of the public debt can be made; no domain can be alienated or exchanged; no raising of men for the army can be ordered; no portion of territory can be exchanged; except by virtue of a law.

Art. 36. No proposal of a tax, of a loan, or of a levy of men, can be made, except in the chamber of representatives.

Art. 37. It is in the chamber of representatives also, that, 1st, the general budget of the state, containing an estimate of the receipts, and the proposal of the funds assigned for the year to each department of the ministry; and, 2dly, an account of the receipts and expenses of the year, or years, preceding; are to be introduced in the first instance.

HEAD IV.
Of ministers and their responsibility.

Art. 38. All the acts of the government must be countersigned by a minister having some department.

Art. 39. The ministers are responsible for the acts of government signed by them, as well as for the execution of the laws.

Art. 40. They may be accused by the chamber of representatives, and are to be tried by that of peers.

Art. 41. Every minister, every commander of an army by land or sea, may be accused by the chamber of representatives, and tried by the chamber of peers, for having compromised the safety or honour of the nation.

Art. 42. In this case the chamber of peers exercises a discretionary power, both in assigning the character of the crime, and in the punishment to be inflicted.

Art. 43. Before it is decided, that a minister shall be put upon his trial, the chamber of representatives must declare, that there are grounds for examining into the charge brought against him.

Art. 44. This declaration can be made only on the report of a committee of sixty members drawn by lot. This committee cannot make its report till at least ten days after its nomination.

Art. 45. When the chamber has declared, that there are grounds for examination, it may summon the minister before it, to demand an explanation of him. This summons cannot take place, till ten days after the committee has made its report.

Art. 46. In all other cases, ministers having departments cannot be summoned or sent for by the chambers.

Art. 47. When the chamber of representatives has declared, that there are grounds for examination against a minister, a new committee is to be formed, of sixty members, drawn by lot as the former; and this committee makes a fresh report on the subject of bringing him to trial. This committee does not make its report till ten days after its nomination.

Art. 48. The bringing to trial cannot be decided upon, till ten days after the report has been read, and distributed among the members.

Art. 49. The accusation being resolved upon, the chamber of representatives names five commissioners, chosen from among its own members, to conduct the charge before the chamber of peers.

Art. 50. Article 75 of head 8 of the constitutional act of the 22d of Frimaire, year 8, declaring, that the agents of the government can be prosecuted only in consequence of a decision of the council of state, shall be modified by a law.

HEAD V.

Of the judicial power.

Art. 51. The Emperor appoints all the judges. They are for life, and irremovable, from the instant of their appointment; the nomination of judges of the peace, and of commerce, excepted, which will take place as heretofore.

The present judges, appointed by the Emperor agreeably to the decree of the senate of the 12th of October, 1807, and whom he may think proper to retain, will receive appointments for life before the 1st of January next.

Art. 52. The institution of juries is retained.

Art. 53. The debating of criminal causes is to be public.

Art. 54. Military crimes alone are amenable to military tribunals.

Art. 55. All other crimes, even if committed by military men, are under the jurisdiction of the civil tribunals.

Art. 56. All crimes and offences, that were amenable to the high imperial court, and the trial of which is not reserved by the present act for the chamber of peers, are to be carried before the ordinary tribunals.

Art. 57. The Emperor has the right of pardoning, even in correctional cases, and of granting amnesties.

Art. 58. The interpretations of laws demanded by the court of cassation shall be given in the form of a law.

HEAD VI.

Rights of citizens.

Art. 59. Frenchmen are equal in the eye of the law, both in contributing to the taxes and public expenses, and in regard to admission to employments civil or military.

Art. 60. No one can be taken out of the hands of the judges assigned him by the law, on any pretence.

Art. 61. No one can be prosecuted, arrested, detained in custody, or banished, except in cases provided for by the law, and according to the forms prescribed.

Art. 62. Freedom in religious worship is guaranteed to all.

Art. 63. All property possessed or acquired agreeably to the laws, and all debts of the state, are inviolable.

Art. 64. Every citizen has a right to print and publish his opinions, he signing them, without any previous censorship; saving that he is legally responsible, after publication, to be tried by a jury, even though the application of a correctional punishment only should be requisite.

Art. 65. The right of petition is secured to all the citizens. Every petition is that of an individual (*est individuelle*). These petitions may be addressed, either to the government, or to the two chambers; nevertheless, even the latter must be superscribed "to his Majesty the Emperor." They must be presented to the chambers under the guarantee of a member, who recommends the petition. They are read publicly; and, if the chamber take them into consideration, they are carried to the Emperor by the president.

Art. 66. No place, no part of the territory, can be declared in a state of siege, except in case of invasion by a foreign power, or of civil disturbance.

In the former case, the declaration is made by an act of the government.

In the second case, it can be made only by the law. However, if the case occur, when the chambers are not assembled, the act of government, declaring the state of siege, must be converted into a proposal for a law in the first fifteen days after the meeting of the chambers.

ART. 67. The French people declare farther, that, in the delegation it has made, and now makes, of its powers, it has not intended, and does not intend, to confer the right of proposing the re-establishment of the Bourbons, or of any prince belonging to that family, on the throne, even in case of the extinction of the imperial dynasty; or the right of re-establishing either the ancient feudal nobility, or feudal and seigniorial rights, or tithes, or any privileged and predominant form of worship; or the power of making any infringement of the irrevocability of the sale of national domains: it formally prohibits the government, the chambers, and the citizens, from every proposal in respect to these.

Done at Paris, the 22d of April, 1815.

(Signed)NAPOLEON.
By the Emperor,
The minister secretary of state,
(Signed) The Duke of Bassano.

This additional act did not answer the general expectation.

The public had hoped, to receive from Napoleon a new constitution, freed from the faults and abuses of the preceding constitutions; and it was surprised, grieved, dissatisfied, when it saw, by the very preamble of the additional act, that it was nothing but a *modification* of the former constitutions, decrees of the senate, and other acts, by which the empire was governed.

What confidence, people cried, can such a production inspire? What guarantee can it afford the nation? Do we not know, that it was by means of these decrees of the senate, that Napoleon sported with our most sacred laws? and, since they are now maintained and confirmed, may he not employ them, as he formerly did, to interpret after his own fashion his additional act, alter its nature, and render it illusory?

It had been to be wished, undoubtedly, that the additional act had not revived the name, and borrowed the assistance, of all the senatorial acts, become on so many accounts objects of the public contempt and derision: but this was impossible[7]. They were the basis of our institutions; and they could not have been proscribed in a body, without arresting the progress of government, and subverting the established order of things from top to bottom.

Besides, the fear of Napoleon's putting them in vigour was founded only on vague suppositions. The oppressive arrangements of the decrees of the senate were annulled, both in fact and in law, by the principles, which the additional act sanctioned: and Napoleon had rendered it impossible for him to augment his authority, or to abuse it, by the immense power, with which he had invested the chambers, the responsibility he had thrown on his agents and ministers, and the inviolable guarantees he had conferred on freedom of opinion and personal liberty. The slightest attempt would have betrayed his secret intentions; and a thousand voices would have been raised, to say to him: "We, who are as good as you, have made you our King, on condition, that you keep our laws: if not, not[8]."

The re-establishment of the chamber of peers, imported from England by the Bourbons, excited no less vividly the public discontent.

It was clear, in fact, that the privileges, and peculiar jurisdiction, which the peers exclusively enjoyed, constituted a manifest violation of the laws of equality; and that the hereditary state of the peerage was a formal infraction of the right of all Frenchmen, to be equally admissible to the offices of the state.

Accordingly the friends of liberty and equality with reason reproached Napoleon for having falsified his promises; and given them, instead of a constitution bottomed on the principles of equality and liberty, which he had solemnly professed, a shapeless act, more favourable than the charter, or any of the preceding constitutions, to the nobility and their institutions.

But Napoleon, when he promised the French a constitution, that might be termed *republican*, had rather followed the political suggestions of the moment, than consulted the welfare of France. Restored to himself, ought he to have adhered strictly to the letter of his promises, or interpreted them merely as an engagement, to give France a liberal constitution, as perfect as possible?

The answer cannot be doubtful.

Now the testimony of the most learned civilians, the experience of England for 125 years, had demonstrated to him, that the government best adapted to the habits, manners, and social relations of a great nation; that which affords the greatest pledge of happiness and stability; in fine, that which best reconciles political liberty with the degree of power necessary to the chief of a state; is a representative monarchical government. It was Napoleon's duty, therefore, as a legislator, and a paternal sovereign, to give this mode of government the preference.

This point granted, and it is incontestable, Napoleon was under the necessity of establishing an hereditary and privileged chamber of peers; for a representative monarchy cannot subsist, without an upper chamber, or chamber of peers; as a chamber of peers cannot subsist without privileges, and without being hereditary.

None therefore but the insincere; or men, who, though good patriots, unconsciously substitute their passions or prejudices in the place of the public welfare; can reproach Napoleon for having introduced this institution into our political organization.

The re-establishment of an intermediate chamber, perhaps, would not have wounded them so deeply, if care had been taken, to give it a name less sullied by feudal recollections: but the revolution had exhausted the nomenclature of public magistracies. Besides, the Emperor thought, that this was the only title answerable to its high destination. Perhaps, too, as Louis XVIII. had had his peers, he was not displeased, to have his also.

A third accusation bore hard on Napoleon. He promised us, it was urged, as a natural consequence of the fundamental truth, *the throne is made for the nation, and not the nation for the throne*, that our deputies, assembled at the *Champ de Mai*, should give to France, jointly with him, a constitution conformable to the interests and wishes of the nation; and by an odious breach of faith, he grants us an additional act, after the manner of Louis XVIII; and this he forces us to adopt in the lump, without allowing us to reject those parts, that may wound our dearest and most sacred rights.

Napoleon had proclaimed, it is true, on the 1st of March, that this constitution should be the work of the nation: but since this period circumstances had altered. It was of importance to the preservation of peace at home, and to the relations between Napoleon and foreign powers, that the state should be speedily established and that Europe should find in its new laws those safeguards against the ambition and despotism of the Emperor, *and perhaps too against the re-establishment of a republic*, that it might deem desirable.

Literally to comply with the words of Napoleon, it would have been necessary, for the electoral colleges to give their deputies written instructions, as in 1789. The assembling of these colleges, the drawing up of their instructions after discussion, the choosing of delegates, their journeying to Paris, the distribution of the labour, the preparation, examination, and discussion of the bases of the constitution, the disputative conferences with the delegates of the Emperor, &c. &c., would have consumed an incalculable portion of time, and left France in a state of anarchy, that would have deprived it of the means or possibility of making peace or war with foreigners.

Thus, then, far from blaming the Emperor for deviating at the moment from this part of his promises, he on the contrary deserves credit for having voluntarily resigned the dictatorship, with which circumstances had invested him, and placed public liberty under the protection of the laws. Had he not been *sincere*; had he not been *honestly* disposed, to restore to the people their rights, and confine his own within proper limits, he would not have been in haste, to publish the additional act: he would have been for gaining time, in hopes that victory or peace, by consolidating the sceptre in his hands, would have enabled him to dictate laws, instead of subjecting himself to them.

In fine, the additional act was reproached with having re-established the confiscations abolished by the charter.

The majority of the counsellors of state and ministers, and M. de Bassano more particularly, strongly opposed this renewed provision of our revolutionary laws. But the Emperor considered the confiscation of estates as the most efficacious means of bridling the royalists; and he persisted obstinately in not giving it up; reserving the power of relinquishing it, when circumstances would permit.

Upon the whole, the additional act was not without blemishes; but these blemishes, easy to be removed, no way affected the beauty or goodness of its basis.

It acknowledged the principle of the sovereignty of the people.

It secured to the three powers of the state the strength and independence necessary, to render their actions free and efficacious.

The independence of the representatives was guarantied by their number, and the mode of their election.

The independence of the peers, by their being hereditary.

The independence of the sovereign by the imperial *veto*, and the happy establishment of the other two powers, which serve him mutually as a safeguard.

The liberties of the people, solidly established, were liberally endowed with all the concessions granted by the charter, and all those subsequently claimed.

The trial of all libels (*délits de la presse*) by a jury, protected and secured freedom of opinion. It defended patriotic writers from the anger of the prince, and the complaisance of his agents. It even assured them of impunity, whenever their writings are in harmony with the secret opinions and wishes of the nation.

Personal liberty was guarantied, not only by the old laws, and the irremoveableness of the judges, but also by two new provisions; one, the responsibility of ministers; the other, the approaching abolition of the impunity, with which public functionaries of all classes had been invested by the constitution of the year 8, and afterward by the regal government.

It was still farther guarantied by the insurmountable barrier opposed to the abuse of the right of banishment, by reducing the jurisdiction of military courts within their natural limits, and by restricting the power of declaring any portion of the country in a state of siege; a power hitherto arbitrary, and by help of which the sovereign suspended at will the authority of the constitution, and placed the citizens, in fact, out of the pale of the law.

The additional act, in fine, by the obstacles it opposed to the usurpations of supreme power, and the innumerable guarantees it secured to the nation, established public and private liberty on foundations not to be shaken; yet, from the most whimsical of all inconsistencies, it was considered as *the work of despotism*, and occasioned Napoleon the loss of his popularity.

The writers most celebrated for their understanding and patriotism took up the defence of Napoleon: but in vain did they quote Delolme, Blackstone, Montesquieu; and demonstrate, that no modern state, no republic, had possessed such liberal and beneficial laws: their eloquence and their erudition were without success. The contemners of the additional act, deaf to the voice of reason, would judge of it only from its title; and as this title displeased and alarmed them, they persisted in blackening and condemning the work on the score of its name, according to the vulgar proverb, *Give a dog a bad name, and hang him*.

Napoleon, far from foreseeing this fatal result, had persuaded himself, on the contrary, that he should receive credit for having so promptly and generously accomplished the hopes of the nation; and he had prepared a long proclamation to the French people in his own hand, in which he sincerely congratulated himself and them on the happiness, that France was about to enjoy under the sway of his new laws.

This proclamation, as may easily be guessed, came to nothing[9]. In its place came a decree for convoking the electoral colleges, in which Napoleon, informed of the public rumours, excused himself, on the ground of the pressure of circumstances, for having abridged the forms he had promised to follow in composing the constitutional act; and announced, that this act, containing in itself the principles of every improvement, might be modified in conformity to the wishes of the nation. By the terms of this decree, the electoral colleges were called on to choose the members of the approaching assembly of representatives; and Napoleon excused himself afresh, for being compelled by the state of affairs, to require them to proceed to the election of deputies previous to the acceptance of the constitution.

It was at the *Champ de Mai*, that the electors of all the departments were to assemble, and proceed to the collection of votes for its rejection or adoption.

The idea of renewing the ancient assemblies of the nation, as it was first formed by the Emperor, was no doubt a grand and generous conception, and singularly calculated to restore to patriotism its energy and lustre; but at the same time, it must be confessed, it bore the stamp of imprudent daring, and might have given Napoleon an irreparable stroke. Was it not to be feared, that, in the equivocal situation in which he was placed, the electors, having every thing to dread from the Bourbons and foreign powers, would not accept so hazardous a mission, and leave the assembly unattended?

Was it not also probable, that no one would covet the dangerous honour of making part of the new national representation, the first act of which must necessarily be, to proscribe for ever the dynasty of the Bourbons, and acknowledge Napoleon, in spite of the foreign powers, the sole and legitimate sovereign of France?

However, so true it is, that with Napoleon events always belied the most sagacious conjectures, the electors hastened in crowds to Paris; and men most respectable for wealth and character entered the lists to be chosen deputies, soliciting votes with as much ardour, as if France had been tranquil and happy[10].

And why was it so? Because, in the eyes of the electors and of the deputies, the object at stake was not the fate of a particular man, but of their country. It was because the critical situation of France, instead of intimidating the partisans of the revolution, awakened in their hearts the most courageous sentiments of patriotism.

They, whom I here call the partisans of the revolution, were not, as certain persons endeavour to persuade the world, those sanguinary beings, who were branded with the title of Jacobins, but that immense body of Frenchmen, who, since the year 1789, have concurred more or less in the destruction of the feudal system, with its privileges and abuses; of those Frenchmen, in fine, who are no strangers to the value of liberty, and the dignity of man.

But was the assembly of the *Champ de Mai* to be deprived of its chief ornament, the Empress and her son? The Emperor was not ignorant, that this princess was carefully watched; and that she had been surprised and threatened into an oath, to communicate all the letters she might receive. He knew, also, that she was surrounded by improper persons: but he thought, that he owed it to himself, and to his affection for the Empress, to exhaust every means of putting an end to her captivity. At first he attempted by several letters, full of feeling and dignity, to move the justice and sensibility of the Emperor of Austria. Entreaties and reclamations proving ineffectual, he resolved, to despatch an officer of the crown to Vienna, to negotiate, or demand publicly, in the name of nature and the law of nations, the deliverance of the Empress and her son. This mission was entrusted to the Count de Flahaut, one of his aides-de-camp. No person was more capable of fulfilling it worthily than this officer. He was a true Frenchman, spirited, amiable, and brave. He shone equally in the field of battle, in a diplomatic conference, and in the drawing-room pleasing every where by the agreeableness and firmness of his character.

M. de Flahaut set out, but could not advance beyond Stutgard. This disgrace converted into painful regret the joy, to which the hope of seeing again the young prince and his august mother had already given birth.

The people who resided near the road they would pass had already made preparations for testifying their love and their respect.

The return of Napoleon had been celebrated by enthusiastic shouts, that resembled the intoxication of victory: that of the Empress would have inspired only tender emotions. Acclamations tempered by tears of joy, the roads strewed with flowers, the village maidens adorned in their best attire and happy looks, would have given this sight the appearance of a family festival; and Marie Louise would have seemed, not the daughter of the Cæsars returning to her territories, but a beloved mother, who, after a long and painful absence, is at length restored to the wishes of her children.

Her son, over whose head such high destinies were then depending, would have excited transports not less vivid, or less affecting. Torn from a throne, and from his country, while yet in his cradle, he had not ceased to turn his eyes and his remembrances toward the land that had given him birth: a number of bold and ingenious expressions had disclosed his regrets and his hopes; and these expressions, repeated and learned by heart, had rendered this august infant the object of the dearest thoughts and affections.

With strange inconsistency, the French had deplored the imperious temper and warlike disposition of Napoleon; yet they loved the son, precisely because he gave promise of possessing the genius and audacity of his father; and because they hoped, that he would at some future day restore to France "the lustre of victories, and the language of a master[11]."

The Emperor was deeply afflicted at the arbitrary detention of his wife and her son. He felt all the importance of it. Offers had been made him several times, to carry them off: I myself was employed, by a very great personage, to make him an offer of this nature. But he obstinately persisted in listening to no proposal of the kind. Perhaps his affection, or his pride, forbade him, to expose to the hazards of such an enterprise persons so dear to him, and whom he felt assured of obtaining in a manner more worthy of him by victory, or by a peace. Perhaps he was apprehensive of endangering their fate, should he succumb in the struggle, that was about to take place between him and Europe; for unhappily this struggle, that had so long remained a matter of doubt, had now ceased to be questionable even to himself.

The indirect overtures made to foreign cabinets, and those renewed in every form by the Emperor, and by the Duke of Vicenza, had completely miscarried.

The efforts made in favour of France in the British parliament, by the generous defenders of the independence and rights of nations, had remained without success.

M. de St. L..... and M. de Mont...., who were returned from Vienna, had announced, that the allies would never depart from the principles manifested in their declaration and treaty of the 13th and 25th of March.

M. de Talleyrand, on whom Napoleon had depended, convinced of the triumph of the Bourbons, had refused to betray or abandon them.

M. de Stassard had been stopped at Lintz, and obliged to return. His despatches, which were seized and sent to the Emperor of Austria, had been shown to the foreign monarchs; and these monarchs had unanimously decreed, that they should not be taken into consideration, and that they adhered anew, and more formally than ever, to their declaration.

The Princess Hortense had received from the Emperor of Russia this laconic answer: "No peace, no truce, with that man: any thing except him[12]."

The agents maintained by the Emperor in foreign countries informed him, that the troops of all the powers were in arms; and that the arrival of the Russians alone was waited for, to commence the campaign[13].

Thus every hope of conciliation was annihilated: the friends of Napoleon began to doubt his safety: he alone contemplated with imperturbable firmness the dangers, with which he was menaced.

The events of 1814 had disclosed to him the importance of the capital; and it may well be presumed, that he did not neglect the means of putting it into a state of defence. When the moment was arrived, for definitively resolving on the work of the fortifications, which he had already sketched out, M. Fontaine, his favourite architect, was with him, and was going to withdraw. "No," said the Emperor to him, "stay here: you shall help me to fortify Paris." He ordered the map of levels to be brought him; examined the sinuosities of the ground; consulted M. Fontaine on the placing of redoubts, and the erection of crown-works, triple crown-works, lunettes, &c. &c.; and in less than half an hour he conceived and settled, under the approbation of his architect, a definitive plan of defence, that obtained the suffrages of the most experienced engineers.

A swarm of workmen soon covered the vicinity of Paris: but to increase the effect, that the fortification of this city would produce both in France and in foreign countries, Napoleon caused it to be suggested to the national guard, to join in the work. Immediately detachments from the legions, accompanied by a number of citizens and federates from the suburbs of St. Antoine, and St. Marceau, repaired to Montmartre and Vincennes, and proceeded to the opening of the trenches with songs. The grenadiers of the guard would not remain idle; and came to take their part in the labour with their band of music at their head. The Emperor, accompanied only by a few of the officers of his household, frequently went to encourage the zeal of the workmen. His presence and his words fired their imagination: they fancied they saw Thermopylæ in every pass they fortified and, like new Spartans, swore with enthusiasm, to defend them till death.

The federates did not stop at these demonstrations of their zeal, empty as they often are; they called for arms, and were angry, at the dilatoriness with which they were given them. They complained no less eagerly, that they had not yet been reviewed by the Emperor.

To pacify them, the Emperor hastened to announce to them, that he would admit them with pleasure to file off before him on the first parade day.

On the 24th of May, they presented themselves at the Tuileries. Their battalions were composed in great part of old soldiers and laborious work people: but some of those vagabonds, who abound in great cities, had crept in among them; and these, with their jailbird countenances, and ragged clothes, recalled to mind but too forcibly those murderous bands, who formerly stained the dwelling of the unfortunate Louis XVI. with blood.

When Louis XIII., and the arrogant Richelieu, invoked the assistance of the corporations of arts and trades, they admitted their deputies to a solemn audience, took them by the hand, and embraced them all, history says, down to the very cobblers. Napoleon, though in a far more critical situation, would not humble himself before necessity: he preserved his dignity, and, in spite of himself, suffered symptoms to escape him of what he felt, at being obliged by circumstances to accept such assistance.

The chiefs of the confederation addressed him in a speech, in which the following passages were principally remarked.

"You, sire, are the man of the nation, the defender of our country: from you we expect independence, and a sage liberty. You will secure to us these two precious possessions; you will render sacred for ever the rights of the people: you will reign according to the constitution and the laws. We come to offer you our arms, our courage, and our blood, for the safety of the capital.

"Ah! sire, why had we not arms at the time when foreign kings, emboldened by treason, advanced up to the walls of Paris? ... we shed tears of rage, at seeing our hands useless to the common cause: ... we are almost all of us old defenders of our country; our country should give arms with confidence to those, who have shed their blood for her. Give us arms in her name ... we are not the instruments of any party, the agents of any faction.... As citizens, we are obedient to our magistrates, and to the laws; as soldiers, we are obedient to our chiefs....

"Long live the nation, long live liberty, long live the Emperor!"

The Emperor answered them in the following terms:

"Soldiers, federates of the suburbs of St. Antoine and St. Marceau: I returned alone, because I reckoned on the people of the towns, the inhabitants of the country, and the soldiers of the army, whose attachment to the honour of the nation I well knew. You have all justified my confidence. I accept your offer. I will give you arms; to lead you, I will give you officers covered with honourable scars, and accustomed to see the enemy flee before them. Your robust limbs, inured to the most laborious work, are better adapted than any other, to handle arms. As to courage, you are Frenchmen: you shall be the skirmishers (*éclaireurs*) of the national guard. I shall be without any anxiety for the capital, while the national guard and you are employed in its defence: and if it be true, that foreigners persist in the impious design of attacking our independence and our honour, I may avail myself of victory, without being checked by any solicitude.

"Soldiers, federates; if there be men among the higher classes of society, who have dishonoured the French name; the love of our country, and the sentiment of national honour, have been preserved entire among the people of our towns, the inhabitants of the country, and the soldiers of the army. I am glad to see you. I have confidence in you: long live the nation!"

Notwithstanding his promise, however, the Emperor, under the pretence, that there was not a sufficient number of muskets, only gave arms to those federates who were on duty; so that they passed daily from one hand to another, and consequently did not remain in the possession of any one. Various motives induced him, to take this precaution. He wished to preserve to the national guard a superiority, which it would have lost, if the whole of the federates had been armed. He was afraid, also, that the republicans, whom he ever considered as his most implacable enemies, would obtain sway over the minds of the federates; and induce them, in the name of liberty, to turn against himself those arms, that he had put into their hands. Fatal prejudice! that induced him to place his reliance elsewhere than on the people, and consequently deprived him of his firmest support.

At the moment when the population of Paris was testifying the most faithful attachment to the Emperor and their country, the alarm-bell of insurrection resounded through the plains of la Vendée.

As early as the 1st of May, some symptoms of commotion had been observed in le Bocage[14]. The brave but unfortunate Travot had effected by his firmness, and by his persuasions, the restoration of order; and every thing appeared quiet, when emissaries arrived from England, to kindle the flames anew.

MM. de la Roche-jaquelin, d'Autichamp, Suzannet, Sapineau, Daudigné, and some others of the chiefs of la Vendée, re-assembled. A civil war was determined on. On the 15th of May, the day appointed, the alarm-bell was heard; energetic proclamations called the inhabitants of Anjou, la Vendée, and Poitou, to arms; and the assembling of a confused body of seven or eight thousand peasants was effected.

The English agents had announced, that the Marquis Louis de la Roche-jaquelin was bringing to the provinces in the West arms, ammunition, and money. The insurgents immediately repaired to Croix de Vic, to favour his landing. A few custom-house officers, assembled in haste, opposed them in vain: la Roche-jaquelin triumphantly delivered into the hands of the unfortunate Vendeans the fatal presents of England[15].

The news of this insurrection, considerably exaggerated by inaccurate accounts, reached the Emperor in the night of the 17th. He called me to his bedside; made me set down on the map the positions of the French and of the insurgents; and dictated to me his commands.

He directed a part of the troops stationed in the neighbouring divisions, to march with all possible speed for Niort and Poitiers; General Brayer, to hasten post to Angers, with two regiments of the young guard; and General Travot, to call in his detachments, and concentrate his force, till he received fresh orders. Experienced officers *d'ordonnances* were appointed, to go and reconnoitre the country; and General Corbineau, whose talents, moderation, and firmness were known to the Emperor, was sent to the spot, to appease the revolt, or preside over the military operations in case of need. All these arrangements being made, the Emperor quietly closed his eyes; for the faculty of tasting at pleasure the sweets of sleep was one of the prerogatives conferred on him by nature.

Telegraphic despatches soon brought more circumstantial and more heartening accounts. "It was known, that the peasants, who had been ordered to furnish merely four men from each parish, had shown hesitation and ill will; and that the chiefs had found great trouble in collecting four or five thousand men, consisting in great part of vagabonds, and workmen out of employ." In fine it was known, that General Travot, having been informed of the landing, and the road the convoy had taken, went in pursuit of the insurgents, came up with them in advance of St. Gilles, killed about three hundred men, and seized the greater part of the arms and ammunition.

The Emperor thought, that this insurrection might be quashed by other means than by force; and, adopting in this respect the conciliatory views proposed by General Travot, he directed the minister of police to invite MM. de Malartie and two other Vendean chiefs, MM. de la Beraudiere and de Flavigny, to repair in the character of pacificators to their ancient companions in arms; and remonstrate with them, that it was not in the plains of the West, the fate of the throne would be decided; and that, the final expulsion or restoration of Louis XVIII. depending neither on their efforts, nor on their defeat, the French blood, which they were about to shed in la Vendée, would be spilt to no purpose.

He sent orders to General Lamarque, whom he had just invested with the supreme direction of this war[16], to favour the negotiations of M. de Malartie to the utmost of his power: at the same time he directed him, to declare formally to la Roche-Jaquelin, and to the other chiefs of the insurgents, that, if they persisted in continuing the civil war, quarter would no longer be given them, and their houses and possessions should be sacked and burned[17].

He likewise recommended to him, to press as closely as possible on the bands of la Vendée, in order to leave them no hope of safety but in prompt submission. But this recommendation was superfluous. By unexpected attacks, skilful marches, and continually increasing successes, General Travot had already struck such terror and alarm into the insurgents, that they took much more pains to shun than to fight him.

In pursuing the movement of concentration, that had been prescribed him, this general accidentally fell in with the royal army by night, at Aisenay. A few musket shots spread dismay and disorder through their ranks; they rushed one upon another, and dispersed so completely, that

MM. de Sapineau and Suzannet were several days without soldiers. M. d'Autichamp, though distant from the place of engagement, experienced the same fate. His troops abandoned him with no less readiness, than he had found difficulty in assembling them.

This defection was not solely the effect of the terror, with which the imperial army could not fail naturally to inspire a body of wretched peasants; it was promoted by several other circumstances. In the first place it resulted from the little confidence of the insurgents in the experience and capacity of their General in chief, the Marquis de la Roche-jaquelin. They did justice to his conspicuous bravery; but he had forfeited their good opinion, by incessantly endangering them through false manœuvres, and by endeavouring to subject them to a regular service, incompatible with their domestic habits, and with their mode of making war.

In the next place it arose from the dissension, that had introduced itself among their generals from the commencement of the war. The Marquis de la Roche-jaquelin, ardent and ambitious, had arrogated to himself the supreme command; and the old founders of the royal army, the Autichamps, Suzannets, and Sapineaus, did not obey without regret the imperious orders of a young officer, hitherto without experience or reputation.

But the first, the fundamental cause of the slackness or inactivity of the Vendeans, was still more the change, that had taken place in the political and military state of France since the coronation of Napoleon. They knew, that the time when they struck terror into the blues, and made themselves masters of their artillery with clubs, was no more. They knew, that the days of terror, of anarchy, were terminated for ever; and that they had no longer to dread those abuses, or those excesses, or those crimes, which had provoked and fomented their first insurrection. As to the attachment for the Bourbon family, which they had inherited from their fathers, this, though not banished from their hearts, was balanced by the fear of seeing the calamities and devastations of the late civil war revived; by the uneasiness they felt from the renewal of the double despotism of the nobles and priests; and perhaps also by the remembrance of the kindness of Napoleon. It was he, who had restored to them their churches and their ministers; who had raised from their ruins their desolate habitations[18]; and who had freed them at once from revolutionary exactions, and from the plunderings of chouanry.

The Emperor, having no doubt of the approaching termination and happy issue of this war, announced it openly at a public audience. "Every thing will soon be finished," said he, "in la Vendée. The Vendeans will not fight any more. They are retiring to their homes one by one; and the fight will be at an end for want of combatants."

The news he received from the King of Naples by no means inspired him with the same satisfaction.

This prince, as I have said above, after having obtained several tolerably brilliant advantages, had advanced to the gates of Placentia; and was preparing, to march through the Piedmontese territory to Milan; when Lord Bentinck notified to him, that England would declare against him, if he did not respect the dominions of the King of Sardinia. Joachim, apprehensive of the English making a diversion against Naples, consented to alter his course. The Austrians had time to come up, and Milan was saved.

While these things were going on, a Neapolitan army, that had penetrated into Tuscany, and driven General Nugent before it, was surprised, and forced to retire precipitately to Florence.

This unexpected check, and the considerable reinforcements, that the Austrians received, determined Joachim to fall back. He retreated slowly to Ancona.

The English, who had hitherto remained neutral, now declared against him, and joined Austria and the Sicilians. Joachim, menaced and pressed on all sides, concentrated his forces. A general engagement took place at Tolentino. The Neapolitans, animated by the presence and valour of their king, briskly attacked General Bianchi, and every thing foreboded victory, when the arrival of General Neipperg, at the head of fresh troops, changed the aspect of affairs. The Neapolitan army was broken, quitted the field of battle, and fled to Macerata.

A second battle, equally disastrous, was fought at Caprano; and the capture of this city by the Austrians opened them an entrance into the kingdom of Naples, while the corps of General Nugent, which had marched from Florence to Rome, penetrated into the Neapolitan territory by another road.

The rumour of the defeat and death of the king, the approach of the Austrian armies, and the proclamations[19] issued by them, excited a sedition at Naples. The Lazaroni, after having assassinated a few Frenchmen, and massacred the minister of police, repaired to the royal palace, with the design of murdering the Queen. This princess, worthy of the blood that circulated in her veins, was not affrighted by their shouts and threats; she courageously made head against them, and obliged them, to return to their obedience.

Joachim, remaining erect amid the ruins of his army, sustained with heroic firmness the efforts of his enemies. Resolved to fall with arms in his hand, he rushed on the battalions, and carried terror and death into the midst of their ranks. But his valour could only ennoble his fall. Still repulsed, still invulnerable, he relinquished the hope of meeting death or victory. In the night of the 19th of March he returned to Naples: the Queen appeared indignant at seeing him. "Madame," said he to her, "I was not able to find death." He departed immediately, that he might not fall into the hands of the Austrians, and came to take refuge in France. The Queen, notwithstanding the dangers, that threatened her life, resolved to remain at Naples, till her fate and that of the army were decided. When the treaty was signed, she withdrew on board an English vessel and repaired to Trieste.

The catastrophe of the King made the most profound impression on the superstitious mind of Napoleon; but the French it inspired with little regret, and no fear. I say no fear, for the nation was familiarised with the idea of war. The patriotism and energy, with which it felt itself animated, filled it with such confidence, that it deemed itself sufficiently strong, to dispense with the support of the Neapolitans, and struggle alone against the coalition. It recalled to mind the campaign of 1814; and, if at that period Napoleon, with sixty thousand soldiers, had beaten and held in check the victorious foreign armies, what might it not hope now, when an army of three hundred thousand fighting men would form, in case of need, only the advanced guard of France? The royalists and their newspapers, by repeating the manifestoes of Ghent and Vienna, enumerating the foreign armies, and exaggerating our dangers, had indeed succeeded in abating the courage of a few, and shaking their opinions; but the sentiments of the bulk of the nation had lost nothing of their vigour and energy. Every day fresh offerings[20] were deposited on the altar of their country; and every day new corps of volunteers, equally numerous and formidable, were establishing, under the names of lancers, partisans, federates, mountain chasseurs, and tirailleurs.

The Parisians, so frequently peaceable spectators of events, participated in this burst of patriotism: not contented with erecting their intrenchments with their own hands, they solicited the honour of defending them; and twenty thousand men, composed of national guards, federates of the suburbs, and citizens of all ranks, were formed into battalions for actual service under the denomination of tirailleurs of the national guard.

Napoleon applauded the noble efforts of the great nation: but unfortunately our arsenals had been plundered in 1814; and, notwithstanding the activity of our workmen, he was grieved to the heart at his inability, to arm every hand raised in his defence. This would have required six hundred thousand muskets; and scarcely could enough be supplied, to arm the troops of the line, and the national guards, that were sent to garrison the fortified towns.

But while Paris was contemplating its ramparts on the one hand, on the other it saw the preparations for the festival of the *Champ de Mai* completing. On both there was an equal crowd; and the French, always the same, always brave and frivolous, traversed with equal pleasure the spots where they were to fight, and those where they expected to amuse themselves.

At length the assembly of the *Champ de Mai*, which several unforeseen circumstances had delayed, took place on the 1st of June. The Emperor believed, that he ought to display at it all the imperial pomp; but in this he was wrong. He was about to appear before old patriots, whom he had deceived; and he should have avoided awakening their memories, and clouding their brows.

His dress, and that of his brothers and his court, made at first a disagreeable impression; but it soon vanished, and gave place to the sensations, that this grand union of the nation excited. What in fact could be more impressive, than the aspect of a people, threatened with a tremendous war, forming peaceably a solemn compact with the sovereign, of whom its enemies were desirous of depriving it; and joining with him, to defend together the honour and independence of its country, in life or death?

An altar was erected in the midst of the vast and superb enclosure of the *Champ de Mars*; and the ceremony commenced with the invocation of the Supreme Being. The homage paid to God in the presence of nature seems more fully to inspire man with religion, confidence, and respect. At the instant of the elevation of the host, this crowd of citizens, soldiers, officers, magistrates, and princes, prostrated themselves in the dust, and implored for France, with a tender and religious emotion, the tutelary protection of the sovereign Arbiter of kings and people. The Emperor himself, usually so absent, displayed a great deal of inward devotion. All eyes were fixed on him: people called to mind his victories and his disasters, his greatness and his fall; they were softened by the fresh dangers, that accumulated round his head; and they put up prayers, truly sincere prayers, that he might triumph over his implacable enemies.

A deputation, composed of five hundred electors, advanced to the foot of the throne; and one of them, in the name of the French people, addressed him in the following terms:

"Sire,

"The French people had decreed you the crown; you laid it down, without their consent their suffrages impose on you the duty of resuming it.

"A new compact is formed between the nation and your Majesty.

"Assembled from all parts of the empire round the tables of the law, on which we are come to inscribe the wish of the people, the wish that constitutes the only legitimate source of power, it is impossible for us, not to proclaim aloud the voice of France, of which we are the immediate organs; and not to say, in the face of Europe, to the august chief of the nation, what it expects of him, and what he has to expect of it.

"Our words are as serious, as the circumstances by which they are inspired.

"What means this league of allied kings, with that preparation for war, with which it appals Europe, and grieves humanity?

"By what act, what transgression, have we provoked their vengeance, or given cause for an attack?

"Have we attempted, to impose laws on them, since the peace? We only wish, to make and follow such, as are adapted to our manners.

"We refuse the chief, whom our enemies choose for us; and we choose him, whom they refuse us.

"They dare to proscribe you personally: you, sire, who, so many times master of their capitals, had generously confirmed them on their tottering thrones! This hatred of our enemies adds to our love of you: were they to proscribe the most insignificant of our citizens, it would be our duty, to defend him with the same energy; he would be, like you, under the aegis of the laws and power of France.

"We are threatened with an invasion; yet, confined within frontiers, which nature did not impose on us; and which victory, and even peace, had extended, long before your reign; we have not overstepped this narrow boundary, out of regard to treaties, which you did not sign, yet have offered to respect.

"Do they demand only guarantees? They have them in our institutions; and in the will of the French people, henceforward united with yours.

"Are they not afraid of reminding us of times, of a state of things, but lately so different, and which may again return?

"It would not be the first time, that we have vanquished Europe in arms against us.

"It is to the French nation, that they dare refuse a second time, in the nineteenth century; in the face of the civilised world, those sacred, imprescriptible rights, which the smallest tribe never claimed in vain at the tribunal of history and justice.

"Because France resolves to be France, must it be degraded, torn to pieces, dismembered and is the fate of Poland reserved for us? Vainly would they conceal their fatal intentions, under the appearance of the sole design of separating you from us, to give us to masters, with whom we have no longer any thing in common, and who can no longer understand us.

"The three branches of the legislature are about to enter into a state of activity: one sentiment will animate them. Confiding in the promises of your Majesty, we resign to you, we resign to our representatives and to the chamber of peers, the care of revising, consolidating, and perfecting in concert, without precipitancy, without concussion, maturely, and with wisdom, our constitutional system, and the institutions that must guaranty it.

"And if, however, we be compelled to fight, let one sole voice resound from every heart. Let us march against the enemy, that would treat us as the lowest of nations. Let us all press around the throne, on which is seated the father and chief of the people and of the army.

"Sire, nothing is impossible: nothing shall be spared, to ensure our honour and independence, possessions dearer than life: every thing shall be attempted, every thing done, to repel an ignominious yoke. We say it to the nations, may their rulers hear us! if they accept your offers of peace, the French people will expect from your strong, liberal, and paternal government, motives of consolation for the sacrifices, which the peace has cost them: but if they leave us no other alternative, than war or disgrace, the whole nation is for war; it is ready to absolve you from the offers, perhaps too moderate, that you have made, in order to spare Europe fresh convulsions. Every Frenchman is a soldier: victory will follow your eagles; and our enemies, who have reckoned on a division, will soon regret their having provoked us."

This speech being ended, the result of the votes[21] was proclaimed, and the acceptance of the constitutional act.

The Emperor then, turning toward the electors, said:

"Gentlemen, electors of the colleges of departments and circles;

"Gentlemen, deputies of the armies by sea and land to the *Champ de Mai*:

"Emperor, consul, soldier, I hold every thing from the people. In prosperity, in adversity; on the field of battle, in the council chamber; on the throne, and in exile; France has been the sole and constant object of my thoughts, and of my actions.

"Like the King of Athens, I sacrificed myself for my people, in the hope of seeing the promise realized, that had been given, to preserve to France its natural integrity, its honours, and its rights.

"Indignation at seeing these sacred rights, acquired by five and twenty years of victory, disregarded, and lost for ever; the cry raised by, French honour disgraced; and the wishes of the nation; have brought me back to the throne, which is dear to me, because it is the palladium of the independence, the honour, and the rights of the people.

"Frenchmen, from the public joy, amid which I traversed the different provinces of the empire, to arrive at my capital, I could not but reckon on a long peace; for nations are bound by the treaties concluded with their governments, be these what they may.

"My thoughts were then turned wholly on the means of establishing our liberty by a constitution conformable to the will and the interests of the people. I convened the *Champ de Mai*.

"It was not long before I learned, that the princes, who have disregarded all principles, and wounded the opinions and dearest interests of so many nations, resolved to make war on us. They purpose, to enlarge the kingdom of the Netherlands, to give it for barriers all our strong places on the North, and to reconcile the differences, which still keep them at variance, by dividing among them Lorraine and Alsace.

"It was necessary, to prepare for war.

"However, before incurring personally the dangers of battle, my first care necessarily was, to consult the nation without delay. The people has accepted the act I have laid before it.

"Frenchmen, when we have repelled these unjust aggressions, and Europe is convinced of what is due to the rights and independence of twenty-eight millions of Frenchmen, a solemn law, made according to the forms willed by the constitutional act, shall combine the different arrangements of our constitutions, that are at present scattered.

"Frenchmen, you are about to return to your departments. Tell the citizens, that the present circumstances are important! That with union, energy, and perseverance, we shall rise victorious from this struggle of a great people against its oppressors; that generations to come will severely scrutinize our conduct; and that a nation has lost every thing, when it has lost its independence. Tell them, that the foreign kings, whom I raised to a throne, or who are indebted to me for the preservation of their crowns; all of whom, in the days of my prosperity, courted my alliance, and the protection of the French people; now direct their blows against my person.

Did I not see, that it is our country at which they really aim, I would place at their mercy this life, against which they appear so exasperated. But tell the citizens also, that, as long as the French retain for me those sentiments of affection, of which they have given me so many testimonies, this rage of our enemies will prove impotent.

"Frenchmen, my will is that of the people: my rights are its rights; my honour, my glory, my happiness, can be no others than the honour, the glory, and the happiness of France."

These words of Napoleon, pronounced with a strong and emphatic voice, produced the most lively sensation. A cry of "Long live the Emperor!" resounded in an instant throughout the immense space of the Champ de Mars, and was repeated from one to another in the places around.

The Emperor, after having sworn on the Gospels, to observe, and cause to be observed, the constitutions of the empire, made the archchancellor proclaim the oath of fealty of the French people, represented by the electors. This oath was spontaneously repeated by thousands and thousands of voices.

The ministers of war and of the navy, in the name of the armies by land and sea, and at the head of their deputations; the minister of the interior, in the name of the national guards of France, and at the head of the electors; the staff of the imperial guard, and that of the national guard; afterwards advanced to take the oath, and receive from the hands of the Emperor the eagles intended for them.

This ceremony ended, the troops, making about fifty thousand men, filed off before Napoleon and the festival concluded, as it had commenced, amid the acclamations of the people, the soldiers, and the majority of the electors: but to the discontent of a certain number of them, who complained, and with reason, that the Emperor had substituted a steril distribution of colours, instead of the grand national congress, which he had convened.

The parties too, that already began to pullulate, were not better satisfied with the issue of the *Champ de Mai*.

The old revolutionists would have wished Napoleon, to have abolished the empire, and re-established a republic.

The partisans of the regency reproached him for not having proclaimed Napoleon II.

And the liberals maintained, that he ought to have laid down the crown, and left to the sovereign nation the right of restoring it to him, or offering it to the most worthy.

Were these different pretensions well founded? No.

The re-establishment of the republic would have ruined France.

The abdication in favour of Napoleon II. would not have saved it. The allies had explained their intentions at Bâle: they would not have laid down their arms, till the Emperor had consented, to deliver himself up. "A circumstance, that, being to a prince the greatest of misfortunes, can never form a condition of peace[22]?"

As to the latter proposition, I confess, that Napoleon, if on the 21st of March, or the 12th of April[23], he had returned into the hands of the French the sceptre, which he had just torn from those of the Bourbons, would have stamped a character completely heroic on the revolution of the 20th of March. He would have disconcerted the foreign powers, augmented his popularity, centuplicated his forces: but on the first of June it was too late: the additional act had appeared.

Unhappily for himself, therefore, Napoleon could do nothing better at the *Champ de Mai*, than what he did: namely, to endeavour to conceal the emptiness of the day under the pomp of a religious and military solemnity, calculated to move the heart, and strengthen by fresh bands the union, already subsisting between him, the people, and the army.

The Emperor had not been able to deliver with his own hands to the electors the eagles of their departments. It had not been concealed from him, that some among them appeared dissatisfied; and he wished to attempt to dissipate their ill-humour, and revive their zeal. Ten thousand persons were assembled in the vast galleries of the Louvre; on one side were seen the deputies and electors of the nation; on the other, its glorious defenders. The eagle of each department, and that of each deputation from the armies, were placed at the head of groups of citizens or warriors; and nothing could exhibit a more animated, and more impressive picture, than this confused assembly of Frenchmen, of all the orders of the state, crowding mutually around the standards and the hero, that were to conduct them to victory and to peace.

The Emperor was polite, affectionate, amiable: with infinite art he accommodated his manners to every body, and almost every body was enchanted with him. He was convinced of the mischief he had done himself by the additional act: and, in order to regain the good opinion of the public, he repeated to satiety, to the representatives and electors, that he would employ himself in concurrence with the two chambers, to collect together those provisions of the constitutional laws, that were not abrogated, and form the whole into one sole constitution, that should become the fundamental law of the nation.

This retraction was the consequence of the remonstrances of his ministers, and particularly of M. Carnot. "Sire," he was incessantly repeating to him, "do not strive, I conjure you, against public opinion. Your additional act has displeased the nation. Promise it, that you will modify it, and render it conformable to its wishes. I repeat to you, Sire, I have never deceived you; your safety and ours depend on your deference to the national will. This is not all, Sire; the French are become a free people. The appellation of 'subject,' which you are continually giving them, wounds and humbles them. Call them citizens, or your children. Neither suffer your ministers, your marshals, your great officers, to be called '*monseigneur:*' there is no *seigneur* in a country, where equality forms the basis of the laws; there are none but citizens."

The Emperor, however, did not see the opening of the chambers approach, without a certain degree of apprehension. His intention was, frankly to submit to the principles and consequences of a representative government; in the first place, because he wished to reign, and was convinced, that he could not retain the throne, unless he governed as the nation demanded.

In the second place, because he was persuaded, that the nation now placed its ideas of happiness on a representative government; and because, greedy of every kind of celebrity, he found, as he told me at Lyons, that it was glorious, to render a great people happy. But, whatever were the sentiments and good inclinations of Napoleon, he had not had time, to divest himself completely of his old notions and ancient prejudices. The remembrance of our preceding assemblies besieged him still in spite of himself: and he appeared to fear, that the French had too much warmth of imagination, instability of will, and propensity to abuse their rights, to be capable of enjoying on a sudden, without any preparation, the benefits of absolute liberty. He feared, too, that the opposition inherent in representative governments would not be rightly comprehended in France, and would make a bad impression; that it would degenerate into resistance; and that it would clog the action of the sovereign power, take from it its illusion, its moral strength, and make of it nothing but an instrument of oppression[24].

Independently of these general considerations, Napoleon had still other motives, to dread the approaching assembly of the chambers. They were going to meet under circumstances, in which it was indispensable, that the chief of the state should govern without contradiction: yet he foresaw, that the representatives, misled by their ardent love of liberty, and by the fear of despotism, would seek to fetter his exercise of authority, instead of seconding its full display.

"When a war has commenced," said he one day, "the presence of a deliberative body is as embarrassing, as it is fatal. *It must have victories.* If the monarch meet with any check, fear seizes the timid, and renders them unconsciously the instruments and accomplices of the audacious. The apprehension of danger, and the desire of withdrawing from it, derange every head. Reason has no longer any sway: *physical feelings are everything.* The turbulent, the ambitious, greedy of rule, of popularity, of making a noise, erect themselves of their own authority into advocates of the people, and advisers of the prince: they want to know all, regulate all, direct all. If no regard be paid to their counsels, from advisers they become censors, from censors factionaries, and from factionaries rebels. The necessary consequence then is, that the prince must either submit to their yoke, or expel them; and in either case he almost always compromises his crown and the state."

Napoleon, tormented by the anxiety, which the sudden and inconsiderate application of the popular system, and the dispositions of the deputies, inspired, rested all his security on the chamber of peers. He hoped, that this chamber would influence the representatives by its example, or check them by its firmness.

The ministers received orders, each to present to him a list of candidates.

M. Delavalette, in whom the Emperor had particular confidence, was also desired to furnish him with a list.

Formerly an aide-de-camp of Napoleon, and connected with him by marriage[25], M. Delavalette had vowed to him an attachment proof against all temptations. Phocion said to Antipater, "I cannot be at once thy flatterer, and thy friend:" and M. Delavalette, thinking like Phocion, had abjured every kind of flattery, to adhere to the rigid language of friendship. Endowed with a cool head, and sound judgment, he appreciated events with skill and sagacity. Reserved in the world, frank and open with Napoleon, he avowed his opinions to him with the freedom of an affectionate, pure, and upright heart. Accordingly Napoleon set much value on his advice; and confessed with noble candour, that he had frequently had to congratulate himself for having followed it.

The lists presented to the Emperor exhibited a complete assortment of ancient nobles, senators, generals, land-holders, and merchants[26]. The Emperor, it is right to say, had only the trouble of choosing, but this was great.

On the one hand he could have wished, both from self-love and a spirit of conciliation, to have had in the chamber of peers some of those great names, that sound so gratefully to the ear. On the other hand he was desirous, as I have said above, that this chamber should hold the deputies in check; and he could not conceal from himself, that, if he introduced into it any of the ancient nobility, it would have no influence over that of the representatives, and probably be on very bad terms with it.

He decided, therefore, to sacrifice his inclinations to the good of the cause; and, instead of granting the peerage to that crowd of parchment nobles, who had humbly solicited it, he conferred it only on a few of them, noted for their patriotism, and their attachment to liberal principles. Many of these illustrious solicitors have since boasted of having refused it. This is very natural, but is it true? I leave it to their own hearts, their own consciences, to answer the question.

The Emperor, fearful of refusals, had taken the precaution to have the inclinations of the doubtful candidates previously sounded. Some hesitated; others plainly refused. Of all these refusals, direct and indirect, which amounted but to five or six at most, no one more painfully disappointed Napoleon, than that of Marshal Macdonald. He had not forgotten the noble fidelity that the Marshal preserved towards him in 1814, to the last moment; and he regretted, that his scruples deprived him of a dignity, to which he was called by his rank, his services, and the public esteem.

The 3d of June being come, the chamber of representatives assembled in the ancient palace of the legislative body, and formed itself provisionally under the presidency of the oldest of its members.

The constitution had left to the representatives the right of choosing their president. The Emperor hoped, that their suffrages would be given in favour of his brother Lucien; and in this hope he did not publish immediately the list of peers, that he might retain the power of comprising this prince in it, or not, according as he should or should not be appointed to the *presidency* [27]. But the chamber, notwithstanding the esteem and confidence, with which the principles and character of Prince Lucien inspired it, thought, that his election would be considered as a deference to the will of the Emperor; and resolved therefore, to make a different choice, in order to prove to France, and to the foreign powers, that it was, and would remain, free and independent. M. Lanjuinais was elected: and Napoleon, who knew that M. Lanjuinais, a malecontent by nature, had never been able to agree with any government[28], was doubly vexed, that Prince Lucien had been rejected, and that such a successor had been given him.

The sitting of the day following gave Napoleon another subject of dissatisfaction. The assembly had expressed its wish the day before, to be acquainted with the list of the members of the Chamber of Peers. The Emperor, from the motive I have mentioned, made answer, that this list would not be fixed, till after the opening of the session. This answer excited violent murmurs: one member proposed, to declare, that the chamber would not proceed to constitute itself definitively, till it was furnished with the list, which it had required. Thus from its entrance on its career, and even before it was installed, the chamber announced its design, of establishing itself in a state of insurrection against the head of the government.

The third sitting witnessed an opprobrium, hitherto unheard of in our national assemblies. The same member, M. Dupin[29], advanced, that the oath to be taken to the sovereign by the nation, in order to be valid and legitimate, should not be administered by virtue of a decree, that emanated from the will of the prince alone, but by virtue of a law, which is the will of the nation constitutionally expressed. In consequence he proposed, to resolve, that no oath could be required of it, but in execution of a law; and that this oath should no way prejudice its right, subsequently to improve the constitution.

This proposal, seconded by M. Roi[30], tended to declare null in law and fact the oath, which the nation and army, represented by their electors and deputies, had just taken to the Emperor and the constitution in the solemnity of the *Champ de Mai*: and as it was this oath, that hitherto formed the only tie binding the nation to the Emperor, and Napoleon to the nation, it followed that the annulling it deprived the Emperor of that character of sovereignty and legitimacy, with which he had been invested, and rendered his rights a subject of deliberation.

The motion of M. Dupin was rejected unanimously: but the chamber, in complaisantly permitting a man, to dare within its walls, to call in question the legitimacy of the Emperor and his authority, and endeavour to render him foreign to the nation, was guilty of an act of weakness and indifference, that deeply grieved Napoleon. "I perceive with sorrow," he said, "that the deputies are not disposed, to act in union with me; and that they let no opportunity escape of seeking a quarrel. Of what have they to complain? What have I done to them? I have given them liberty with an unsparing hand; I have given them perhaps too much; for kings in the present day have more need than nations of guarantees. I will act with them as long as I can: but if they think to make of me a King Log, or a second Louis XVI., they are mistaken; I am not a man to receive the law from counsellors[31], or to allow my head to be cut off by factionaries."

The hostile disposition of the representatives would have given him no uneasiness at any other time: the constitution conferred on him the right of dissolving the chamber, and he would have availed himself of it: but on the eve of a war, and in the critical situation in which he was placed, he could not have recourse to such an expedient, without endangering the fate of France. He resolved, therefore, to conceal his vexation and ill humour, and permit what he could not prevent.

On the 7th of June he repaired to the legislative body, to open the chambers; and, after having received the oaths of the peers and deputies, delivered the following speech:

"Gentlemen of the chamber of peers, and gentlemen of the chamber of representatives:

"Circumstances, and the confidence of the people, have invested me these three months with unlimited power. To-day the most urgent desire of my heart is accomplished: I come to commence the constitutional monarchy.

"Men are too feeble, to ensure the future: institutions alone fix the fate of nations. Monarchy is necessary in France, to guaranty the liberty, the independence, and the rights of the people.

"Our constitution is made up of scattered parts: one of our most important occupations will be, to unite them within one frame, and arrange them in one simple design. This labour will transmit the fame of the present period to future generations.

"I am ambitious of seeing France enjoy all the liberty possible: I say possible, because anarchy always leads to an absolute government.

"A formidable coalition of kings aims at our independence: their armies are arriving on our frontiers.

"The frigate *la Melpomène* has been attacked and taken in the Mediterranean, after a bloody engagement, by an English seventy-four. Blood has been shed during peace[32].

"Our enemies reckon upon our intestine divisions. They are exciting and fomenting civil war. Meetings have taken place; and a communication is kept up with Ghent, as in 1792 it was with Coblentz. Legislative measures are indispensable: to your patriotism, your intelligence, and your attachment to my person, I confide myself without reserve.

"The liberty of the press is inherent in our present constitution: no change can be made in this, without altering our whole political system: but we want repressive laws, particularly in the present state of the nation. I recommend this important subject to your consideration.

"The ministers will make known to you the state of our affairs.

"The finances would be in a satisfactory condition, were it not for the increased expense, which the present circumstances have required.

"Still we might answer the whole, if the sums to be received, included in the budget, could all be realised in the course of the year; and my minister of finance will turn your attention to the means of attaining this result.

"It is possible, that the first duty of a prince may soon call me, to fight for our country at the head of the children of the nation. The army and I will do our duty.

"Do you, peers and representatives, set the nation an example of confidence, energy, and patriotism: and, like the senate of the great people of antiquity, resolve rather to die, than to survive the dishonour and degradation of France. The sacred cause of our country will be triumphant!"

This speech, full of moderation and reason, made a profound impression on the assembly. Shouts of "Long live the Emperor!" much more numerous than had burst out at his arrival, were heard, and continued long after his departure.

The next day, the chamber of representatives was employed in drawing up its address.

An indiscreet admirer of Napoleon, after having observed, that flattery had decreed the surname of Desired to a prince, whom the nation had neither called nor expected, moved, that the title of Saviour should be decreed to Napoleon, who had come to save France from regal slavery. This ridiculous motion, smothered by ironical laughter, gave rise to a multitude of sarcasms and offensive reflections, which were reported to Napoleon, and which, without personally wounding him, for he had too high a sense of his glory, to think it affected by such clamours, injured him in the opinion of France.

Napoleon, like all great men, loved praise: public censure, when he thought it unjust, made no impression on him. This indifference did not arise from the pride of the diadem; it was the result of the contempt he felt for the judgment of men in general. "He was accustomed to look for the reward of the pains and labours of life only in the opinion of posterity."

The assembly rejected the adulatory proposal of M. *****; and in this it did right. But it did wrong, not to express its decision so as to soften what there was in it of harsh, unjust, and disagreeable to the Emperor, who had not provoked it.

This rudeness did not surprise him: experience had already convinced him, that the chamber would let no opportunity of vexing him escape it.

This chamber, notwithstanding, was composed entirely of partisans of the 20th of March: but all the deputies were not partisans of Napoleon, if they were of the revolution; some in consequence of personal enmity, others from remembrance of his despotism, and fear of its return.

The enemies of Napoleon, disguising their hatred under the cloak of a love of liberty, had insinuated themselves into the minds of the patriots; and, with the additional act in their hands, had drawn them into their ranks, under the apparent pretence of combating and bridling the incurable tyranny of the Emperor.

On the other hand, the friends of Napoleon, while they refused to join in this coalition, did not attempt to break it; because they inwardly dreaded the encroachments of the imperial power, and were not sorry to leave to others the task of opposing it.

Thus the whole assembly, though instigated by different motives, joined to set themselves in a state of hostile opposition to the head of the government; without perceiving, that this inconsiderate, unjust, and ill-timed opposition, would occasion anxiety, mistrust, and irresolution, in the minds of all; and destroy that national harmony, that union of interests, wills, and sentiments, the only source of strength to Napoleon, of safety to France.

Be this as it may, the chamber of deputies, after having spent two days in discussing the substance and style of its address, was admitted, as well as the chamber of peers, to appear at the foot of the throne.

The chamber of peers spoke first, and said:

"Sire; your readiness to subject to constitutional forms and rules that absolute power, which circumstances, and the confidence of the people, had imposed on you; the past guarantee given to the rights of the nation; the devotion, that leads you into the midst of the perils, which the army is about to brave; penetrate every heart with profound gratitude. The peers of France are come to offer to your Majesty the homage of this sentiment.

"You have manifested, Sire, principles, that are those of the nation: they must necessarily be ours. Yes, all power proceeds from the people, is instituted for the people; a constitutional monarchy is necessary for the French nation, as a guarantee of its liberty, and of its independence.

"Sire, while you shall be on the frontiers, at the head of the children of the country, the chamber of peers will concur with zeal in all the legislative measures, that circumstances may require, to compel foreigners to acknowledge the independence of the nation, and render the principles sanctioned by the will of the people triumphant at home.

"The interest of France is inseparable from yours. If fortune should deceive your efforts, disasters, Sire, will not weaken our perseverance, and would redouble our attachment to you.

"If success should correspond to the justice of our cause, and the hopes; we are accustomed to conceive from your genius and the valour of our armies, France desires no other fruit from it than peace. Our institutions are a pledge to Europe, that the French government can never be hurried on by the seductions of victory."

The Emperor answered:

"The contest in which we are engaged is serious. The ardour of prosperity is not the danger that threatens us at present. Foreigners are desirous of making us pass under the *Caudine forks*!

"The justice of our cause, the public spirit of the nation, and the courage of the army, are potent grounds, to hope for success; but, if we should experience disasters, then in particular I should wish, to see all the energy of this great people displayed; then I should find in the chamber of peers proofs of attachment to their country, and to myself.

"It is in times of difficulty, that great nations, like great men, display all the energy of their character, and become an object of admiration to posterity[33].

"Mr. President and gentlemen deputies of the chamber of peers, I thank you for the sentiments which you have expressed to me in the name of the chamber."

Count Lanjuinais, at the head of the deputation of the chamber of representatives, then delivered the following speech:

"Sire, the chamber of representatives received with profound emotion the words pronounced from the throne at the solemn sitting, when your Majesty, laying down the extraordinary power you were exercising, proclaimed the commencement of a constitutional monarchy.

"The principal bases of this monarchy, the guardian of the liberty, equality, and happiness of the people, have been acknowledged by your Majesty, who, voluntarily meeting every scruple, as well as every wish, has declared, that the care of collecting together our scattered constitutions, and arranging them in one whole, was among the most important occupations reserved for the legislature. Faithful to its mission, the chamber of representatives will fulfil the task that is devolved to it, in this noble work: it demands, that, to satisfy the will of the public, as well as the wishes of your Majesty, the deliberations of the nation shall rectify, as soon as possible, what the urgency of our situation may have produced defective, or left imperfect, in the whole of our constitutions.

"But at the same time, Sire, the chamber of representatives will not show itself less eager, to proclaim its sentiments and its principles with regard to the terrible conflict, that threatens to ensanguine the fields of Europe. After a series of disastrous events, invaded France appeared listened to for a moment on the establishment of its constitution, only to see itself almost immediately subjected to a royal charter, emanating from absolute power, to a system of reformation, in its nature always revocable....

"Resuming now the exercise of its rights; rallying round the hero, whom its confidence invests anew with the government of the state; France is astonished and grieved, to see sovereigns in arms demand of it the reason of an internal change, which is the result of the national will, and affects neither its existing connexions with other governments, nor their security. France cannot admit the distinctions, under which the coalized powers endeavour to cloak their aggression. To attack the monarch of its choice is to attack the independence of the nation. It is entirely in arms, to defend this independence; and to repel every family, and every prince, that they may dare wish to impose on it. No ambitious project enters into the thoughts of the French people: even the will of a victorious prince would be impotent, to carry the nation beyond the limits of its own defence. But to protect its territory, to maintain its liberty, its honour, its dignity, it is ready to make any sacrifice. Why are we not allowed, Sire, still to hope, that these preparations for war, caused perhaps by the irritations of pride, and by illusions that every day must weaken, will vanish before the want of a peace necessary to all the nations of Europe; and which would restore to your Majesty your consort, to the French the heir to the throne? But already blood has been shed: the signal of battles, prepared against the independence and liberty of the French, has been given in the name of a people, who carry to the highest point their zeal for independence and liberty. No doubt among the communications, which your Majesty has promised us, the chambers will find proofs of the efforts you have made, to maintain the peace of the world. If all these efforts must remain useless, may the calamities of the war fall on those, by whom it has been provoked!

"The chamber of deputies waits only for the documents, that have been announced to it, to concur with all its power in the measures, that the success of a war so legitimate may demand. It is eager, to be acquainted with the wants and resources of the state, in order to enunciate its wishes: and while your Majesty, opposing to the most unjust aggression the valour of our national armies, and the force of your genius, seeks in victory only the means of arriving at a durable peace, the chamber of representatives is persuaded, that it shall be proceeding toward the same end, by labouring unremittingly at the compact, the perfecting of which must cement still more closely the union between the people and the throne; and strengthen in the eyes of Europe the pledge of our engagements, by the improvement of our institutions."

The Emperor answered:

"I find with satisfaction my own sentiments, in those you express to me. Under our present weighty circumstances, my thoughts are absorbed by the imminent war, to the success of which are attached the honour and independence of France.

"I shall set out this night, to place myself at the head of my armies: the movements of the different corps of the enemy render my presence there indispensable. During my absence, I shall see with pleasure, that a committee named by each chamber is meditating on our constitution.

"The constitution is our rallying point: it should be our pole-star in this season of tempests. Every public discussion, that would tend, directly or indirectly, to diminish the confidence we ought to have in its arrangements, would be a misfortune to the state: we should find ourselves in the midst of shoals, without a compass, and without a chart. The crisis in which we are engaged is violent. Let us not imitate the example of the Lower Empire, which, pressed on all sides by the barbarians, rendered itself the laughing-stock of posterity, by engaging in abstract discussions, at the moment when the battering ram was bursting open the gates of the city.

"Independently of the legislative measures, which internal circumstances require, you will deem it useful perhaps, to occupy yourselves on regulating laws, calculated to render the constitution active. These may be subjects of your public labours without any inconvenience.

"Mr. President, and gentlemen deputies of the chamber of representatives, the sentiments expressed in your address sufficiently demonstrate the attachment of the chamber to my person, and all the patriotism, with which it is animated. In all events my course will ever be straight and firm. Assist me to save our country. The first representative of the people, I have contracted the obligation, which I renew, of employing, in times of greater tranquillity, all the prerogatives of the crown, and the little experience I have acquired, to second you in the improvement of our institutions."

The voice of Napoleon, naturally emphatic, gave prominence to the masculine thoughts, that sparkled throughout both these speeches: and when he arrived at this passage, "every public discussion, that would tend to diminish the confidence," &c.; and at this, "let us not imitate the Lower Empire;" he gave these salutary exhortations with a penetrating look, that made the instigators of discord cast down their eyes. The sound part of the representatives approved the Emperor's answer: the rest considered it as a lecture offensive to the dignity of the chamber. There are some men, who think they may be allowed to push remonstrance to insult, yet cannot listen to the most prudent and temperate advice, without being offended.

The Emperor set out, as he had announced, in the night of the 12th of May.

The question of deciding, whether he ought to be the first, to give the signal for hostilities, or not, had frequently recurred to his reflections.

By attacking the enemy, he had the advantage of engaging before the arrival of the Russians, and of carrying the war out of the French territories. If he were victorious, he might raise up Belgium, and detach from the coalition a part of the old confederation of the Rhine, and perhaps Austria.

By waiting to be attacked, he retained it in his power to choose his field of battle, to increase his means of resistance in an infinite degree, and of carrying the strength and devotion of his army to the highest pitch. An army of Frenchmen, fighting under the eyes of their mothers, their wives, and their children, for the preservation of their well-being, and in defence of the honour and independence of their country, would have been invincible. It was the latter alternative, to which Napoleon gave the preference: it agreed with the hope he involuntarily cherished of coming to an agreement with the foreign powers, and with his fear of gaining the ill-will of the chamber, if he commenced the war without previously exhausting all means of obtaining peace.

But Napoleon felt, that, to render a war national, all the citizens must be united in heart and will with their chief: and convinced, that the untoward disposition of the chamber would increase daily, and introduce division and trouble into the state, he resolved to commence the war; hoping, that fortune would favour his arms, and that victory would reconcile him to the deputies, or furnish him with the means of reducing them to order.

The Emperor entrusted the government during his absence to a council, composed of the fourteen persons following:

>Prince Joseph, president.
>
>Prince Lucien.
>
>*Ministers.*
>
>Prince Cambacérès.
>
>The prince of Eckmuhl.

The duke of Vicenza.

The duke of Gaëta.

The duke of Decrès.

The duke of Otranto.

Count Mollien.

Count Carnot.

Ministers of State [34].

Count Défermon.

Count Regnaud de St. Jean d'Angeli.

Count Boulay de la Meurthe.

Count Merlin.

He said to them: "To-night I set off: do your duty: the French army and I will do ours: I recommend to you union, zeal, and energy."

It appeared strange, in a representative monarchy, where responsibility bore hard on ministers, to see ministers of state, who were not responsible, associated in the government.

This was remarked to the Emperor, and he answered, that he had added ministers of state to the council, that they might be the interpreters of the government to the chamber of deputies; that he wished the ministers at the head of particular offices, to appear in this chamber as little as possible, as long as their constitutional education was incomplete; that they were not familiarized to the tribune[35]; that they might there disclose opinions or principles, without intending it, that government could not avow; and that it would be inconvenient and difficult, to contradict the words of a minister, while those of a minister of state might be disavowed, without implicating the government, or wounding its dignity.

Were these the only motives? I think not. He distrusted the perfidy of the Duke of Otranto, and the indifference of more ministers than one; and he was glad to find a reason, or a pretence, for introducing into the council of regency the four ministers of state, whose devotion and unshaken fidelity appeared to him an additional guarantee. When he made known his intention of commencing the war, the Duke of Vicenza solicited the favour of attending him to the army, "If I do not leave you at Paris," answered Napoleon, "on whom can I depend?" How much is expressed in these few words!

The day after his departure, the ministers of the interior and for foreign affairs repaired to the chamber of peers. M. Carnot laid before it a statement of the situation of the Emperor and the empire.

"His Majesty," said he, "enlightened by past events, has returned, having at heart the full desire and hope of preserving peace abroad, and of governing paternally at home....

"If the Emperor were less secure of the firmness of his character, and the purity of his resolutions, he might consider himself as placed between two shoals, the partisans of the expelled dynasty, and those of the *republican system*. But the former, having been unable to retain what they possessed, must be still less capable of seizing on it anew: the latter, undeceived by long experience, and bound by gratitude to the prince, who has been their deliverer, are become his most zealous defenders; their candour, as well known as their philanthropic ardour, surround the throne occupied by the august founder of a new dynasty, who glories in having issued from the ranks of the people."

After this declaration, to which the republican opinions of M. Carnot gave great weight, he entered into an examination of the several branches of the public administration in succession.

He disclosed the state, to which the calamities of the times, and the mismanagement of the regal government, had reduced the finances of the communes, the hospitals, religious worship, public works, mines, manufactures, commerce, and public instruction; and made known the system of improvement, which the Emperor had formed, and already commenced, to restore to the communes and hospitals their former resources, to public works their activity, to commerce its scope, to the university its lustre, to manufactures their prosperity, to the clergy that respect and easiness of circumstances, which it had forfeited through the persecutions, directed by it, at the instigation of the emigrants, against the pretended spoilers of their property.

When come to the war department, he announced, that the Emperor had re-established on its old foundations the army, the elements of which had been intentionally dispersed by the late government. That since the 20th of March our forces had been raised by voluntary enlistments, and the recall of the ancient soldiery, from a hundred thousand men, to three hundred and seventy-five thousand. That the imperial guard, the noblest ornament of France during peace, and its strongest rampart during war, would soon amount to forty thousand men. That the artillery, notwithstanding the twelve thousand six hundred pieces of ordnance delivered to the enemy by the fatal convention of the 23d of April, 1814, had risen from its ruins, and now reckoned a hundred batteries, and twenty thousand horses. That our disorganised arsenals had resumed their labours, and were replacing the army stores. That our manufactories of arms, lately abandoned and empty, had made or repaired four hundred thousand muskets in the course of two months. That a hundred and seventy fortified towns, or fortresses, both on the frontiers and in the interior, had been provisioned, repaired, and put into a condition, to resist an enemy. That the national guard, completely re-organised, had already supplied for the defence of the frontiers two hundred and forty battalions, or a hundred and fifty thousand men; and that the successive formation of the other battalions of flank companies would produce more than two hundred thousand men. That the volunteers in the walled towns, and the pupils of the Lyceums and *special* schools[36], had been formed into companies of artillery, and constituted a body of more than twenty-five thousand excellent gunners. So that eight hundred and fifty thousand Frenchmen would defend the independence, the liberty, and the honour of the country; while the sedentary national guards were preparing themselves in the interior, to furnish fresh resources for the triumph of the national cause.

In fine, after having taken a hasty view of the hostile dispositions of our enemies, of the interior disturbances they had excited, and of the means the Emperor had adopted to suppress them, M. Carnot concluded his report by expressing a wish, that the two chambers might soon bestow on France, in concert with the Emperor, those organising laws, which were necessary *to prevent licentiousness from assuming the place of liberty, and anarchy that of order.*

This report, in which M. Carnot did not totally conceal the apprehensions, with which the progress of that spirit of insubordination and demagogism, manifested by certain members of the chamber, inspired the Emperor and the nation, was immediately followed by one from the Duke of Vicenza, on the menacing dispositions of foreign powers, and the fruitless efforts, that the Emperor had made, to bring them to moderate and pacific sentiments. Their hostile resolutions he ascribed chiefly to the suggestions of the cabinet of London. He afterward made known the military preparations of the four great powers, the leagues renewed or recently formed against us, and concluded thus:

"To believe it possible, to maintain peace, at present, therefore, would be a dangerous blindness: war surrounds us on all sides, and it is on the field of battle alone, that peace can be regained by France. The English, the Prussians, the Austrians, are in line of battle; the Russians are in full march. It becomes a duty, to hasten the day of engagement, when too long hesitation might endanger the welfare of the state."

These two reports were presented to the chamber of deputies by ministers of state, at the same time when the ministers were making them known to the chamber of peers. Instead of impressing upon the representatives the necessity of frankly joining the Emperor, and, as one of them observed, of not entering into a contest with the government, at a moment when the blood of Frenchmen was about to be shed, they suggested to them only steril discussions of the impropriety of the connexion of ministers of state with the chamber, and of the urgency of appointing a committee, to remould the additional act. An immoderate desire of speechifying, and of making laws, had seized the greater number of the deputies: but a state is not to be saved by empty words, and schemes of a constitution. The Romans, when their country was in danger, instead of deliberating, suspended the sway of the laws, and gave themselves a dictator.

The next day, the 17th, a new report, made to the Emperor by the minister of police, on the moral state of France, was communicated to the two chambers.

"Sire," said this minister, "it is my duty, to tell you the whole truth. Our enemies are emboldened by instruments without, and supporters within. They wait only for a favourable moment, to realize the plan they conceived twenty years ago, and which during these twenty years has been continually frustrated, of uniting the camp of Jalès to Vendée, and seducing a part of the multitude into that confederacy which extends from the Mediterranean to the Channel.

"In this system, the plains on the left bank of the Loire, the population of which it is most easy to mislead, are the principal focus of the insurrection; which, by the help of the wandering bands of Britanny, is to spread into Normandy, where the vicinity of the islands, and the disposition of the coasts, will render communication more easy. On the other side it rests on the Cevennes, to extend thence to the banks of the Rhone by the revolts, that may be excited in some parts of Languedoc and Provence. Bordeaux has been the centre of the direction of these movements from the beginning.

"This plan is not abandoned. Nay more: the party has been increased, at every change in our revolution, by all the malecontents, that events have produced; by all the factious, that a certainty of amnesty has encouraged; and by all the ambitious, who have been desirous of acquiring some political importance in the changes they foreboded.

"...... It is this party, that now disturbs the interior. Marseilles, Toulouse, and Bordeaux, are agitated by it. Marseilles, where the spirit of sedition animates even the lowest classes of the population; where the laws have been disregarded: Toulouse, which seems still under the influence of that revolutionary organisation, which was imparted to it some months ago: Bordeaux, where all the germs of revolt are deposited, and intensely fermenting.

"It is this party, which by false alarms, false hopes, distribution of money, and the employment of threats, has succeeded in stirring up peaceable agriculturists, throughout the territory included between the Loire, la Vendée, the ocean, and the Rhone. Arms and ammunition have been landed there. The hydra of rebellion revives, re-appears wherever it formerly exercised its ravages, and is not destroyed by our successes at St. Gilles and Aisenay. On the other side of the Loire, bands are desolating the department of Morbihan, and some parts of those of Isle and Vilaine, the Coasts of the North, and Sarthe. They have invaded in a moment the towns of Aurai, Rhedon, and Ploermel, and the plains of Mayenne as far as the gates of Laval; they stop the soldiers and sailors, that are recalled; they disarm the land-holders; increase their numbers by peasants, whom they compel to march with them; pillage the public treasures, annihilate the instruments of administration, threaten the persons in office, seize the stage coaches, stop the couriers, and for a moment intercepted the communication between Mans and Angers, Angers and Nantes, Nantes and Rennes, and Rennes and Vannes.

"On the borders of the Channel, Dieppe and Havre have been agitated by seditious commotions. Throughout the whole of the 15th division, the battalions of the national militia have been formed only with the greatest difficulty. The soldiers and sailors have refused, to answer their call; and have obeyed it only by compulsion. Caen has twice been disturbed by the resistance of the royalists; and in some of the circles of the Orne bands are formed as in Britanny and Mayenne.

"In fine, all kinds of writings, that can discourage the weak, embolden the factious, shake confidence, divide the nation, bring the government into contempt; all the pamphlets, that issue from the printing-offices of Belgium, or the clandestine presses of France; all that the foreign newspapers publish against us, all that the party-writers compose; are distributed, hawked about, and diffused with impunity, for want of restrictive laws, and from the abuse of the liberty of the press.

"Firm in the system of moderation, which your Majesty had adopted, you have thought it right, to wait for the meeting of the chambers, that legal precautions only might be opposed to manœuvres, which by the ordinary course of law are not always punishable, and which it could neither foresee, nor prevent......"

The Duke of Otranto, entering on the subject, then discussed the laws, which, issued under analogous circumstances, might have been applied on the present occasion; and, as these laws appeared to him, impolitic, dangerous, and inadequate, he concluded, that it was indispensable for the chambers, immediately to set about framing new laws, which were necessary to check the licentiousness of the press, and circumscribe personal liberty, till internal peace and order were restored.

This report did not make the impression, that might have been expected from it. The deputies, accurately acquainted with what was passing in their departments, knew, that facts had been misrepresented. They persuaded themselves, that the melancholy picture of the situation of France, presented to them by M. Fouché, had been drawn up by order of the Emperor, with the view to alarm them, and render them more docile to his will.

The separate committees of the chamber rung with the contradictions, more or less direct, that each representative gave to the assertions of the minister. One of the members of the deputation from Calvados, would not rest satisfied with this civil way of giving him the lie, but declared openly from the tribune, that the agents of the minister had deceived their principal, by describing to him a personal quarrel of no consequence, and quelled on the spot, as a general insurrection of the royalists. They might have spared themselves the trouble of telling M. Fouché, that his report exaggerated the truth, and transformed private occurrences into public events: he knew this. Already devoted to the cause of the Bourbons, he had intentionally distorted facts, with the design of giving hope and consistency to the royalists, and of intimidating, cooling, and dividing, the partisans of Napoleon[37].

The chamber, instead of occupying itself on laws and measures for promoting the public safety, the introduction of which had been referred to them, left to the minister the task of proposing them. It preferred the resumption of its discussions on its favourite subject, the additional act; and I shall leave it, to waste its time in abstract dissertations, while I return to Napoleon.

The Emperor, who set out on the 12th at three in the morning, had gone over the fortifications of Soissons and Laon in his way, and arrived at Avesnes on the 13th. His anxious thoughts were incessantly turned toward Paris. Placed as it were between two fires, he seemed less to dread the enemies he had before him, than those he left behind.

On the 14th of June the whole of his forces amounted to three hundred thousand men; of which only a hundred and fifty thousand infantry, and thirty-five thousand cavalry, were in a state to take the field.

These hundred and eighty-five thousand men he had formed into four armies, and four corps of observation.

The first, under the name of the grand army, was intended to act immediately under his own orders. This was subdivided into five principal corps, commanded

The 1st by Count d'Erlon;

The 2d by Count Reille;

The 3d by Count Vandamme;

The 4th by Count Gérard;

The 5th (called the 6th) by Count de Lobau[38]:

And into a corps of cavalry commanded by Marshal Grouchy.

This army, exclusive of the imperial guard, which was 4500 horse, and 14,000 foot, amounted to a hundred thousand men, or thereabouts, of whom sixteen thousand were cavalry.

The second, entitled the army of the Alps, was commanded by Marshal the Duke of Albuféra. It was to occupy the passes of Italy, and the border country of the Pays de Gex. Its strength might be twelve thousand men.

The third, styled the army of the Rhine, had at its head General Count Rapp; and its business was, to protect the frontiers of Alsace. It was estimated at eighteen thousand men.

The fourth, called the army of the West, was employed in La Vendée; and, after that country was quieted, it was to be incorporated in the grand army. It consisted of seventeen thousand men; and General Lamarque was its commander-in-chief.

The first corps of observation, stationed at Béford, was commanded by General Lecourbe. It had to defend the passages from Switzerland, and Franche Comté; and to form a communication, according to circumstances, by its left with the army of the Alps, or by its right with the army of the Rhine[39].

The other three corps, the commanders of which were Marshal Brune at Marseilles, General Clausel at Bordeaux, and General Decaen at Toulouse, were to maintain the tranquillity of the country; and, in case of need, to oppose any invasion, that the Spaniards might attempt on the one side, or the Piedmontese and English on the other.

These four corps of observation amounted together to about twenty thousand men.

They were to be supported and reinforced by ten thousand soldiers, and fifty thousand national guards receiving pay.

The two armies of the Rhine and of the Alps were to be the same, fifty thousand men of the line, and a hundred thousand chasseurs and grenadiers of the national guard.

In fine, the army commanded by the Emperor in person was to be augmented by a hundred thousand national guards, who would have been stationed in a second line; and by sixty thousand regulars, who, as well as those mentioned above, were daily forming in the *dépôts*.

All these resources, when they should be disposable, and they might be before the end of the campaign, would have mounted the strength of the acting army to more than three hundred thousand fighting men; and that of the army of reserve, namely the national guards in the second line, or in the fortified towns, to four hundred thousand men. They would have been recruited, the first by levies from the conscriptions of 1814 and 1815; the second, by calling into service fresh battalions of the flank companies.

The whole army was superb, and full of ardour: but the Emperor, more a slave, than could have been believed, to his remembrances and habitudes, committed the fault of replacing it under the command of its former chiefs. Most of these, notwithstanding their addresses to the King, had not ceased to pray for the triumph of the imperial cause; yet they did not appear disposed to serve it with the ardour and devotion, that circumstances demanded. They were not now the men, who, full of youth and ambition, were generously prodigal of their lives, to acquire rank and fame; they were men tired of war, and who, having reached the summit of promotion, and being enriched by the spoils of the enemy or the bounty of Napoleon, had no further wish, than peaceably to enjoy their good fortune under the shade of their laurels.

The colonels and generals, who entered on their career subsequent to them, murmured at finding themselves placed under their tutelage. The soldiers themselves were dissatisfied: but this dissatisfaction did not abate their confidence of victory, for Napoleon was at their head[40].

On the 14th the Emperor directed the following proclamation, to be issued in the orders of the day.

"Avesnes, June 14, 1815.

"Soldiers,

"This is the anniversary of Marengo and of Friedland, which twice decided the fate of Europe: then, as after Austerlitz, as after Wagram, we were too generous! We trusted to the protestations and oaths of the princes, whom we left on the throne! Now, however, in coalition against us, they aim at the independence and the most sacred rights of France, They have commenced the most unjust of aggressions. Let us then march to meet them: are not they and we still the same men?

"Soldiers, at Jena, against these same Prussians, now so arrogant, you were but one to three, and at Montmirail one to six! Let those among you, who were prisoners to the English, give you an account of their hulks (*pontons*), and of the dreadful miseries they endured.

"The Saxons, the Belgians, the Hanoverians, the soldiers of the confederation of the Rhine, groan at being obliged to lend their arms to the cause of princes, who are enemies to justice, and to the rights common to all people. They know, that this coalition is insatiate. After having devoured twelve millions of Polanders, twelve millions of Italians, a million of Saxons, six millions of Belgians, it would devour all the states of the second order in Germany.

"Madmen! a moment of prosperity has blinded them. The oppression and humiliation of the French people are out of their power! If they enter France, they will find in it their graves.

"Soldiers, we have forced marches to make, battles to fight, hazards to run; but, with firmness, victory will be ours: the rights, the honour, and the happiness of our country will be reconquered.

"To every Frenchman, who has any heart, the moment is come, to conquer or die!"

The plan of the campaign adopted by the Emperor was worthy the courage of the French, and the high reputation of their chief.

Information given by a hand to be depended upon, and agents furnished by the Duke of Otranto[41], had made known the position of the allies in all its particulars. Napoleon knew, that the army of Wellington was dispersed over the country from the borders of the sea to Nivelles: that the right of the Prussians rested on Charleroy; and that the rest of their army was stationed in échélon indefinitely as far as the Rhine. He judged, that the enemies' lines were too much extended; and that it would be practicable for him, by not giving them time to close up, to separate the two armies, and fall in succession on their troops thus surprised.

For this purpose he had united all his cavalry into a single body of twenty thousand horse, with which he intended to dart like lightning into the midst of the enemies' cantonments.

If victory favoured this bold stroke, the centre of our army would occupy Brussels on the second day, while the corps of the right and of the left drove the Prussians to the Meuse, and the English to the Scheldt. Belgium being conquered, he would have armed the malecontents, and marched from success to success as far as the Rhine, where he would have solicited peace anew.

On the 14th, in the night, our army, the presence of which the Emperor had taken care to conceal, was to commence its march: nothing indicated, that the enemy had foreseen our irruption, and every thing promised us grand results; when Napoleon was informed, that General Bourmont, Colonels Clouet and Villoutreys, and two other officers, had just deserted to the enemy.

He knew from Marshal Ney, that M. de Bourmont, at the time of the occurrences at Besançon, had shown some hesitation, and was backward to employ him. But M. de Bourmont, having given General Gérard his word of honour, to serve the Emperor faithfully; and this general, whom Napoleon highly valued, having answered for Bourmont; the Emperor consented, to admit him into the service. How could he have supposed, that this officer, who had covered himself with glory in 1814, would, in 1315, go over to the enemy on the eve of a battle?

Napoleon immediately made such alterations in his plan of attack, as this unexpected treason rendered necessary, and then marched forward.

On the 15th, at one in the morning, he was in person at Jumiguan on the Eure.

At three, his army moved in three columns, and debouched suddenly at Beaumont, Maubeuge, and Philippeville.

A corps of infantry, under General Ziethen, attempted to dispute the passage of the Sambre. The fourth corps of chasseurs, supported by the ninth, broke it sword in hand, and took three hundred prisoners. The sappers and mariners of the guard, sent after the enemy, to repair the bridges, did not allow them time to destroy them. They followed them as sharp shooters, and penetrated with them into the great square. The brave Pajol soon arrived with his cavalry, and Charleroy was ours. The inhabitants, happy at seeing the French once more, saluted them unanimously with continued shouts of "Long live the Emperor! France for ever!"

General Pajol immediately sent the hussars of General Clary in pursuit of the Prussians, and this brave regiment finished its day by the capture of a standard, and the destruction of a battalion, that ventured to resist it.

During this time, the second corps passed the Sambre at Marchiennes, and overthrew every thing before it. The Prussians, having at length rallied, attempted to oppose some resistance to it; but General Reille broke them with his light cavalry, took two hundred prisoners, and killed or dispersed the rest. Beaten in every part, they retired to the heights of Fleurus, which had been so fatal to the enemies of France twenty years before[42].

Napoleon reconnoitred the ground at a glance. Our troops rushed on the Prussians full gallop. Three squares of infantry, supported by several squadrons and some artillery, sustained the shock with intrepidity. Wearied of their immoveableness, the Emperor ordered General Letort, to charge them at the head of the dragoons of the guard. At the same moment General Excelmans fell upon the left flank of the enemy; and the twentieth of dragoons, commanded by the brave and young Briqueville, rushed on the Prussians on one side, while Letort attacked them on the other. They were broken, annihilated; but they sold us the victory dear: Letort was killed.

This affair, of little importance in its results, for it cost the enemy only five pieces of artillery, and three thousand men killed or taken prisoners, produced the happiest effects on the army. The sciatica of Marshal Mortier[43], and the treason of General Beaumont, had given birth to sentiments of doubt and fear, which were entirely dissipated by the successful issue of this first battle.

Hitherto each chief of a corps had retained its immediate command, and it is easy to suppose, what their ardour and emulation must have been: but the Emperor fell into the error of overturning the hopes of their courage and their ambition; he placed General Erlon and Count Reille under the orders of Marshal Ney, whom he brought forward too late; and Count Gérard, and Count Vandamme, under those of Marshal Grouchy, whom it would have been better to have left at the head of the cavalry.

On the 16th, in the morning, the army, thus distributed, occupied the following positions.

Marshal Ney, with the 1st and 2d corps, the cavalry of General Lefevre-Desnouettes, and that of General Kellerman, had his advanced guard at Frasnes, and the other troops disseminated round Gosselies[44].

Marshal Grouchy, with the 3d and 4th corps, and the cavalry of Generals Pajol, Excelmans, and Milhaud, was placed on the heights of Fleurus, and in advance of them.

The 6th corps and the guard were in échélon between Fleurus and Charleroi.

The same day the army of Marshal Blucher, ninety thousand strong, collected together with great skill, was posted on the heights of Bry and Sombref, and occupied the villages of Ligny and St. Amand, which protected his front. His cavalry extended far in advance on the road to Namur[45].

The army of the Duke of Wellington, which this general had not yet had time to collect, was composed of about a hundred thousand men scattered between Ath, Nivelle, Genappe, and Brussels.

The Emperor went in person, to reconnoitre Blucher's position; and penetrating his intentions, resolved to give him battle, before his reserves, and the English army, for which he was endeavouring to wait, should have time to unite, and come and join him.

He immediately sent orders to Marshal Ney, whom he supposed to have been on the march for Quatre Bras, *where he would have found very few forces*, to drive the English briskly before him, and then fall with his main force on the rear of the Prussian army.

At the same time he made a change in the front of the imperial army: General Grouchy advanced toward Sombref, General Gérard toward Ligny, and General Vandamme toward St. Amand.

General Gérard, with his division, five thousand strong, was detached from the 2d corps, and placed in the rear of General Vandamme's left, so as to support him, and at the same time form a communication between Marshal Ney's army and that of Napoleon.

The guard, and Milhaud's cuirassiers, were disposed as a reserve in advance of Fleurus.

At three o'clock the 3d corps reached St. Amand, and carried it. The Prussians, rallied by Blucher, retook the village. The French, entrenched in the churchyard, defended themselves there with obstinacy; but, overpowered by numbers, they were about to give way, when General Drouot, who has more than once decided the fate of a battle, galloped up with four batteries of the guard, took the enemy in the rear, and stopped his career.

At the same moment Marshal Grouchy was fighting successfully at Sombref, and General Gérard made an impetuous attack on the village of Ligny. Its embattled walls, and a long ravine, rendered the approaches to it not less difficult than dangerous: but these obstacles did not intimidate General Lefol, or the brave fellows under his command; they advanced with the bayonet, and in a few minutes the Prussians, repulsed and annihilated, quitted the ground.

Marshal Blucher, conscious that the possession of Ligny rendered us masters of the event of the battle, returned to the charge with chosen troops: and here, to use his own words, "commenced a battle, that may be considered as one of the most obstinate mentioned in history." For five hours two hundred pieces of ordnance deluged the field with slaughter, blood, and death. For five hours the French and Prussians, alternately vanquished and victors, disputed this ensanguined post hand to hand, and foot to foot, and seven times in succession was it taken and lost.

The Emperor expected every instant, that Marshal Ney was coming to take part in the action. From the commencement of the affair, he had reiterated his orders to him, to manœuvre so as to surround the right of the Prussians; and he considered this diversion of such high importance, as to write to the marshal, and cause him to be repeatedly told, *that the fate of France was in his hands.* Ney answered, that "he had the whole of the English army to encounter, yet he would promise him, to hold out the whole day, but nothing more." The Emperor, better informed, assured him, "that it was Wellington's advanced guard alone, that made head against him;" and ordered him anew, "to beat back the English, and make himself master of Quatre Bras, cost what it might." The marshal persisted in his fatal error. Napoleon, deeply impressed with the importance of the movement, that Marshal Ney refused to comprehend and execute, sent directly to the first corps an order, to move with all speed on the right of the Prussians; but, after having lost much valuable time in waiting for it, he judged, that the battle could not be prolonged without danger, and directed General Gérard, who had with him but five thousand men, to undertake the movement, which should have been accomplished by the twenty thousand men of Count Erlon; namely, to turn St Amand, and fall on the rear of the enemy.

This manœuvre, ably executed, and seconded by the guard attacking in front, and by a brilliant charge of the cuirassiers of General Delore's brigade and of the horse grenadier guards, decided the victory. The Prussians, weakened in every part, retired in disorder, and left us, with the field of battle, forty cannons and several standards.

On the left, Marshal Ney, instead of rushing rapidly on Quatre Bras, and effecting the diversion, that had been recommended to him, had spent twelve hours in useless attempts, and given time to the Prince of Orange to reinforce his advanced guard. The pressing orders of Napoleon not allowing him, to remain meditating any longer; and desirous, no doubt, of repairing the time he had lost; he did not cause either the position or the forces of the enemy, to be thoroughly reconnoitred, and rushed on them headlong. The division of General Foy commenced the attack, and drove in the sharpshooters, and the advanced posts. Bachelu's cavalry, aided, covered, and supported by this division, pierced and cut to pieces three Scotch battalions: but the arrival of fresh reinforcements, led by the Duke of Wellington, and the shining bravery of the Scotch, the Belgians, and the Prince of Orange, suspended our success. This resistance, far from discouraging Marshal Ney, revived in him an energy, which he had not before shown. He attacked the Anglo-Hollanders with fury; and drove them back to the skirts of the wood of Bassu. The 1st of chasseurs and 6th of lancers overthrew the Brunswickers; the 8th of cuirassiers defeated two

Scotch battalions, and took from them a flag. The 11th, equally intrepid, pursued them to the entrance of the wood: but the wood, which had not been examined, was lined with English infantry. Our cuirassiers were assailed by a fire at arm's length, which at once carried dismay and confusion into their ranks. Some of the officers, lately incorporated with them, instead of appeasing the disorder, increased it by shouts of "Every one for himself (*sauve qui peut!*)" This disorder, which in a moment spread from one to another as far as Beaumont, might have occasioned greater disasters, if the infantry of General Foy, remaining unshaken, had not continued to sustain the conflict with equal perseverance and intrepidity.

Marshal Ney, who had with him only twenty thousand men, was desirous of causing the first corps, which he had left in the rear, to advance: but the Emperor, as I have said above, had sent immediate orders to Count Erlon, who commanded it, to come and join him, and this general had commenced his march. Ney, when he heard this, was amid a cross fire from the enemy's batteries. "Do you see those bullets?" exclaimed he, his brow clouded with despair: "I wish they would all pass through my body.". Instantly he sent with all speed after Count Erlon, and directed him, whatever orders he might have received from the Emperor himself, to return, Count Erlon was so unfortunate and weak as to obey. He brought his troops back to the marshal; but it was nine o'clock in the evening, and the marshal, dispirited by the checks he had received, and dissatisfied with himself, and others, had discontinued the engagement.

The Duke of Wellington, whose forces had increased successively to more than fifty thousand men, retired in good order during the night to Genappe.

Marshal Ney was indebted to the great bravery of his troops, and the firmness of his generals, for the honour of not being obliged, to abandon his positions.

The desperation, with which this battle was fought, made those men shudder, who were most habituated to contemplate with coolness the horrors of war. The smoking ruins of Ligny and St. Amand were heaped with the dead and dying: the ravine before Ligny resembled a river of blood, on which carcasses were floating: at Quatre Bras there was a similar spectacle! the hollow way, that skirted the wood, had disappeared under the bloody corses of the brave Scotch and of our cuirassiers. The imperial guard was every where distinguished by its murderous rage: it fought with shouts of "The Emperor for ever! No quarter!" The corps of General Gérard displayed the same animosity. It was this, that, having expended all its ammunition, called out aloud for more cartridges and more Prussians.

The loss of the Prussians, rendered considerable by the tremendous fire of our artillery, was twenty-five thousand men. Blucher, unhorsed by our cuirassiers, escaped them only by a miracle.

The English and Dutch lost four thousand five hundred men. Three Scotch regiments, and the black legion of Brunswick, were almost entirely exterminated. The Prince of Brunswick himself, and a number of other officers of distinction, were killed.

We lost, in the left wing, near five thousand men, and several generals. Prince Jerome, who had already been wounded at the passage of the Sambre, had his hand slightly grazed by a musket shot. He remained constantly at the head of his division, and displayed a great deal of coolness and valour.

Our loss at Ligny, estimated at six thousand five hundred men, was rendered still more to be regretted by General Gérard's receiving a mortal wound. Few officers were endued with a character so noble, and an intrepidity so habitual. More greedy of glory than of wealth, he possessed nothing but his sword; and his last moments, instead of resting with delight on the remembrance of his heroic actions alone, were disturbed by the pain of leaving his family exposed to want.

The victory of Ligny did not entirely fulfil the expectations of the Emperor. "If Marshal Ney," said he, "had attacked the English with all his forces, he would have crushed them, and have come to give the Prussians the finishing blow: and if, after having committed this first fault, he had not been guilty of his second folly, in preventing the movement of Count Erlon, the intervention of the 1st corps would have shortened the resistance of Blucher, and rendered his defeat irreparable: his whole army would have been taken or destroyed."

This victory, though imperfect, was not the less considered by the generals as of the highest importance. It separated the English army from the Prussians, and left us hopes of being able to vanquish it in its turn.

The Emperor, *without losing time,* was for attacking the English on one side at daybreak, and pursuing Blucher's army without respite on the other. It was objected to him, that the English army was intact, and ready to accept battle; while our troops, harassed by the conflicts and fatigue of Ligny, would not perhaps be in a condition, to fight with the necessary vigour. In fine, such numerous objections were made, that he consented to let the army take rest. Ill success inspires timidity. If Napoleon, as of old, had listened only to the suggestions of his own audacity, it is probable, it is certain, and I have heard General Drouot say it, that he might, according to his plan, have led his troops to Brussels on the 17th; *and who can calculate what would have been the consequences of his occupying that capital?*

On the 17th therefore, the Emperor contented himself with forming his army into two columns; one of sixty-five thousand men, headed by the Emperor, after having joined to it the left wing, followed the steps of the English. The light artillery, the lancers of General Alphonse Colbert, and of the intrepid Colonel Sourd, kept close after them to the entrance of the forest of Soignes, where the Duke of Wellington took up his position.

The other, thirty-six thousand strong, was detached under the orders of Marshal Grouchy, to observe and pursue the Prussians. It did not proceed beyond Gembloux.

The night of the 17th was dreadful, and seemed to presage the calamities of the day. A violent and incessant rain did not allow the army, to take a single moment's rest. To increase our misfortunes, the bad state of the roads retarded the arrival of our provision, and most of the soldiers were without food: however, they gaily endured this double ill luck; and at daybreak announced to Napoleon by repeated acclamations, that they were ready to fly to a fresh victory.

The Emperor had thought, that Lord Wellington, separated from the Prussians, and foreseeing the march of General Grouchy, who, on passing the Dyle, might fall on his flank, or on his rear, would not venture to maintain his position, but would retire to Brussels[46]. He was surprised, when daylight discovered to him, that the English army had not quitted its positions, and appeared disposed, to accept battle. He made several generals reconnoitre these positions; and, to use the words of one of them, he learned, that they were defended "by an army of cannons, and mountains of infantry."

Napoleon immediately sent advice to Marshal Grouchy, that he was probably about to engage in a grand battle with the English, and ordered him, to push the Prussians briskly, to approach the grand army as speedily as possible, and to direct his movements so as to be able to connect his operations with it[47].

He then sent for his principal officers, to give them his instructions.

Some of them, confident and daring, asserted, that the enemy's position should be attacked and carried by main force. Others, not less brave, but more prudent, remonstrated, that the ground was deluged by the rain; that the troops, the cavalry in particular, could not manœuvre without much difficulty and fatigue; that the English army would have the immense advantage of awaiting us on firm ground in its intrenchments; and that it would be better, to endeavour to turn these. All did justice to the valour of our troops, and promised, that they would perform prodigies; but they differed in opinion with regard to the resistance, that the English would make. Their cavalry, said the generals who had fought in Spain, are not equal to ours; but their infantry are more formidable, than is supposed. When intrenched, they are dangerous from their skill in firing: in the open field, they stand firm, and, if broken, rally again within a hundred yards and return to the charge. Fresh disputes arose; and, what is remarkable, *i never entered into any one's head*, that the Prussians, pretty numerous parties of whom had been seen towards Moustier, might be in a situation to make a serious diversion on our right.

The Emperor, after having heard and debated the opinions of all, determined, on considerations to which all assented, to attack the English in front. Reiterated orders were despatched to Marshal Grouchy; and Napoleon, to give him time to execute the movement he had enjoined, spent the whole morning in arranging his army.

The English army was reconnoitred anew by the Emperor in person. Its central position, resting on the village of Mont St. Jean, was supported on the right by the farm of Hougoumont, on the left by that of La Haie Sainte. Its two wings extended beyond the hamlets of Terre la Haie and Merkebraine. Hedges, woods, ravines, an immense quantity of artillery, and eighty-five or ninety thousand men, defended this formidable position.

The Emperor disposed his army[48] in the following order.

The 2d corps, of which Prince Jerome always made a part, was posted opposite the woods, that surrounded Hougoumont.

The 1st corps opposite La Haie Sainte.

The 6th corps was sent to the extremity of the right, so as to be able to form a communication with Marshal Grouchy, when he should appear.

The light cavalry and cuirassiers were flanked in a second line, behind the first and second corps.

The guard and cavalry were kept in reserve on the heights of Planchenois.

The old division of General Gérard was left at Fleurus.

The Emperor, with his staff, took his station on a little knap, near the farm of La Belle Alliance, which commanded the plain, and whence he could easily direct the movements of the army, and observe those of the English.

At half after twelve, the Emperor, persuaded that Marshal Grouchy must be in motion, caused the signal for battle to be given.

Prince Jerome, with his division, proceeded against Hougoumont. The approaches were defended by hedges and a wood; in which the enemy had posted a number of artillery. The attack, rendered so difficult by the state of the ground, was conducted with extreme impetuosity. The wood was alternately taken and retaken. Our troops and the English, most frequently separated by a single hedge, fired on each other reciprocally, their muskets almost touching, without retreating a single step. The artillery made fearful ravages on both sides. The event was doubtful, till General Reille ordered Foy's division to support the attack of Prince Jerome, and thus succeeded in compelling the enemy, to abandon the woods and orchards, which they had hitherto so valiantly defended and kept possession of.

It was one o'clock. A few moments before, an intercepted despatch informed the Emperor of the near approach of thirty thousand Prussians, commanded by Bulow[49].

Napoleon thought, that the strength of this corps, some of the skirmishers of which had appeared on the heights of St. Lambert, was exaggerated; and persuaded too, that Grouchy's army was following it, and that it would soon find itself between two fires, it gave him but little uneasiness. However, rather from precaution than from fear, he gave orders to General Domont, to advance with his cavalry and that of General Suberwick, to meet the Prussians and directed Count de Lobau, to be ready to support General Domont in case of necessity. Orders were despatched at the same time to Marshal Grouchy, to inform him of what was passing, and enjoin him *anew*, to hasten his march, to pursue, attack, and crush Bulow.

Thus by drawing off the divisions of Domont and Suberwick, and by the paralyzation of the 6th corps, our army was reduced to less than fifty-seven thousand men: but it displayed so much resolution, that the Emperor did not doubt its being sufficient, to beat the English.

The second corps, as I have already said, had effected the dislodgment of the English from the woods of Hougoumont; but the first corps, notwithstanding the continual play of several batteries, and the resolution of our infantry and of the light horse of General Lefevre Desnouettes and Guyot, had been unable to force either La Haie Sainte, or Mont St. Jean. The Emperor ordered Marshal Ney, to undertake a fresh attack, and to support it by eighty pieces of cannon. A tremendous fire of musketry and artillery then took place throughout the whole line. The English, insensible to danger, supported the charges of our foot and of our horse with great firmness. The more resistance they displayed, the more furiously did our soldiers engage. At length the English, driven from one position to another, evacuated La Haie Sainte and Mont St. Jean, and our troops seized on them with shouts of "Long live the Emperor!"

To sustain them there, Count d'Erlon immediately sent the second brigade of General Alix. A body of English horse intercepted the passage, threw the brigade into disorder, and then, falling on our batteries, succeeded in dismounting several pieces of artillery. The cuirassiers of General Milhaud set off at a gallop, to repulse the English horse. A fresh division of these came and fell upon our cuirassiers. Our lancers and chasseurs were sent to their assistance. A general charge ensued, and the English, broken, overthrown, cut down, were forced to retire in disorder.

Hitherto the French army, or, to speak more properly, the forty thousand men of Generals Reille and d'Erlon, had obtained and preserved a marked superiority. The enemy, driven back, appeared hesitating on their movements. Dispositions had been observed, that seemed to indicate an approaching retreat. The Emperor, satisfied, joyfully exclaimed: "They are ours: I have them:" and Marshal Soult, and all the generals, considered, as he did, the victory certain[50]. The guard had already received orders to put itself in motion, to occupy the ground we had gained, and finish the enemy, when General Domont sent to inform the Emperor, that Bulow's corps had just formed in line, and was advancing rapidly on the rear of our right. This information changed the design of Napoleon; and, instead of employing his guard to support the first and second corps, he kept it in reserve; ordering Marshal Ney to maintain his ground in the woods of Hougoumont, at La Haie Sainte, and at Mont St. Jean, till the event of the movement, which Count Lobau was about to make against the Prussians, was known.

The English, informed of the arrival of Bulow, resumed the offensive; and endeavoured to drive us from the positions, that we had taken from them. Our troops repulsed them victoriously. Marshal Ney, carried away by his boiling courage, forgot the orders of the Emperor. He charged the enemy at the head of Milhaud's cuirassiers and the light cavalry of the guard, and succeeded, amid the applauses of the army, in establishing himself on the heights of Mont St. Jean, till then inaccessible.

This ill-timed and hazardous movement did not escape the Duke of Wellington. He caused his infantry to advance, and fell upon us with all his cavalry.

The Emperor immediately ordered General Kellerman and his cuirassiers, to hasten to extricate our first line. The horse grenadiers and dragoons of the guard, either from a misconception of Marshal Ney, or spontaneously, put themselves in motion, and followed the cuirassiers, without its being possible to stop them. A second conflict, more bloody than the first, took place at all points. Our troops, exposed to the incessant fire of the enemy's batteries and infantry, heroically sustained and executed numerous brilliant charges during two hours, in which we had the glory of taking six flags, dismounting several batteries, and cutting to pieces four regiments; but in which we also lost the flower of our intrepid cuirassiers, and of the cavalry of the guard.

The Emperor, whom this desperate engagement vexed to the heart, could not remedy it. Grouchy did not arrive: and he had already been obliged to weaken his reserves by four thousand of the young guard, in order to master the Prussians, whose numbers and whose progress were still increasing.

Mean time our cavalry, weakened by a considerable loss, and unequal contests incessantly renewed, began to be disheartened, and to give ground. The issue of the battle appeared to become doubtful. It was necessary to strike a grand blow by a desperate attack.

The Emperor did not hesitate.

Orders were immediately given to Count Reille, to collect all his forces, and to fall with impetuosity on the right of the enemy, while Napoleon in person proceeded, to attack the front with his reserves. The Emperor had already formed his guard into a column of attack, when he heard, that our cavalry had just been forced, to evacuate in part the heights of Mont St. Jean. Immediately he ordered Marshal Ney, to take with him four battalions of the middle guard, and hasten with all speed to the fatal height, to support the cuirassiers by whom it was still occupied.

The firm countenance of the guard, and the harangues of Napoleon, inflamed their minds: the cavalry, and a few battalions, who had followed his movement to the rear, faced about towards the enemy, shouting "The Emperor for ever!"

At this moment the firing of musketry was heard[51]. "There's Grouchy!" exclaimed the Emperor: "the day is ours!" Labedoyère flew to announce this happy news to the army: in spite of the enemy, he penetrated to the head of our columns: "Marshal Grouchy is arriving, the guard is going to charge: courage! courage! 'tis all over with the English."

One last shout of hope burst from every rank: the wounded, who were still capable of taking a few steps, returned to the combat; and thousands of voices eagerly repeated, "Forward! forward!"

The column commanded by the bravest of the brave, on his arrival in face of the enemy, was received by discharges of artillery, that occasioned it a terrible loss. Marshal Ney, weary of bullets, ordered the batteries to be carried by the bayonet. The grenadiers rushed on them with such impetuosity, that they neglected the admirable order, to which they had been so often indebted for victory. Their leader, intoxicated with intrepidity, did not perceive this disorder. He and his soldiers rushed on the enemy tumultuously. A shower of balls and grape burst on their heads. Ney's horse was shot under him, Generals Michel and Friant fell wounded or dead, and a number of brave fellows were stretched on the ground. Wellington did not allow our grenadiers time to recollect themselves. He caused them to be attacked in flank by his cavalry, and compelled them to retire in the greatest disorder. At the same instant the thirty thousand Prussians under Ziethen, who had been taken for Grouchy's army, carried by assault the village of La Haye, and drove our men before them. Our cavalry, our infantry, already staggered by the defeat of the middle guard, were afraid of being cut off, and precipitately retreated. The English horse, skilfully availing themselves of the confusion, which this unexpected retreat had occasioned, pierced through our ranks, and rendered them completely disordered and disheartened. The other troops of the right, who continued to resist with great difficulty the attacks of the Prussians, and who had been in want of ammunition above an hour, seeing some of our squadrons pell mell, and some of the guards running away, thought all was lost, and quitted their position. This contagious movement was communicated in an instant to the left; and the whole army, after having so valiantly carried the enemy's strongest posts, abandoned them with as much eagerness, as they had displayed ardour in conquering them.

The English army, which had advanced in proportion as we retreated, and the Prussians, who had not ceased to pursue us, fell at once on our scattered battalions; night increased the tumult and alarm; and soon the whole army was nothing but a confused crowd, which the English and Prussians routed without effort, and massacred without pity.

The Emperor, witnessing this frightful defection, could scarcely believe his eyes. His aides-de-camp flew to rally the troops in all directions. He also threw himself into the midst of the crowd. But his words, his orders, his entreaties, were not heard. How was it possible for the army to form anew under the guns, and amid the continual charges of eighty thousand English, and sixty thousand Prussians, who covered the field, of battle?

However, eight battalions, which the Emperor had previously collected, formed in squares, and stopped the way against the Prussian and English armies. These brave fellows, resolute and courageous as they were, could not long resist the efforts of an enemy twenty times their number. Surrounded, assaulted, cannonaded on all sides, most of them at length fell. Some sold their lives dearly: others, exhausted with fatigue, hunger, and thirst, had no longer strength to fight, and suffered themselves to be killed, without being able to make any defence. Two battalions[52] alone, whom the enemy were unable to break, retreated disputing the ground, till, thrown into disorder and hurried along by the general movement, they were obliged themselves to follow the stream.

One last battalion of reserve, the illustrious and unfortunate remains of the granite column of the fields of Marengo, had remained unshaken amid the tumultuous waves of the army. The Emperor retired into the ranks of these brave fellows, still commanded by Cambronne! He formed them into a square, and advanced at their head, to meet the enemy. All his generals, Ney, Soult, Bertrand, Drouot, Corbineau, de Flahaut, Labedoyère, Gourgaud, &c. drew their swords, and became soldiers. The old grenadiers, incapable of fear for their own lives, were alarmed at the danger that threatened the life of the Emperor. They conjured him to withdraw. "Retire," said one of them: "you see, that Death shuns you." The Emperor resisted, and ordered them to fire. The officers around him seized his bridle, and dragged him away. Cambronne and his brave fellows crowded round their expiring eagles, and bade Napoleon an eternal adieu. The English, moved by their heroic resistance, conjured them to surrender. "No," said Cambronne, "the guard can die, but not yield!" At the same moment they all rushed on the enemy, with shouts of "Long live the Emperor!" Their blows were worthy of the conquerors of Austerlitz, Jena, Wagram, and Montmirail. The English and Prussians, from whom they still detained the field of victory, united against this handful of heroes, and cut them down. Some, covered with wounds, fell to the ground weltering in their blood; others, more fortunate, were killed outright: in fine, they whose hopes were not answered by death, shot one another, that they might not survive their companions in arms, or die by the hands of their enemies.

Wellington and Blucher, thus become quiet possessors of the field of battle, traversed it as masters. But at what expense of blood was this unjust triumph purchased! Never, no never, were the blows of the French more formidable or more deadly to their adversaries. Thirsting after blood and glory, they rushed daringly on the blazing batteries of their enemy; and seemed to multiply in number, to seek, attack, and pursue them in their inaccessible intrenchments. Thirty thousand English or Prussians[53] were sacrificed by their hands on that fatal day; and when it is considered, that this horrible carnage was the work of fifty thousand men[54], dying with fatigue and hunger, and striving in miry ground against an impregnable position and a hundred and thirty thousand fighting men, we cannot but be seized with sorrowful admiration, and decree to the vanquished the palm of victory.

At the moment, when Bulow's corps penetrated our right, I was at head-quarters at the farm of Caillou.

One of the grand marshal's aides-de-camp came from him, to inform the Duke of Bassano, that the Prussians were proceeding in that direction. The duke, having received orders from the Emperor to remain there, would not quit the place, and we resigned ourselves to wait the event. In fact, the enemy's dragoons soon made themselves masters of the little wood, that covered the farm, and attacked our people sword in hand. Our guard repulsed them with their muskets; but, returning in greater number, they assailed us anew, and compelled us, in spite of the stoicism of M. de Bassano, to yield up the place to them very speedily. The imperial carriages, furnished with able horses, carried us rapidly from the enemy's pursuit. The duke was not so fortunate: his carriage, having poor horses, received several shots; and he was at length forced to escape on foot, and take refuge in mine.

The cessation of the firing, and the precipitate retreat of the wreck of the army, too powerfully confirmed to us the fatal issue of the battle. We inquired on all sides after the Emperor, but no one could satisfy our painful anxiety. Some assured us, that he had been taken prisoner; others, that he was killed. To put an end to the anxiety that overwhelmed us, I took the horse of the principal of our attendants (*chef de nos équipages*), and, accompanied by one of our principal *piqueurs*, named Chauvin, who had returned with Napoleon from the island of Elba, I hastened back toward Mont St. Jean. After having in vain wearied a multitude of officers with questions, I met a page, young Gudin, who assured me, that the Emperor must have quitted the field of battle. I still pushed on. Two cuirassiers, raising their sabres, stopped me. "Where are you going?"—"I am going to meet the Emperor."—"You lie; you are a royalist; you are going to rejoin the English." I know not how the business would have ended, had not a superior officer of the guard, sent by heaven, fortunately known me, and extricated me from the difficulty. He assured me, that the Emperor, whom he had escorted a long way, must be before. I returned to the Duke of Bassano. The certainty, that the Emperor was safe and sound, alleviated our sorrows for a few moments: but they soon resumed all their strength. He must have been no Frenchman, who could behold with dry eyes our dreadful catastrophe. The army itself, after recovering from its first impressions, forgot the perils with which it was still menaced, to meditate with sadness on the future. Its steps were dejected, its looks dismayed; not a word, not a complaint, was heard to interrupt its painful meditations. You would have said it was accompanying a funeral procession, and attending the obsequies of its glory and of its country.

The capture and plundering of the baggage of the army had suspended for a moment the enemy's pursuit. They came up with us at Quatre Bras, and fell upon our equipage. At the head of the convoy marched the military chest, and after it our carriage. Five other carriages, that immediately followed us, were attacked and sabred. Ours, by miracle, effected its escape. Here were taken the Emperor's clothes: the superb diamond necklace, that the princess Borghese had given him; and his landau, that in 1813 had escaped the disasters of Moscow.

The Prussians, raging in pursuit of us, treated with unexampled barbarity those unfortunate beings, whom they were able to overtake. Except a few steady old soldiers, most of the rest had thrown away their arms, and were without defence; but they were not the less massacred without pity. Four Prussians killed General ...... in cold blood, after having taken from him his arms. Another general, whose name also I cannot call to mind, surrendered to an officer: and this officer had the cowardice still more than the cruelty, to run him through the body. A colonel, to avoid falling into their hands, blew out his brains. Twenty other officers, of various ranks, imitated the example. An officer of cuirassiers, seeing them approach, said: "They shall have neither me, nor my horse." With one of his pistols he shot his horse dead; with the other, himself[55]. A thousand acts of despair, not less heroic, illustrate this fatal day.

We continued our retreat to Charleroi. The further we advanced, the more difficult it became. They who preceded us, whether to impede the enemy, or through treachery, obstructed the way, and at every step we had to break through barricades. When halting for a moment, I heard cries and moanings at our side. I went to the place, and found they came from a ditch on the road-side, into which two large waggon-loads of wounded men had been overturned. These unfortunate people, tumbled in a heap under the waggons, that were upset upon them, implored the compassion of those who passed by; but their feeble voices, drowned by the noise of the carriages, had not been heard. We all set to work, and succeeded in extricating them from their tombs. Some were still breathing; but the greater number were stifled. The joy of these poor wretches affected us to tears; but it was of short duration—we were forced to leave them.

Still pursued and harassed by the enemy, we arrived at Charleroi, which place was so encumbered, and in such confusion, that we were obliged to leave behind us our carriage and our baggage. The secret portfolio of the cabinet was carried off by the keeper of the portfolio; the other important papers were destroyed; and we left only some letters and reports of no moment, which were afterwards printed at Brussels[56]. The Duke of Bassano and I were continuing our journey on foot, when I saw some *piqueurs* with led horses of the Emperor's, and I ordered them, to bring them to us. Such was the respect of the duke for every thing belonging to Napoleon, that he hesitated to avail himself of this good fortune. Happily for him, I succeeded in overcoming his scruples; for the Prussians had come up with us, and the firing of musketry informed us, that they were engaging only a few paces behind us. We were equally obliged to abandon the military chest. The gold in it was distributed among the Emperor's domestics; all of whom faithfully delivered it to him.

The Emperor, accompanied by his aides-decamp and a few orderly officers, on quitting the field of battle, had taken the road to Charleroi. On his arrival at this place, he attempted to rally a few troops; but his efforts were vain, and, after having given orders to several generals, he continued his course.

Count Lobau, the generals of the guards Petit and Pelet de Morvan, and a number of other officers, equally endeavoured to form the army anew. With swords drawn, they stopped the troops on their way, and forced them, to draw up in order of battle; but scarcely were they formed, when they dispersed again immediately. The artillery, that had been able to be brought off, alone preserved its structure unshaken. The brave gunners, feeling the same attachment to their guns as soldiers to their colours, followed them quietly. Obliged by the roads being so much encumbered, to halt at every step, they saw the tide of the army flow by them without regret: it was their duty, to remain by their guns; and they remained, without considering, that their devotion might cost them their liberty or their lives.

By chance M. de Bassano and I took the road to Philippeville. We learned, with a joy of which we did not think ourselves any longer susceptible, that the Emperor was in the town. We ran to him. When he saw me, he condescended to present me his hand. I bathed it with my tears. The Emperor himself could not suppress his emotion: a large tear, escaping from his eyes, betrayed the efforts of his soul.

The Emperor caused orders to be despatched to generals Rapp, Lecourbe, and Lamarque, to proceed by forced marches to Paris, and to the commanders of fortified towns, to defend themselves to the last extremity. He afterward dictated to me two letters to Prince Joseph. One, intended to be communicated to the council of ministers, related but imperfectly the fatal issue of the battle: the other, for the prince alone, gave him a recital, unhappily too faithful, of the rout of the army. He concluded however: "All is not lost. I suppose I shall have left, on re-assembling my forces, a hundred and fifty thousand men. The federates and national guards, who have heart, will supply me with a hundred thousand men; the *dépôt* battalions, with fifty thousand. Thus I shall have three hundred thousand soldiers, to oppose to the enemy immediately. I shall supply the artillery with horses by means of those kept as articles of luxury. I shall levy a hundred thousand conscripts. I shall arm them with the muskets of the royalists and ill-disposed national guards. Dauphiny, the Lyonese, Burgundy, Lorraine, and Champagne, I shall levy in mass. I shall overwhelm the enemy: but it is necessary for me to be assisted, and not perplexed. I am going to Laon. No doubt I shall find men there. I have heard nothing of Grouchy; if he be not taken, as I am afraid he is, in three days time I may have fifty thousand men. With these

I could keep the enemy employed, and give time to Paris and France, to do their duty. The English march slowly. The Prussians are afraid of the peasantry, and dare not advance too far. Every thing may yet be repaired. Write me word of the effect, that the horrible result of this rash enterprise produces in the chamber. I believe the deputies will feel, that it is their duty on this great occasion, to join with me, in order to save France. Prepare them, to second me worthily."

The Emperor added with his own hand: "Courage, and firmness."

While I was despatching these letters, he dictated to M. de Bassano instructions for the major-general. When he had finished, he threw himself on a sorry bed, and ordered preparations to be made for our departure.

A postchaise half broken to pieces, a few waggons and some straw, had just been prepared, as nothing better was to be had, for Napoleon and us; when some carriages belonging to Marshal Soult entered the town. These we seized upon. The enemy having already some scouts in the neighbourhood of Philippeville and Marienbourg, two or three hundred fugitives of all sorts were collected, to form an escort for the Emperor. He set off with General Bertrand in a calash. It was thus Charles XII. fled before his conquerors after the battle of Pultowa.

The Emperor's suite was in two other calashes. One, in which I was, contained M. de Bassano, General Drouot, General Dejean, and M. de Canisy, first equerry: the other was occupied by Messrs. de Flahaut, Labedoyère, Corbineau, and de Bissi, aides-de-camp.

The Emperor stopped beyond Rocroi, to take some refreshment. We were all in a pitiable state: our eyes swelled with tears, our countenances haggard, our clothes covered with blood or dust, rendered us objects of compassion and horror to one another. We conversed on the critical situation, in which the Emperor and France would find themselves. Labedoyère, in the abundant candour of a young and inexperienced heart, persuaded himself, that our dangers would unite all parties, and that the chambers would display a grand and salutary energy. "The Emperor," said he, "without stopping on the road, should repair directly to the seat of the national representation; frankly avow his disasters; and, like Philip Augustus, offer to die as a soldier, and resign the crown to the most worthy. The two chambers will revolt at the idea of abandoning Napoleon, and join with him, to save France."—"Do not imagine," answered I, "that we live still in those days, when misfortune was sacred. The chamber, far from pitying Napoleon, and generously coming to his assistance, will accuse him of having ruined France, and endeavour to save it by sacrificing him."— "Heaven preserve us from such a misfortune!" exclaimed Labedoyère: "if the chambers separate themselves from the Emperor, all is over with us. The enemy will be at Paris in a week. The next day we shall see the Bourbons; and then what will become of liberty, and of all those who have embraced the national cause? As for me, my fate is not doubtful. *I shall be the first man shot.*"—"The Emperor is a lost man, if he set his foot in Paris:" replied M. de Flahaut: "there is but one step he can take, to save himself and France; and this is, to treat with the allies, and cede the crown to his son. But, in order to treat, he must have an army; and perhaps at this *very* moment, while we are talking, most of the generals are already thinking of sending in their submissions to the king[57]."—"So much the more reason is there," resumed Labedoyère, "why he should hasten to make common cause with the chambers and the nation; and set out without loss of time."—"And I maintain with M. de Flahaut," rejoined I, "that the Emperor is lost, if he set foot in Paris. He has never been forgiven for having abandoned his army in Egypt, in Spain, at Moscow: still less would he be pardoned for leaving it here, in the centre of France."

These different opinions, blamed or approved, supplied us with subjects for discussion; when a person came to inform us, that the English were at la Capelle[58], four or five leagues from us. With this General Bertrand was instantly made acquainted: but the Emperor continued talking with the Duke of Bassano, and we had infinite trouble, to make him resume his journey.

We arrived at Laon. The Emperor alighted at the foot of the walls. Our defeat was already known. A detachment of the national guard came to meet the Emperor. "Our brothers and sons," said the commanding officer to him, "are in the garrison towns, but dispose of us, sire; we are ready to die for our country, and for you." The Emperor thanked him heartily. Some peasants came round us, and gaped at us with stupid looks: they often shouted, "Long live the Emperor!" but these shouts annoyed us. In prosperity they are pleasing; after a battle lost they wound the heart.

The Emperor was informed, that a considerable number of troops were perceived at a distance. He sent one of his aides-de-camp, to reconnoitre them. They were about three thousand Frenchmen, horse and foot, whom Prince Jerome, Marshal Soult, General Morand, and Generals Colbert, Petit, and Pelet de Morveau, had succeeded in rallying. "Then," said Napoleon, "I will remain at Laon, till the rest of the army joins. I have given orders for all the scattered soldiers to be sent to Laon and Rheims. The gendarmerie and national guard shall scour the country, and collect the laggers; the good soldiers will join of themselves; in four and twenty hours we shall have a nucleus of ten or twelve thousand men. With this little army I will keep the enemy in check, and give Grouchy time to arrive, and the nation to face about." This resolution was strongly combated. "Your Majesty," it was urged, "has seen with your own eyes the complete rout of the army. You know, that the regiments were confounded together; and it is not the work of a few hours, to form them anew. Even supposing, that a nucleus of ten thousand soldiers could be collected, what could your Majesty do with such a handful of men, for the most part destitute of arms and stores? You might stop the enemy at one point; but you could not prevent their advancing at another, as all the roads are open to them. The corps of Marshal Grouchy, if he have crossed the Dyle, must have fallen into the hands of Blucher or of Wellington: if he have not crossed it, and attempt to effect his retreat by way of Namur, the Prussians must necessarily arrive at Gembloux or at Temploux before him, and oppose his passage; while the English will proceed through Tilly and Sombref to his right flank, and cut off all hopes of his saving himself. In this state of things, your Majesty cannot reasonably reckon upon any assistance from his army: he has none. France can only be saved by herself. It is necessary, that all the citizens take arms: and your Majesty's presence at Paris is requisite, to repress your enemies, and animate and direct the zeal of the patriots. The Parisians, when they see your Majesty, will fight without hesitation. If your Majesty remain at a distance from them, a thousand false reports concerning you will be spread: now it will be said, that you are killed; anon, that you are made prisoner, or surrounded. The national guard and federates, disheartened by the fear of being abandoned or betrayed, as they were in 1814, will fight heartlessly, or not at all."

These considerations induced the Emperor, to change his resolution. "Well!" said he, "since you deem it necessary, I will go to Paris; but I am persuaded, that you make me act foolishly. My proper place is here. Hence I could direct what is to be done at Paris, and my brothers would see to the rest."

The Emperor then retired into another room with M. de Bassano and me; and, after having despatched fresh orders to Marshal Soult on the rallying and movements of the army, he put the finishing hand to the bulletin of Mont St. Jean, which had been already sketched at Philippeville. When it was ended, he sent for the grand marshal, General Drouot, and the other aides-de-camp. "Here," said he, "is the bulletin of Mont St. Jean: I wish you to hear it read: if I have omitted any essential circumstances, you will remind me of them; it is not my intention, to conceal any thing. Now, as after the affair of Moscow, the whole truth[59] must be disclosed to France. I might have thrown on Marshal Ney," continued Napoleon, "the blame of part of the misfortunes of that day: but the mischief is done; no more is to be said about it." I read this new twenty-ninth bulletin: a few slight changes, suggested by General Drouot, were assented to by the Emperor; but, from what whim I know not, he would not confess, that his carriages had fallen into the hands of the enemy. "When you get to Paris," said M. de Flahaut to him, "it will be plainly seen, that your carriages have been taken. If you conceal this, you will be charged with disguising truths of more importance; and it is necessary, to tell the whole, or say nothing." The Emperor, after some demur, finally acceded to this advice.

I then read the bulletin a second time; and, every person agreeing in its accuracy, M. de Bassano sent it off to Prince Joseph by a courier extraordinary.

At the moment when it arrived, Paris was resounding with transports of joy, to which the splendid victory of Ligny, and the good news received from the armies of the West and of the Alps, had given rise.

Marshal Suchet, always fortunate, always able, had made himself master of Montmelian, and from one triumph had proceeded to another, till he had driven the Piedmontese from the passes and valleys of Mount Cenis.

General Desaix, one of his lieutenants, had driven back from the side of Jura the enemy's advanced posts, taken Carrouge, crossed the Arva, and, in spite of the difficulty of the country, made himself master of all the defiles in the twinkling of an eye.

The war of la Vendée had justified the Emperor's conjectures.

The Marquis of Roche-jaquelin, ashamed of the defeat at Aisenay, awaited with impatience an opportunity for redeeming the disgrace. Informed, that a fresh English fleet was bringing him arms and stores, he thought this opportunity was arrived; and immediately made preparations to favour the landing announced, and, if necessary, to give battle to the imperialists.

These preparations, badly contrived, and badly ordered, did not obtain the unanimous assent of the army. Part of the generals, and of the troops, already wearied and disgusted by marches and countermarches without end and without utility, executed with ill will the orders given them. Another part, questioning the reality of the disembarkation, hesitated. In fine, the corps of M. d'Autichamp, one of the most considerable, plainly refused, to take any part in this hazardous expedition; and this example, for which the other divisions waited, was soon imitated by MM. de Sapineau and Suzannet. La Roche-jaquelin, too proud to retract, too presumptuous to be sensible of the danger and folly of his resolutions, saw in the resistance opposed to him nothing but odious treachery; and, in the delirium of his anger, announced, as master, the dismissal of the rebellious generals. One division alone, that of his brother, remaining faithful to him, he put himself at its head, and rashly plunged into the Marsh[60], where fresh disasters and death awaited him.

General Lamarque had penetrated at a glance the designs of his imprudent adversary, and given orders to the formidable Travot, to quit Nantes, and advance with all speed on the rear of the royal army. This bold scheme was ably executed. Travot's advanced guard bore down every thing that opposed its way, made itself master of St. Gilles, kept off the English fleet, and obstructed the disembarkation. Travot, with the rest of his troops, at the same time crossed the river Vic at Bas-Oupton, and closed the road against La Roche-jaquelin. The Vendeans, pressed on all sides, retreated, and took post at St. Jean de Mont. Orders were given to General Esteve, to attack them. They awaited him with firmness; and Esteve, knowing the inexperience of their leader, feigned a retreat. The Vendeans, deceived by this, came out of the intrenchments, by which they were protected. The imperialists suddenly faced about, and soon dispersed their credulous and unfortunate enemies with the bayonet. La Roche-jaquelin, his brains turned, and in despair, ran about every where to give orders, to which no one would listen, which no one would follow, and at length got himself killed[61].

La Roche-jaquelin had been the principal instigator of this war from zeal and from ambition; and it was supposed, that his death would be followed by peace: but news of the approaching commencement of hostilities revived the courage of the Vendeans, restored concord among their chiefs, and they prepared for fresh battles.

General Lamarque, informed that MM. de Sapineau, de Suzannet, and d'Autichamp, were united to favour a third disembarkation, went in pursuit of them, at the head of the divisions of General Brayer and Travot. He came up with them at la Roche Servière. Their position appeared impregnable: but the imperial troops, animated to fight by the news of the battle of Ligny received by the telegraph, performed prodigies of valour; and had it not been for their generals, who were sparing of French blood, it is probable, that the royal army, driven from its intrenchments, defeated, and put to the rout, would have been entirely annihilated.

This fratricidal victory, the last France should have to deplore, left the Vendeans no other resource than peace. This they demanded, and in a few days obtained. If the talents, the vigour, of Generals Lamarque, Travot, and Brayer, &c., added new lustre to their military reputation, their humanity and moderation acquired them still more glorious claims to national gratitude. In hands less truly French, this war would have covered the insurgent country with a funeral pall; in their tutelary hands, it deprived the nation only of a few of its sons.

So many joint successes, magnified too by report, had diffused confidence and intoxication throughout Paris. The fears disseminated by malevolence, or conceived by the anxious solicitude of the patriots, were diminished. People began to contemplate the future with security; they gave themselves up to the hope, that fortune was becoming once more propitious to France; when this deceitful dream was suddenly broken by the news of the misfortunes of our army, and by the arrival of the Emperor.

On alighting at the Elyseum, the Emperor was received by the Duke of Vicenza, his censor in prosperity, his friend in adversity. He appeared sinking under grief and fatigue: his breast was affected, his respiration difficult. After a painful sigh, he said to the duke: "The army performed prodigies; a panic terror seized it; all was lost.... Ney conducted himself like a madman; he got my cavalry massacred for me.... I can say no more.... I must have two hours rest, to enable me to set about business: I am choking here:" and he laid his hand upon his heart.

He gave orders for a bath to be prepared for him; and, after a few moments' silence, resumed: "My intention is, to assemble the two chambers in an imperial sitting. I will describe to them the misfortunes of the army: I will demand from them the means of saving their country: after that, I will set out again."—"Sire," answered the Duke of Vicenza, "the news of your disasters has already transpired. Men's minds are in great agitation: the dispositions of the deputies appear more hostile than ever: and, since your Majesty deigns to listen to me, it is my duty to say, that it is to be feared the chamber will not act agreeably to your expectations. I am sorry, Sire, to see you in Paris. It would have been better, not to have separated from your army: that constitutes your strength, your safety."—"I have no longer an army," replied the Emperor: "I have nothing but fugitives. I shall find men, but how are they to be armed? I have no muskets left. However, with unanimity every thing may be repaired. I hope the deputies will second me; that they will feel the responsibility, that will rest upon them. I think you have formed a wrong judgment of their spirit: the majority is good; it is French. I have against me only Lafayette, Lanjuinais, Flaugergues, and a few others. These would fain have nothing to do with me, I know. I am a restraint upon them. They would labour for themselves ... I will not let them. My presence here will control them."

The arrival of Prince Joseph and Prince Lucien in succession interrupted this discourse. They confirmed the Duke of Vicenza's opinion respecting the ill disposition of the chamber; and advised the Emperor, to defer the convocation of an imperial session, and allow his ministers to act first.

While the Emperor was in the bath, the ministers and great officers of state hastened to the Elyseum, and eagerly questioned the aides-de-camp and officers, who were returned from Mont St. Jean. The spectacle of the rout and destruction of the army was still present to their eyes: they omitted no particular, and imprudently conveyed terror and discouragement into every heart. They said aloud, that it was all over with Napoleon; and whispered, that he had no other means of saving France than by his abdication.

The Emperor, recovered from his fatigue, assembled his council. He made the Duke of Bassano read the bulletin of the battle of Mont St. Jean, and said: "Our misfortunes are great. I am come to repair them: to impress on the nation, on the army, a great and noble movement. If the nation rise, the enemy will be crushed: if disputation be substituted instead of levies, instead of extraordinary measures, all is lost. The enemy is in France. To save the country it is necessary, that I should be invested with great power, *with a temporary dictatorship*. For the good of the country I might seize on this power: but it would be advantageous, and more national, that it should be given me by the chambers." The ministers held down their heads, and made no answer. The Emperor then called upon them, to give their opinion on the measures, that circumstances required to be taken for the public safety.

M. Carnot was of opinion, that it was necessary, to declare the country in danger, call the federates and national guards to arms, place Paris in a state of siege, defend it, at the last extremity retire behind the Loire, form intrenchments there, recall the army of La Vendée and the corps of observation in the South, and keep the enemy in check, till a sufficient force had been collected and organized, to resume acting on the offensive, and drive them out of France.

The Duke of Vicenza recalled to mind the events of 1814, and maintained, that the occupation of the capital by the enemy would decide the fate of the throne a second time. That it was necessary for the nation to make a grand effort, to preserve its independence: that the safety of the state did not depend on this or that measure; the question was in the chambers, and their union with the Emperor.

The Duke of Otranto, and several other ministers, joined in this opinion; and thought, that by acting towards the chambers with confidence and good faith, they would be brought to feel, that it was their duty to join with the Emperor, that by energetic measures they might together preserve the honour and independence of the nation.

The Duke Decrès declared plainly, that they were wrong to flatter themselves with the hope of gaining the deputies; that they were ill-disposed, and appeared decided, to proceed to the most violent extremes.

Count Regnault added, he did not think, that the representatives would consent to second the views of the Emperor; they seemed persuaded, that it was no longer in his power, to save the country; and he was afraid, that a great sacrifice would be necessary.—"Speak plainly," said the Emperor to him: "it is my abdication they want, is it not?"—"I believe so, Sire," replied M. Regnault: "painful as it is to me, it is my duty, to open your Majesty's eyes to your true situation. I will add, it is even possible, that, if your Majesty should not resolve to offer your abdication of your own accord, the chamber would venture to demand it."

Prince Lucien warmly replied: "I have already found myself placed in circumstances of difficulty; and I have seen, that, the more important the crisis, the greater the energy we ought to display. If the chamber will not second the Emperor, he will dispense with its assistance. The safety of our country ought to be the first law of the state; and since the chamber does not appear disposed, to join the Emperor in saving France, he must save it alone. He must declare himself dictator, place France in a state of siege, and call to its defence all the patriots, and all good Frenchmen."

Count Carnot declared, it appeared to him indispensable, that, during this crisis, the Emperor should be invested with great and imposing authority.

The Emperor then took up the discourse, and said: "The presence of the enemy on their native land will, I hope, bring the deputies to a sense of their duty. The nation did not send them to displace, but to support me. I do not fear them. Let them do what they will, I shall still be the idol of the people and of the army. Were I to say a single word, they would be all knocked on the head. But, while I fear nothing on my own account, I fear every thing for France. If we quarrel, instead of preserving a good understanding with each other, we shall experience the fate of the Lower Empire: all will be lost.... The patriotism of the nation, its hatred to the Bourbons, its attachment to myself, offer us still immense resources: our cause is not desperate."

He then, with admirable skill and strength of expression, passed successively in review the means of repairing the disasters of Mont St. Jean; and delineated with a bold pencil the innumerable calamities, with which discord, the foreigners, and the Bourbons threatened France. Every thing he said carried conviction to the minds of his ministers; their opinions, hitherto divided, were tending to an agreement; when the council was interrupted by a message from the chamber of representatives, containing the following resolutions.

"The chamber of representatives declares, that the independence of the nation is threatened.

"The chamber declares itself in a state of permanence. Any attempt to dissolve it is a crime of high treason: whoever shall be guilty of such an attempt will be a traitor to his country, and immediately condemned as one.

"The army of the line and national guard, who have fought, and still fight, in defence of the liberty, the independence, and the territory of France, have deserved well of their country.

"The ministers at war, of foreign affairs, and of the interior, are desired, to repair immediately to the assembly[62]."

These resolutions had been adopted, almost at the first dash, on the proposal of M. de Lafayette. Each of the articles was an infringement of the constitution, and an usurpation of sovereign authority. The Emperor at once foresaw all the consequences. "I was right in thinking," said he with vexation, "that I ought to dismiss those fellows, before I departed. It is all over; they are on the point of ruining France." He broke up the sitting, adding: "I see Regnault did not deceive me: *If it must be so, I will abdicate.*" This imprudent and fatal speech, which was reported immediately to the enemies of Napoleon, strengthened their designs, and increased their boldness. Scarcely had the Emperor uttered the words, however, but he was aware of their impropriety; and, returning, announced, that, previously to taking any decided step, it would be proper, to know, *where all this would end*. Accordingly he directed M. Regnault, to repair to the chamber, endeavour to calm it, and feel the ground. "You will announce to them, that I am returned; that I have just convened the council of ministers; that the army, after a signal victory, has fought a great battle; that all was going on well; that the English were beaten; and that we had taken from them six pair of colours; when some ill-disposed persons excited a panic. That the army is assembling together; that I have given orders, to stop the fugitives; that I am come, to concert measures with my ministers, and with the chambers; and that I am this moment engaged on those steps, which circumstances require for the public safety."

By the Emperor's orders, M. Carnot set out at the same moment, to make a similar communication to the chamber of peers. It was listened to there with suitable calmness: but M. Regnault, with his utmost efforts, could not moderate the impatience of the representatives; and they imperiously renewed their desire to the ministers, by a second message, to appear at their bar.

The Emperor, offended at the chamber's arrogating to itself an authority over his ministers, forbade them to stir. The deputies, finding they did not come, considered their delay as *a contempt for the nation*. Some, to whom contempt both of the Emperor and of constitutional principles was already familiar, moved, that the ministers should be ordered to attend the assembly, setting all other business aside. Others, alarmed by their own consciences, and, fearing a politic stroke, created phantoms of their own imagination. Persuaded, that Napoleon was marching troops, to maim and dissolve the national representation, they demanded with loud cries, that the national guard should be summoned, to protect the chamber. Others moved, that the command of this guard should be taken from the Emperor and General Durosnel, and conferred on General Lafayette.

The Emperor, weary of all this noise, authorised his ministers, to inform the president, that they should soon be with him: but not choosing to let it be thought, that they obeyed the injunctions of the chamber, he deputed them to it as bearers of an imperial message drawn up for the purpose. Prince Lucien was appointed to accompany them, under the title of commissioner general. That this innovation might not hurt the feelings of the ministers, the Emperor said to them, that Prince Lucien, by means of his temporary office of commissioner general, might answer the interrogatories of the representatives, without its having any future consequences, and without giving the chamber a right to assert, that their power of sending for the ministers and interrogating them had been acknowledged and conceded. But this was not the real motive. The Emperor had not been satisfied with the lukewarmness, which the majority of the ministers had displayed; and he was desirous of placing in hands more to be depended on the task of defending his person and his throne. At six o'clock the ministers, with Prince Lucien at their head, were introduced into the chamber.

The Prince announced, that the Emperor had appointed him commissioner extraordinary, to concert with the representatives prudential measures: he laid on the president's desk the commission and message of the Emperor, and demanded, that the assembly would think proper to form itself into a secret committee.

This message contained a brief sketch of the disasters experienced at Mont St. Jean. It recommended to the representatives, to join the head of the state to preserve their country from the misfortune of falling again under the yoke of the Bourbons, or becoming, like the Poles, the prey of foreigners. In fine it announced, that it appeared necessary for the two chambers, to appoint each a committee of five members, to concert with ministers the proper measures for securing the public safety, and treating for a peace with the combined powers.

Scarcely was the reading finished, when questions put to the ministers from all parts of the hall instantly threw the deliberations of the assembly into confusion. All the deputies, who had risen, addressed to them at once questions as absurd as they were arrogant, and were astonished, indignant, that they did not satisfy their eager and insatiable curiosity.

The disturbance being calmed, one member, M. Henry Lacoste, was able to make himself heard. "The veil then is torn," said he: "our misfortunes are made known; but, fearful as these disasters are, perhaps they are not yet entirely disclosed to us. I shall not discuss the communications made to us: the moment is not come, to call the head of the state to account for the blood of our brave soldiers, and the loss of the honour of the nation: but I require him, in the name of the public safety, to disclose to us the secret of his thoughts, of his policy; to teach us the means of closing the abyss, that yawns beneath our feet. Ministers of Napoleon, you talk to us of the national independence, you talk to us of peace; but what new basis will you give to your negotiations? What new means of communication have you in your power? You know, as well as we, that Europe has declared war against Napoleon alone! Will you henceforth separate the nation from Napoleon? For my part, I declare, that I see but one man between us and peace. Let him speak, and the country will be saved."

Prince Lucien attempted, to answer this violent attack. "What!" said he, "shall we still have the weakness to believe the words of our enemies? When victory was for the first time faithless to us, did they not swear, in the presence of God and man, that they would respect our independence and our laws? Let us not fall a second time into the snare, that they have set for our confidence, for our credulity. Their aim, in their endeavour to separate the nation from the Emperor, is, to disunite us, in order to vanquish us, and replunge us more easily into that degradation and slavery, from which his return delivered us. I conjure you, citizens, by the sacred name of our country, rally all of you round the chief, whom the nation has so solemnly replaced at its head. Consider, that our safety depends on our union; and that you cannot separate yourselves from the Emperor, and abandon him to his enemies, without ruining the state, without being faithless to your oaths, without tarnishing for ever the national honour."

This speech, uttered amid the coil of parties, was drowned, interrupted, by the tumultuous noise of the assembly: few of the deputies listened to it, or heard it: their minds, however, astonished by the blow aimed at Napoleon, appeared disquieted and irresolute. The Duke of Vicenza, and the Prince of Eckmuhl, had given satisfactory explanations, one of the means of coming to an understanding with the allies, the other of the imaginary approach of troops intended to act against the national representation. The friends of the Emperor had succeeded in bringing over to his cause a majority of the assembly, and every thing seemed to presage a favourable issue, when one of the Emperor's enemies, M. de la Fayette, obtained a hearing. "You accuse us," said he, addressing Prince Lucien, "of failing in our duties towards our honour, and towards Napoleon. Have you forgotten all that we have done for him? have you forgotten, that we followed him in the sands of Africa, in the deserts of Russia, and that the bones of our sons and brothers every where attest our fidelity? For him we have done enough: it is our duty now, to save our country." A number of voices rose together in confusion, to accuse or defend Napoleon. M. Manuel, M. Dupin, displayed the dangers, with which France was threatened. They hinted at the means of preserving it, but durst not pronounce the word abdication: so difficult it is to overcome the respect, that a great man inspires.

In fine, after a long debate, it was agreed, conformably to the conclusions of the message, that a committee of five members, consisting of the president and vice-presidents of the chamber, Monsieur Lanjuinais, and MM. de la Fayette, Dupont de l'Eure, Flaugergues, and Grenier, should concert measures with the council of ministers, and with a committee of the chamber of peers (if this chamber should think proper to appoint one), to collect every information respecting the state of France, and propose every means that might be conducive to the public safety.

Prince Lucien, in the same capacity of commissioner extraordinary, repaired immediately to the chamber of peers; and this chamber, after having heard the imperial message, hastened also to appoint a committee; which was composed of Generals Drouot, Dejean, and Andréossy, and MM. Boissy d'Anglas, and Thibaudeau.

On his return to the Elyseum, the prince did not conceal from the Emperor, that the chamber had declared itself too strongly, to allow any hope of ever reclaiming it: *and that it was necessary, either to dissolve it immediately, or submit to an abdication.* Two of the ministers present, the Duke of Vicenza and the Duke of Bassano, remonstrated, that the chamber had acquired too great hold of the public opinion, for an act of authority to be attempted against it. They respectfully hinted to Napoleon, that it was more prudent to submit: that, if he hesitated, the chamber would indubitably decree his deposition, and perhaps he would not have it in his power, to abdicate in favour of his son.

Napoleon, without promising, without refusing, without giving any indication of his resolves, contented himself with the answer of the Duke of Guise: "They dare not." But it was easy to perceive, that he stood in fear of the chamber; that he thought his abdication inevitable; and that he only sought, in the hope of some favourable event, to put off the catastrophe as long as possible.

The committees of the two chambers, the ministers, and the ministers of state, met the same day at eleven in the evening, Prince Lucien being present.

It was decided by a majority of sixteen against five:

1st, That the safety of the country required the Emperor to consent, that the two chambers should appoint a committee, to negotiate directly with the combined powers, on the condition of their respecting the independence of the nation, and the right every people have, to give themselves such a constitution, as they may deem proper.

2dly, That it was advisable, to back these negotiations by the complete display of the national force.

3dly, That the ministers of state should propose suitable measures for supplying men, horses, and money; as well as those necessary for curbing and repressing domestic enemies.

This resolution was combated by M. de la Fayette. He stated, that it did ot answer the general expectation; that the most certain, the most speedy 1eans of putting an end to the state of crisis, in which France found itself, ested solely and exclusively in the abdication of Napoleon; and that it was necessary to call upon him, in the name of the country, to lay down the crown.

Prince Lucien declared, that the Emperor was ready, to make any sacrifice, which the safety of France might require: but that the time for recurring to this desperate resource was not yet arrived; and that it was advisable, with a view to the interests of France itself, to wait the result of the overtures, that should be made to the allied powers.

The assembly agreed in this opinion, and broke up from weariness at three o'clock in the morning.

General Grenier was appointed by his colleagues, to give the chamber an account of the result of this conference: an embarrassing mission, since the principal object of the conference, which, in the opinion of the representatives, ought to have been, to determine on the abdication of Napoleon, had been eluded, and left out of sight. M. ***, whom I refrain from naming, advised him, to speak out plainly, and to declare, that the committee, though it had not formally declared it, felt the necessity of desiring the Emperor to abdicate. But the inflexible and virtuous Dupont de l'Eure, always the friend of rectitude and sincerity, raised his voice like a man of honour against this shameful suggestion; and protested, that he would ascend the tribune, to declare the truth, if the reporter dared to disregard or falsify it. Accordingly General Grenier confined himself, to giving a faithful account of the sitting of the committee: but he added, from instructions just given him by the ministers of state, that the chamber would presently receive a message, by which the Emperor would declare, that he approved of the assembly's appointing ambassadors, to send to the allies; and that, if he were an insuperable obstacle to the nation's being admitted to treat of its independence, he should always be ready, to make the sacrifice required of him.

This explanation answered every end: but, instead of calming the minds of the representatives, it excited the irascibility of all those, who, from fear of the enemy, from ambition, or from a mistaken patriotism, considered Napoleon's immediate abdication necessary. They did not perceive, that on the contrary it was of importance, to leave Napoleon nominally on the throne, in order to give the negotiators an opportunity of bartering with the foreign powers his abdication in exchange for peace.

M. Regnault, witnessing the irritation that prevailed, went to acquaint the Emperor, that the chamber appeared disposed, to pronounce his deposition, if he did not abdicate immediately. The Emperor, not accustomed to receive the law, was indignant at the force attempted to be put upon him: "Since this is the case," said he, "I will not abdicate. The chamber is composed of Jacobins, fanatics, and ambitious men, who thirst after places and disturbance. I ought to have denounced them to the nation, and expelled them: the time lost may be repaired...."

The Emperor's agitation was extreme. He strode about his closet, and muttered broken phrases, that it was impossible to comprehend. "Sire," at length answered M. Regnault, "do not endeavour, I conjure you, to struggle any longer against the stream of events. Time passes on: the enemy is advancing. Do not give the chamber, do not give the nation, room to accuse you of having prevented it from obtaining peace. In 1814 you sacrificed yourself for the common safety; repeat to-day this great, this generous sacrifice."

The Emperor pettishly replied: "I shall see: it has never been my intention, to refuse to abdicate. I was a soldier; I will become one again: but I want to be allowed, to think of it calmly, with a view to the interests of France and of my son: tell them to wait."

During this conversation, the chamber was extremely agitated. The president, informed by M. Regnier of the disposition of the Emperor, announced, that a message would presently satisfy the wishes of all. But, impatient to enjoy its work, it was unwilling, even to leave Napoleon the merit of sacrificing himself freely for the safety of his country.

M. Duchène, who was the first to interrupt General Grenier's report by his murmurs, moved, that the Emperor should be desired, in the name of the safety of the state, to declare his abdication.

General Solignac proposed, to send a deputation to him, to express the urgency of his decision.

M. de la Fayette, who seems called by fate to be the scourge of kings, exclaimed, that, if Napoleon did not decide, he would move for his deposition.

A number of members, among whom General Sébastiani rendered himself conspicuous by his violence, insisted, that Napoleon should be compelled, to abdicate immediately.

At length it was agreed, "in order to save the honour of the head of the state," to grant him an hour's grace; and the sitting was suspended.

Fresh importunities immediately assailed the Emperor. General Solignac, I believe, and other deputies, came to summon him to abdicate. Prince Lucien, who had never ceased to conjure the Emperor, to make head against the storm, now thought the time was passed, and that it was necessary to submit. Prince Joseph united with him, and their joint advice at length overcame the resistance of the Emperor. This determination he announced to the ministers, and said to the Duke of Otranto with an ironical smile, "Write to those gentlemen, to make themselves easy: they shall soon be satisfied[63]."

Prince Lucien then took up the pen, and wrote, from the dictation of his august brother, the following declaration.

"Declaration to the French People.

"In commencing a war, to maintain the independence of the nation, I reckoned on the joint efforts of all, the unanimity of all, and the concurrence of all the national authorities. From these I had reason, to hope for success; and I set at defiance all the declarations of foreign powers against me.

"Circumstances appear to me to be changed: I offer up myself as a sacrifice to the animosity of the enemies of France: may they prove themselves sincere in their declarations, and that they really aimed at me personally alone! My political life is at an end: and I proclaim my son, under the title of Napoleon II., Emperor of the French.

"The present ministers will form provisionally the council of government. The interest I feel in what concerns my son induces me, to desire the chambers, to form a regency without delay by a law.

"Unite, all of you, for the public safety, and to remain an independent nation.

(Signed) "Napoleon."
"Palace of the Elyseum,
June the 22d, 1815."

The minute of Prince Lucien was put into my hands by the Duke of Bassano, to make two copies of it. When they were presented to the Emperor, they still exhibited traces of my sorrow. He perceived them, and said to me, with a very expressive look, "They would have it so."

The Duke of Bassano observed to him, that he made a great sacrifice to peace; but that perhaps the allies would not deem it sufficiently complete.—"What do you mean?" asked the Emperor.—"It is possible, they may require the renunciation of the crown by your Majesty's brothers."—"What! by my brothers Ah, Maret, then you would dishonour us all!"

The Duke of Otranto, the Duke of Vicenza, the Duke Decrès, were immediately employed, to carry the Emperor's declaration to the chamber of deputies; and the Duke of Gaëta, Count Mollien, and M. Carnot, to carry it to that of the peers.

The Prince of Eckmuhl had been sent previously to the former by the Emperor, to give it information respecting the army, and amuse it till the abdication should arrive.

Scarcely was the abdication sent off, when the Count de la Borde, adjutant-general of the national guard, ran to inform the Emperor, that there was not a moment to be lost, as they were going to put the deposition to the vote. The Emperor, tapping him on the shoulder, said: "These good people are in great haste, then: tell them to be easy; I sent them my abdication a quarter of an hour ago." The ministers and M. de la Borde had passed each other on the way.

When they appeared before the chamber, the president, apprehensive that the enemies of Napoleon would insult his misfortunes by cowardly applauses, reminded it, that its regulations prohibited every sign of approbation or disapprobation: he then read the declaration.

The Duke of Otranto, who had been in secret one of the instigators of the rage of certain deputies, pretended to be affected at the fate of Napoleon, and recommended him to the attention and protection of the chambers. This simulation of generosity disgusted every pure heart in the assembly; it was reserved for the unfortunate Regnault, to rouse their feelings. He reminded them of the benefits and victories of Napoleon with so much eloquence and sensibility; he drew them a picture so true, so affecting, so pathetic, of the misfortunes, to which this great man, the hero of the nation, was about to devote himself without reserve, and without conditions, to ransom his country; that the eyes of his most obdurate enemies were moistened with tears, and the whole assembly remained for some moments plunged in a sad and painful silence. This silence, perhaps the noblest homage, that Napoleon ever obtained, was at length interrupted: and the chamber unanimously decreed, that a solemn deputation should wait on Napoleon, to express to him, in the name of the nation, "the respect and gratitude, with which they accepted the noble sacrifice he had made to the independence and happiness of the French people."

Napoleon received coldly the congratulations of the deputies of the chamber. What value could empty words have in his eyes? He answered them[64]:

"I thank you for the sentiments you express towards me: I wish, that my abdication may procure the happiness of France; *but I have no expectation of it*; it leaves the state without a head, without political existence. The time wasted in overturning the monarchy might have been employed in putting France into a condition to crush the enemy. I recommend to the chamber, speedily to reinforce the armies: whoever is desirous of peace ought to prepare for war. Do not leave this great nation at the mercy of foreigners: be on your guard against being deceived by your hopes. *There lies the danger.* In whatever situation I may find myself, I shall always be at ease, if France be happy. I recommend my son to France. I hope it will not forget, that I abdicated only for him. I have made this great sacrifice also for the good of the nation; it is only with my dynasty, that it can expect to be free, happy, and independent."

The Emperor delivered this answer in such a noble and affecting tone, that all present were deeply moved, and M. Lanjuinais himself could not refrain from tears.

Count Regnault was congratulating himself on being the first interpreter of the sentiments and gratitude of the nation; when the Emperor interrupted him: "Since this deliberation is your work," said he to him, "you ought to have remembered, that the title of Emperor is never lost[65]:" and he turned his back upon him.

The chamber of peers hastened, to follow the example of the deputies. The Emperor received it with kindness, and recommended to it, not to forget that he had abdicated only in favour of his son.

The abdication of Napoleon gave free scope to the political speculations of the representatives every one of them thought himself called upon, to give the state a government and a head.

The republicans, still the dupes of their own illusions, flattered themselves with the hope of introducing a federal government into France.

The Bonapartists, confident in the wishes of the nation, and the promises of foreign powers, reckoned on decreeing the crown to Napoleon II., and the regency to Maria Louisa.

The partisans of the Duke of Orleans, in whose ranks were found the most distinguished personages and the ablest orators of the assembly, secretly flattered themselves with seating on the throne the son of kings and of the republic.

Some of the deputies, seduced by the brilliant reputation of the one, or by the valour and family connexions of the other, inclined for the Prince of Sweden, or the Prince of Orange.... In a word, they would have any body, except the legitimate sovereign.

A small number of the deputies only remained neutral. Free from ambition and personal interest, attentive to their country alone, they thought of availing themselves of the passing events, only to turn them to the advantage of liberty and the nation.

The parties, that thus divided the chamber, were not slow in entering on their career.

M. Dupin, too skilful to manifest directly the intention of not acknowledging Napoleon II., and declaring the throne vacant, took a circuitous course. He proposed to the chamber, to form itself into a national assembly to send ambassadors to negotiate for peace; to form an executive committee, selected from the members of the two chambers; and to give it in charge to another committee, to prepare the plan of the new constitution, and to settle the conditions, on which the throne might be filled by the prince, whom the people should choose.

M. Scipio Morgues, though not sitting under the same banners with M. Dupin, took up the proposition; and, carrying it still farther, moved, that the chamber should form itself into a constituent assembly: that the government of the state should be entrusted provisionally to the ministers, who should act in conjunction with a committee of five members belonging to the chamber, with the president at their head[66]; and that the throne should be declared vacant, till the will of the people was known: so that the sovereign people would have had the power of changing the established form of government, and rendering France a republic, or a monarchy, as they pleased.

M. Regnault represented, that either of these propositions would tend to throw the state into the labyrinth of a complete disorganization; that they could not be adopted, without announcing to the foreign powers, that there was no established order of things in France, no acknowledged rights, no fixed principles, no basis for a government: yet, soon falling himself into the error of his opponents, he proposed, 1st, to name, instead of the council of regency, prescribed by the fundamental laws, to which he had just referred, an executive committee of five members, two from the chamber of peers, and three from that of deputies, who should exercise the functions of government provisionally.

2dly. In order not to disturb the unity of power, to leave to this committee the choice and direction of the commissioners, to be sent to negotiate with the allies.

In times of doubt and fear, a middle course is always most agreeable to the majority; and the majority of the chamber adopted the sort of conduct proposed by M. Regnier, without perceiving its inconsistency: for, to elude the acknowledgment of the Emperor Napoleon II. was to declare to foreigners, *what it had been desirous of avoiding*, that there were no established rights in France, and that the throne and even the government were vacant.

In the existing state of things there were only two courses to be pursued: either to proclaim Napoleon II. constitutionally, as its essence, its duty, its interest, prescribed:

Or, if, from a cowardly condescension, it would not decide any thing without the assent of the allies, to unite the two chambers into a national assembly, and wait the course of events. In this case it would not have placed the fate of the revolution of the 20th of March in the hands of five individuals; it would have acquired an imposing and national character, which would have given to its acts, its negotiations, and even its resistance, a degree of strength and dignity, that the unusual kind of government, to which it had just given birth, could never obtain.

The resolution taken by the representatives was immediately carried to the chamber of peers.

Prince Lucien was the first who rose to combat it. He eloquently exposed the principles, on which hereditary monarchies are founded. He invoked the constitution, the solemn oaths taken in the *Champ de Mai*, and conjured the peers, the faithful guardians of the fealty sworn, and of the constituent laws of the monarchy, to reject this unconstitutional resolution, and proclaim Napoleon II. Emperor of the French.

M. de Pontécoulant strongly resisted this proposal; declaring, that he never would consent to acknowledge as sovereign a Prince not in France, and a captive as regent. "Besides," added he, "by what right does the Prince of Cannino come to speak within these walls? is he a Frenchman?"

"If I be not a Frenchman in your eyes," exclaimed Prince Lucien, "I am in the eyes of the whole nation."

Labedoyère darted rapidly to the tribune. "I have seen," said he, "round the throne of the prosperous sovereign, men, who now shun it, because he is in adversity. They are at this moment ready to receive any prince, that foreigners may think proper to impose on them. But, if they reject Napoleon II., the Emperor ought to have recourse to his sword, and to those brave men, who, covered as they are with blood and scars, still cry 'Long live the Emperor!' It was, in favour of his son, that he abdicated: his abdication is void, if Napoleon II. be not acknowledged. Shall French blood have been spilt again, only to make us pass a second time under a foreign yoke? to bow the head beneath a degraded government? to see our brave warriors drink the cup of bitterness and humiliation, and deprived of the rewards due to their services, their wounds, their glory? There are still here perhaps generals," turning his eyes toward Marshal Ney, "who meditate new treasons; but woe to all traitors: may they be devoted to infamy! may their houses be rased, their families proscribed!" At these words the most lively expressions of displeasure burst out in the assembly. Labedoyère, interrupted, impiously exclaimed: "*Great God!* is it then decreed, that the voices of baseness alone shall be heard within these walls?"

This exclamation excited fresh murmurs. "We have already a foreign war," said M. Boissy d'Anglas: "must we have a civil war also? Unquestionably the Emperor has made the greatest of sacrifices to our country, but the proposal, to proclaim Napoleon II. is unseasonable and impolitic. I move the order of the day."

Messrs. de Ségur, de Flahaut, and Roederer, opposed this, and strenuously maintained the rights of Napoleon II. "If the Emperor had been killed," said they, "his son would succeed him as a matter of right. He is politically deceased why should not his son succeed him? The monarchy is composed of three branches: one of these branches is dead; it must be replaced. We are strong only within the sphere of our duties: let us not step out of the constitution, let us not give the foreign powers a right to say to us, you are no longer any thing! They have declared, that Napoleon alone was the obstacle to a peace: let us put their good faith to the test. It is besides as advantageous, as it is just and politic, to acknowledge Napoleon II., and to govern in his name. Look at the soldiers, look at the people of Alsace, Franche Comté, Lorraine, Burgundy, and Champagne, for whom, and in whose name, have they lavished their generous blood? At home, the acknowledgment of Napoleon II. would justify the nation and the army; abroad it would reconcile us to Austria. Could the Emperor view us with the eyes of an enemy, when we had adopted for our sovereign a child of his own blood?"

"The 67th article of the constitution," said M. Thibaudeau, "is still the law of the two chambers: neither the chamber, nor the nation, nor the provisional government we shall form, thinks of bringing back the government, under which we groaned a whole year; but the proposal for acknowledging Napoleon II. cannot be discussed at the present moment. Let us leave things as they are, and adopt the resolution of the chamber of deputies, *without prejudging any thing in regard to the entirety of the abdication of Napoleon.*"

The chamber, delighted at having discovered a method of preserving the rights of Napoleon, without placing itself in manifest opposition to the representatives, adopted this suggestion, and proceeded immediately to the nomination of the two members to the committee of government.

The Duke of Vicenza and Baron Quinette had the suffrages in their favour.

M. Carnot, the Duke of Otranto, and General Grenier, were at the same time chosen by the other chamber.

The committee of government immediately entered on its functions under the presidency of the Duke of Otranto.

Though the question of the entirety of the abdication remained untouched upon, the Emperor nevertheless considered the creation of a committee of government as a manifest violation of its conditions. He reproached the ministers of state, and particularly M. Regnault, with not having maintained the rights of his son: and made them sensible, that it was incumbent on them, as they regarded their honour and duty, to oblige the chambers to declare themselves. "I have not abdicated," said he, "in favour of a new directory. I abdicated in favour of my son. If they do not proclaim him, my abdication must be null, and not made. The chambers well know, that the people, the army, public opinion, desire it, will it; but the foreigners check them. It is not by presenting themselves before the allies with their ears hanging down, and their knee on the ground, that they will compel them to acknowledge the independence of the nation. Had they been sensible of their situation, they would spontaneously have proclaimed Napoleon II. The foreign powers would then have seen, that you know how to have but one will, one object, one rallying point: they would have seen, that the 20th of March was not a party affair, the attempt of a faction; but the result of the attachment of the French to me and to my dynasty. The unanimity of the nation would have had more effect upon them, than all your mean and degrading deference."

The effect produced by the sitting of the chamber of peers, in spite of the pains taken to misrepresent it, roused the attention of the Duke of Otranto, and of the Anti-Napoleon faction, of which he was become the director and the head.

On the other hand the army of Marshal Grouchy, which was supposed to be destroyed, had just re-entered France[67]. Prince Jerome, Marshal Soult, Generals Morand, Colbert, Poret, Petit, and a number of other officers, whom I regret not being able to name, had succeeded in rallying the wreck of Mont St. Jean; and the army already formed a body of fifty or sixty thousand men, whose sentiments in favour of the Emperor had undergone no alteration.

The Duke of Otranto and his party then perceived the necessity of keeping terms with Napoleon and in a secret conference, which took place at the house of the minister of police, and at which M. Manuel and the deputies of most weight in the party of the Duke of Otranto were present, it was confessed, that it appeared neither prudent nor possible, to prevent the acknowledgment of Napoleon II.; and that they would exert themselves merely to retain the authority in the hands of the committee.

The next day, as had been foreseen, Count Defermont, dexterously availing himself of a debate on the oath to be taken by the committee, asked the assembly, in whose name the committee was to act? how the titles of its acts should run? and, in fine, whether Napoleon II. were, or were not, Emperor of the French? (*Yes, yes, yes!*) "The abdication of Napoleon I. calls to the succession him," said he, "who in the order established by the constitution is designated beforehand as his heir." (Here a single voice called out, *The order of the day!*) "On this fundamental point the slightest hesitation cannot exist. If it did exist, it would be our duty, to put an end to it. We must not allow people, to go and persuade the national guard of Paris, or the armies, that we are waiting for Louis XVIII., and that we all share the same sentiment." (*A great majority of the members rose, and exclaimed, "Long live Napoleon II.!" These shouts were repeated with transport by the tribunes, and by the officers of the line and of the national guard, who were at the entrance of the hall.*)

"It must frankly be confessed," said another member, M. Boulay de la Meurthe, "that doubts have been started: some newspaper writers have gone so far as to say, that the throne is vacant. Were such our misfortune, this assembly, and our liberties, would be at an end. In fact, what should we be? By what mandate are we here? We exist only through the constitution.... It is the same constitution, that proclaims Napoleon II. Emperor. His father has abdicated: you have accepted his abdication without restriction the contract is formed, Napoleon II. is Emperor by the course of events." (*Yes, yes! we ought not even to deliberate.*) "Besides, the Emperor gave his abdication only under the express condition (*murmurs*).... These murmurs do not terrify me: I have long made the sacrifice of my life. I will speak the whole truth in presence of the nation. There exists a faction, that would persuade us we have declared the throne vacant, in the hope of filling up this vacancy immediately by the Bourbons. (*No, no! never, never!*) This faction is that of the Duke of Orleans. It has seduced some patriots, not too clear-sighted, who do not perceive, that the Duke of Orleans would accept the throne only to resign it to Louis XVIII. The assembly must speak out, and instantly declare, that it acknowledges Napoleon II. as Emperor of the French."

Count Regnault spoke to the same purpose; but threw cold water on the debate, by unskilfully introducing the mention of the foreign powers, and asking in whose name the army was to fight.

The members of the opposition, who had hitherto confined themselves to a few murmurs, and calling for the order of the day, now began to speak. M. Dupin first endeavoured to prove, that the safety of the country was the first thing to be considered. "Why," said he afterward, "has the Emperor abdicated? Because he felt, that it was no longer in his power, to save France. Now, I ask you, if Napoleon I. could not save the state, how can Napoleon II. save it? Besides, are not this prince and his mother captives? Have you any hope, that they will be restored to you?

"What have been our ideas? We have wished, instead of a name, which our enemies object to us, as the sole motive of the war, to bring forward the French nation. Yes, it is in the name of the nation, that we would fight, and that we would treat. It is from the nation we await the choice of a sovereign. The nation precedes all governments, and survives them all."

"Why do you not propose a republic?" a single voice exclaimed.

Numerous and violent murmurs had often interrupted M. Dupin. M. Manuel, more adroit, felt the necessity of being also more temperate. He appeared at first uncertain on the determination it would be proper to take; and, after having brought all the parties on the stage, and placed in the balance the hopes and fears, with which each might inspire the nation, he exclaimed: "But is it an individual, then, is it a family, that is in question? No; it is our country. Why should we deprive ourselves of the means of saving it? Already we have made one great stride[68]: but do we know, whether it will be great enough, whether it will be sufficiently complete, to obtain from it the results we wish? Let us leave it to time to act. In accepting the abdication of Napoleon, you accepted the condition it carries with it; and we ought to acknowledge Napoleon II., since the forms of the constitution require it: but, in conforming to them in this respect, it is impossible for us not to deviate from them, when the object is to secure our independence; and it is to attain this object, that you have thought proper, to place authority in the hands of men, who particularly possess your confidence; in order that this or that prince, appointed by the laws the guardian of the sovereign during a minority, may not claim his rights, and become the arbiter of the fate of France.

"I move, therefore, the order of the day, for the following reasons: 1st, that Napoleon II. is become Emperor of the French, by the fact of the abdication of Napoleon I., and by virtue of the constitution of the empire.

"2dly, That the two chambers have willed and intended, by naming a committee of government, to secure to the nation the guarantees it requires, under the extraordinary circumstances, in which it is placed, to preserve its liberty and tranquillity."

This specious proposal seduced the assembly. It was adopted amid the most vociferous acclamations, and shouts of "Long live Napoleon II." a thousand times repeated; without its suspecting, that this order of the day, which appeared to it so decisive, signified nothing, except that it proclaimed Napoleon II. because the constitution required it; but that it declared, at the same time, that it was merely a matter of form, and that it would be ready to give it up, when the provisional government should deem it necessary.

This was the second time of the chamber's being the dupe of its eagerness: yet it reckoned among its members men of great judgment and talents; but the greater number, and it is the majority always that gives the law, never having had a seat in our assemblies, allowed themselves to be subjugated by the illusions of eloquence, and with so much the more facility, because there existed in the assembly no fixed notion, no paramount will, that might serve it as a beacon and guide.

The provisional government, influenced by M. Fouché, soon evinced, that it had caught the true sense of M. Manuel's proposal. Two days after, its acts were issued in the name of the French people. This insult to the sincerity of the chamber, and to the sovereign it had acknowledged, excited its astonishment, and its complaints. The capital and the patriots murmured. The president of the government was summoned, to explain and justify this strange proceeding. He answered: "That it had never been the intention of the committee, to disavow Napoleon II.; but this prince not having been yet acknowledged as sovereign of France by any of the foreign powers, they could not treat with them in his name; and the committee had thought it its duty, to act provisionally in the name of the French people, in order to deprive the enemy of every pretext for refusing to admit the negotiation."

This explanation, strengthened by the hacknied support of the potent words, our country, the public safety, foreign armies, appeared plausible; and no more was said.

The Emperor himself, stunned by the force and rapidity of the blows, that his enemies inflicted on him, thought no longer of defending himself; and seemed to leave to Providence the care of watching over him and his son. He complained: but his dissatisfaction expired on his lips, and excited in him none of those resolutions, that might have been expected from the fire and energy of his character.

The Duke of Otranto, however, and the deputies who had concurred with him in pulling down Napoleon from his throne, did not look on his residence at the Elyseum without alarm. They dreaded, lest, emboldened by the daring counsels of Prince Lucien, by the attachment the army retained for him, by the acclamations of the federates, and citizens of all classes, who assembled daily under the walls of his palace, he should attempt to renew a second 18th Brumaire. They demanded of the chamber, therefore, by the mouth of M. Duchesne, that the *ex-Emperor* should be desired, in the name of their country, to remove from the capital. This demand having no effect, recourse was had to other means. Endeavours were made to frighten him. Every day officious advisers warned him, that attempts were making against his life: and to give more probability to this clumsy scheme, his guard was suddenly reinforced. Nay, one night, we were roused out of our beds by a messenger from the commandant of Paris, General Hulin, who warned us to be on our guard, as the Elyseum was going to be attacked, &c. But so great was our contempt for these wretched impositions, we did not even think it necessary, to mention it to Napoleon; and saw the return of day, without having lost a single moment's rest. Nothing however could have been more easy, than to carry off or assassinate Napoleon. His palace, which ten days before could scarcely contain the bustling crowd of ambitious men and courtiers, was now one vast solitude. All those men, destitute of faith and honour, whom power attracts, and adversity keeps at a distance, had deserted it. His guard had been reduced to a few old grenadiers: and a single sentry, scarcely in uniform, watched the gate of that Napoleon, that king of kings, who lately reckoned millions of soldiers under his banners.

Napoleon himself, however, was aware, that his presence at Paris, and in an imperial palace, might give the allies room to question the sincerity of his abdication, and be detrimental to the re-establishment of peace. He determined, therefore, to remove.

His private correspondence with the sovereigns, and some original letters, concealed from their search in 1814, he caused to be delivered into his own hands. He then directed us to burn the petitions, letters, and addresses, that had been received since the 20th of March. I was employed in this business one day, when Napoleon passed through the closet. He came up to me, and took a letter I had in my hand. It was one from the Duke of …. He ran it over, and said to me with a smile: "Don't burn this: keep it for yourself. It will be an excellent recommendation, if you find yourself in any trouble. * * * [**TN: Missing words in the book] will not fail to swear to those people, that he has maintained his fidelity toward them inviolate; and when he knows, that you have in your hands substantial proof of his having laid himself at my feet, and that I refused both him and his services, he will be ready to quarter himself to serve you, for fear you should blab." I thought the Emperor was jesting: he perceived it, and resumed: "No, I tell you; don't burn that letter, or any of those from persons of the same description: I give them to you for your protection."—"But, Sire, they will accuse me of having stolen them."—"If they complain, threaten, that you will print them all as they are, and they will say no more: I know them."—"Since it is your Majesty's desire, I will keep them." I did, in fact, set aside a certain number of these letters. After the return of the king, I had the complaisance, to restore some of them to the writers. This is not said gratuitously: scarcely had their authors, whom I could name, these letters in their possession, when they extolled their pretended fidelity to the skies; and became the most virulent detractors, both in their conversation and writing, of all who had embraced or served the cause of the 20th of March.

On the 25th, at noon, Napoleon set off for Malmaison. He was received there by the Princess Hortensia. This princess, so odiously calumniated, and so worthy of respect, set us an example of courage and resignation. Her situation, and that of Napoleon, must have wounded her to the heart: yet she found sufficient strength of mind, to suppress her sorrows, and console ours. She was attentive to the Emperor, she was attentive to us, with such constant solicitude, such perfect courteousness, that you would have supposed, she had nothing to think of but the misfortunes of others. If the fate of Napoleon and of France drew from us groans or imprecations, she ran to us; and, restraining her own tears, reminded us with the wisdom of a philosopher, and the sweetness of an angel, that we should surmount our sorrows and regrets, and submit with docility to the decrees of Providence.

Napoleon was roused by the shock, that his departure from the Elyseum gave him. At Malmaison he recovered his spirit, his activity, his energy. Accustomed to see all his wishes, all his enterprises, crowned with success, he had not learned, to contend against the sudden attacks of misfortune; and, notwithstanding the firmness of his character, they threw him occasionally into a state of irresolution, during which a thousand thoughts, a thousand designs, jostled each other in his mind, and deprived him of the possibility of coming to any decision. But this moral catalepsy was not the effect of a cowardly dejection, as has been asserted. His great mind remained erect amid the temporary numbness of his faculties; and Napoleon, when he awoke, was but so much the more terrible, and the more formidable.

A few minutes after his arrival, he was desirous of addressing once more his old companions in arms, and expressing to them for the last time his sentiments and regrets. The affection he bore them, and his despair at being unable to avenge at their head the affront received at Mont St. Jean, made him forget in his first sketch of a proclamation, that he had broken with his own hands his sceptre and his sword. He soon perceived, that the impassioned style, in which he addressed his army, was not such, as his abdication imposed on him: and accordingly he substituted the following address in the place of the too animated effusions of his heart.

"*Napoleon to the brave Soldiers of the Army before Paris.*

"Malmaison, June the 25th, 1815.

"Soldiers,

"While I yield to the necessity, that compels me to retire from the brave French army, I carry with me the pleasing certainty, that it will justify, by the eminent services its country expects from it, those praises, which our enemies themselves cannot refuse it.

"Soldiers, though absent, I shall mark your steps. I know all the corps; and no one of them can obtain a signal advantage over the enemy, without my doing justice to the courage it displays. Both you and I have been calumniated. Men not worthy to judge of your actions have seen, in the proofs of attachment you have given me, a zeal, of which I was the sole object: let your future successes teach them, that it was your country you served more especially in obeying me; and that, if I had any share in your affection, I owe it to my ardent love for France, our common mother.

"Soldiers, yet a few efforts, and the coalition is dissolved. Napoleon will know you by the blows you strike.

"Save the honour, the independence of France: continue to the end such as I have known you these twenty years, and you will be invincible."

The Emperor, who perhaps had intended by this proclamation, to turn the remembrance and concern of his ancient soldiers toward himself, inquired after the effect it had produced. He was informed, as was the truth, that it had not been published in the Moniteur, and that the army knew nothing of it. He showed no mark of vexation or discontent, and began to talk of the two chambers.

Since the abdication, the peers and deputies had rivalled each other, in their zeal and endeavours, to put France into a state, to awe its enemies at home and abroad.

They had declared the war national, and summoned all Frenchmen to their common defence.

They had authorized the government, to make requisitions in kind, for victualling the army, and the conveyance of subsistence.

To raise the conscription of 1815.

To suspend the laws respecting personal liberty; and to arrest, or place under inspection, every person charged with exciting disturbances, or conveying intelligence to the enemy.

In fine, they had voted it an immense credit, for defraying provisionally the expense of equipping and paying the army.

The committee, on its part, took, and executed with indefatigable care, every measure, that circumstances demanded. Its task, it must be confessed, was as difficult as perilous. Never was a government placed in similar circumstances. They required, at least in the majority of its members, great courage, great devotion, great patriotism: they required an heroic disregard of ease, of liberty, of life, to assume the responsibility incurred by power, and by events, towards the nation, and towards the king.

The first act of the committee was, to replace in the hands of the Prince of Essling the command in chief of the national guard, which had before devolved on the Emperor. The Duke of Otranto was desirous of taking the post of second in command from General Durosnel, whose rectitude was embarrassing to him, in order to bestow it on M. T**, who appeared to him no doubt more tractable. The Duke of Vicenza and M. Carnot opposed this; and it was left with General Durosnel, to the satisfaction of the national guard, which had already learned how to value the excellent character of this officer.

Marshal Soult not choosing to accept the command, and General Rapp having resigned his, the committee appointed Marshal Grouchy commander of the army of the North.

General Reille was appointed commander of the 1st, 2d, and 6th corps, united into one:

General Drouot commander of the guards:

Marshal Jourdan commander of the army of the Rhine.

Orders were given in all quarters, to replace the stores of the army, remount the cavalry, march out the dépôts, and oblige the straggling soldiers, to return to their colours.

In fine, the committee, after having had recourse to every possible means of supporting the negotiations, by the simultaneous display of the national forces, appointed MM. de la Fayette, de Pontécoulant, de la Forêt, d'Argenson, Sébastiani, and Benjamin Constant, the last being added in the character of secretary, to repair to the allied sovereigns and their generals, to negotiate a suspension of hostilities, and treat of peace.

The day on which these plenipotentiaries departed, M. S*** came to congratulate Napoleon. "The allies," answered the Emperor, "are too deeply interested in imposing the Bourbons on you, to give you my son. My son will reign over France, but his time is not yet arrived. The instructions given the deputies, I have been assured, are in favour of my dynasty: if this be true, other persons should have been chosen to defend it. La Fayette, Sébastiani, Pontécoulant, and Benjamin Constant, have conspired against me. They are my enemies: and the enemies of the father will never be the friends of the son. Besides, the chambers have not sufficient energy, to display an independent will: they obey the directions of Fouché. If they had bestowed on me what they lavish on him, I would have saved France. My presence alone at the head of the army would have done more, than all your negotiations. I would have obtained my son, as the price of my abdication: you will not obtain him. Fouché is not sincere: he has sold himself to the Duke of Orleans. He will make fools of the chambers; the allies will make a fool of him; and you will have Louis XVIII. He thinks himself able, to manage every thing as he pleases; but he is mistaken. He will find, that it requires a hand of a different stamp from his, to guide the reins of a nation, particularly when an enemy is in the land.... The chamber of peers has not done its duty: it has behaved like a chicken. It has suffered Lucien to be insulted, and my son to be dethroned. If it had stood firm, it would have had the army on its side: the generals there would have given it to it[69]. Its order of the day has ruined France, and brought you back the Bourbons, I alone could repair all: but your party-leaders will never consent to it: they would rather be swallowed up in the gulf, than join with me to close it."

The complaints, the regrets, the menaces, that Napoleon allowed continually to escape him, alarmed the promoters of his fall more and more. In the first moments of their warmth they had displayed some boldness; but after their heads had grown cool, they appeared themselves to be astonished at their own courage. They turned pale at the very name of Napoleon and conjured the government night and day, to make him embark as speedily as possible.

From the very day of his abdication, the Emperor had thought of seeking an asylum in a foreign country. Accustomed to powerful emotions, to extraordinary events, he familiarized himself to this idea without difficulty; and appeared to take a momentary pleasure in calculating the hazards of the present, and the chances of the future; and balancing the fictions of hope against the dangers of reality.

The Emperor had never confounded the English nation with the political system of its government. He considered the heart of a Briton as the inviolable sanctuary of honour, generosity, and all the public and private virtues, that stamp on man loftiness and dignity. This high opinion prevailed in his mind over the fears, with which the known principles and sentiments of the cabinet of London could not fail to inspire him: and his first intention was, to retire to England, and there place himself under the protection of hospitality and the laws. He opened his mind to the Dukes of Bassano and Vicenza. The former did not appear to relish this determination. The latter, without condemning of approving it, advised him, if he persisted in taking this step, to go on board a smuggling vessel; and, as soon as he landed, to present himself to the magistrate of the place, and declare, that he came with confidence to invoke the protection of the English nation. Napoleon appeared, to relish this advice; but the counsels of other persons induced him, to incline to the United States. He then sent to the minister of marine for an account of the American vessels, that were in our ports. The minister sent it to him immediately. "Take notice, Sire," he wrote, "of the vessel at Havre. Her captain is in my antechamber; his postchaise at my door. He is ready to depart. I will answer for him. To-morrow, if you please, you may be out of the reach of your enemies."

M. de Vicenza pressed the Emperor, to avail himself of this opportunity. "I am well aware," answered the Emperor, "that there are people, who wish me already gone; who want to get rid of me, and to have me taken prisoner." The duke gave signs of surprise and reproach. "Ah! Caulincourt, it is not you I am speaking of." The Duke of Vicenza replied, that his advice came from his heart; and that he had no other motive, than to see him safe from the dangers, with which he was threatened by the approach of the allies.—The Emperor stopped him. "What have I to fear? I have abdicated; *it is the business of France to protect me!*"

Several Americans, who were at Paris, wrote of their own accord to Napoleon, to offer him their services, and assure him, in the name of their fellow-citizens, that he would be received at Washington with the sentiments of respect, admiration, and devotion, that were his due. Napoleon refused their offers. Not that he had any intention of withdrawing himself from the effects of his abdication: but he had changed his opinion; and considered, that it was his duty, not to quit the country, unless it were exacted of him, till it was no longer in danger.

The government, however, yielding to the continual importunities of the deputies, and of M. Fouché, caused it to be hinted to him, that it was proper he should come to some decision. The Emperor then declared, that he was ready to repair with his family to the United States; and that he would embark, as soon as two frigates were placed at his disposal. The minister of marine was immediately authorized, to fit out these two frigates. Baron Bignon received orders, to demand from Lord Wellington the necessary passports and safeconducts: but the committee, under pretence of not exposing the *frigates* to fall into the enemy's hands, decreed, that they should not put to sea, till the safeconducts were arrived: a singular condition, that cannot be explained honourably but by the supposition, that the government was not desirous at bottom of letting Napoleon depart; no doubt considering his presence in France as a circumstance, that would render the allies more docile, and less exacting.

The promise made by the Emperor, and the measures taken to ensure his departure, were not sufficient, to quiet the apprehensions of his enemies. They were afraid, that he would avail himself of the delay, which must take place before the safeconducts could arrive, to seize on the sovereign authority by main force. Accordingly, they returned to the charge; and the government, to put an end to their importunate fears, and answer by anticipation the objections of the foreign powers, consented to appoint a guardian to the late head of the state. General Count Beker, a member of the chamber of deputies, was named commander of the Emperor's guard; and, under this pretext, directed, to repair to Malmaison, "to watch over the preservation (*conservation*) of the person of Napoleon, and the respect due to him; and to prevent ill-disposed persons from making use of his name, to excite disturbances[70]."

When the general made his appearance at Malmaison, it was supposed, that he came to arrest Napoleon. An exclamation of sorrow escaped from every heart. Gourgaud and some other officers swore, that no one should lay a sacrilegious hand off the Emperor. I ran to inform Napoleon of what was passing. He came out of his closet, and appeared to our eyes

> Avec cet air serein, ce front majestueux,
> Tels que dans les combats, maître de son courage,
> Tranquille, il arrêtait ou pressait le carnage[71].

The Emperor ordered us, to respect the person and mission of General Beker, and let him know, that he might appear without scruple, and without fear. But this officer had already explained the purpose of his journey; and a person came to inform the Emperor, that the object of his mission was, not to arrest him, but to watch over the safety of his person, placed under the protection of the national honour[72].

This declaration deceived no one. It grieved us profoundly. The Princess Hortensia's heart was torn by it. "O, my God!" said she, sorrowfully lifting her eyes to Heaven; "was I born, to see the Emperor a prisoner to the French in Malmaison?"

M. Fouché and his followers did not stop at this first precautionary step; and, to deprive the Emperor of the means "of forming plots," they took from him in succession, under one pretence or other, most of the officers, on whose attachment he could depend. Some were sent for to be about the government, others received missions or commands. All were spoken to in the sacred name of their country, and all obeyed. I too was not forgotten and I received orders, as well as my colleague, Baron Fain, to repair to Paris. I informed the Emperor of it. "Go," said he: "you have my consent. You will know what passes there, and will acquaint me with it. I am sorry, that we did not think of sending you in the suite of the plenipotentiaries: you would have reminded Metternich of what was said at Bâle: you would have informed him, that Fouché is labouring for the Duke of Orleans, &c. &c. Perhaps it may not yet be too late. See Caulincourt from me, and tell him, to give you some mission."

As soon as I arrived at the Tuileries, I expressed to the president of the committee, and to M. de Vicence, a wish to make part of the embassy. I reminded them of the proposals of M. Werner, &c. &c. M. de Vicence thought, that my services might be very useful. The Duke of Otranto answered me, that I must give up all thoughts of that; and nothing more was said about it.

Thus Napoleon remained at Malmaison almost alone[73]; and there retired, as Achilles to his tent, he was cursing his state of idleness, when the minister of marine came to announce to him, in the name of the government, that the enemy was at Compiègne; that the committee, apprehensive for his safety, dispensed with his waiting for the safeconducts, and requested him to depart incognito. The Emperor promised to depart: but, when he heard at a distance the first report of a cannon, his whole body thrilled, and he lamented in a tone of despair, that he was condemned to remain far from the field of battle. He ordered General Beker to be called: "The enemy is at Compiègne; at Senlis!" said he to him: "to-morrow he will be at the gates of Paris. I cannot conceive the blindness of the government. A man must be mad, or a traitor to his country, to question the bad faith of the foreign powers. These people understand nothing of affairs." General Beker made a motion with his head, which Napoleon took for a sign of approbation, and he went on: "All is lost: is it not so? In this case, let them make me general; I will command the array; I will immediately demand this (*speaking in an authoritative tone*): General, you shall carry my letter; set off immediately a carriage is ready for you. Explain to them, that it is not my intention, to seize again the sovereign power: that I will fight the enemy, beat them, and compel them by victory, to give a favourable turn to the negotiations: that afterward, this great point obtained, I will pursue my journey. Go, general, I depend on you; you shall quit me no more."

General Beker, overcome by the ascendancy of his prisoner, set off immediately. The letter, the former part of which I am sorry I cannot warrant to be exact, was in substance as follows:

"*To the Committee of Government.*

"In abdicating the sovereign authority, I did not renounce the noblest right of a citizen, the right of defending my country.

"The approach of the enemy to the capital leaves no doubt of their intentions, of their bad faith.

"Under these weighty circumstances, I offer my services as general, still considering myself as the first soldier of my country."

The Duke of Otranto read this letter aloud, and exclaimed: "Is he *laughing* at us?"

M. Carnot appeared to be of opinion, that the Emperor should be replaced at the head of the army.

The Duke of Otranto replied, that the Emperor no doubt had spared the committee this trouble; that he had probably *stolen away*, the moment General Beker departed; and was already haranguing the soldiers, and reviewing them.

General Beker pledged himself, that Napoleon would await his return.

The president of the committee observed then, that the recall of Napoleon would destroy for ever all hope of conciliation: that the enemy, indignant at our Punic faith, would no longer grant us either truce or quarter: that the character of Napoleon would not allow any confidence, to be placed in his promises; and that, if he should meet with any success, he would re-ascend the throne, and bury himself under its ruins, rather than descend from it a second time, &c.

These observations united all their suffrages, and the members of the committee answered the Emperor, "That their duty toward their country, and the engagements the plenipotentiaries had entered into with the foreign powers, did not permit them, to accept his offer." They appointed M. Carnot, to go to Malmaison; explain to the Emperor his situation, and that of France; and conjure him, to spare those calamities, that he appeared desirous of bringing upon France and upon himself.

The proposal of Napoleon was soon known all over Paris. It was first reported, that he had wished, to resume the command; and at last, that he had resumed it. In fact, immediately after the departure of General Beker, Napoleon ordered his chargers to be saddled; and for three hours it was supposed, that he was going to the army. But he had no thought of basely availing himself of the absence of his guardian, to make his escape. Such an idea was beneath a man, who had come to attack and invade a kingdom with eight hundred soldiers.

General Beker returned to Malmaison. The Emperor snatched the answer of the committee, ran it hastily through, and exclaimed: "I was sure of it; these people have no energy. Well, general, since it is so, let us be gone, let us be gone." He ordered M. de Flahaut to be called; and directed him, to go to Paris immediately, and concert measures for his departure and embarkation with the members of the committee.

The Prince of Eckmuhl was at the Tuileries when M. de Flahaut made his appearance there. In the mission of this general he saw nothing but a subterfuge of the Emperor, to defer his departure. "This Bonaparte of yours," said he to him in a tone of anger and contempt, "will not depart: but we must get rid of him: his presence hampers us, is troublesome to us; it is injurious to the success of our negotiations. If he hope, that we shall take him again, he deceives himself: we will have nothing more to do with him. Tell him from me, that he must go; and if he do not depart instantly, I will have him arrested, *I will arrest him myself.*" M. de Flahaut, burning with indignation, answered: "I could not have believed, M. marshal, that a man, who was at the knees of Napoleon but a week ago, could to-day hold such language. I have too much respect for myself, I have too much respect for the person and misfortunes of the Emperor, to report to him your words; go yourself, M. marshal, it will befit you better than me."—The Prince of Eckmuhl, irritated at this, reminded him, that he was speaking to the minister at war, to the general in chief of the army: and enjoined him, to repair to Fontainebleau, where he should receive his orders.—"No, sir," replied Count de Flahaut briskly, "I will not go; I will not abandon the Emperor I will preserve to the last moment that fidelity to him, which so many others have sworn."—"I will have you punished for your disobedience."—"You have no longer the right to do so. From this moment I give in my resignation. I can no longer serve under your orders, without disgracing my epaulettes."

He went away. The Emperor perceived on his return, that something had cut him to the heart. He questioned him; and at length brought him to confess all that had passed. Accustomed since his abdication, to be surprised at nothing, and to endure every thing without complaint, Napoleon appeared neither astonished nor displeased at the insults of his former minister. "Let him come," answered he coolly: "*I am ready, if he desire it, to hold out my throat to him.* Your conduct, my dear Flahaut, touches me; but your country wants you: remain in the army, and forget, like me, the Prince of Eckmuhl and his dastardly menaces."

History, more rigid, will not forget them. Respect for misfortune has always been placed in the foremost rank of military virtues. If the warrior, who insults his disarmed enemy, lose the esteem of the brave, what sentiment should he inspire, who abuses, insults, and threatens, his friend, his benefactor, his prince, when under misfortunes?

In the bosom of faithful friendship the Emperor disburdened his mind of the chagrin, that the refusal of his services by the committee occasioned him. "Those people," said he to M. de Bassano, "are blinded by their avidity of enjoying power, and continuing to act the sovereign. They feel, that, if they replaced me at the head of the army, they would be no longer any thing more than my shadow; and they are sacrificing me and their country to their pride, to their vanity. They will ruin every thing." After a few moments silence he added: "But why should I let them reign? I abdicated, to save France, to save the throne of my son. If this throne must be lost, I had rather lose it in the field of battle than here. I can do nothing better for all of you, for my son, and for myself, than throw myself into the arms of my soldiers. My presence will electrify the army, will be a clap of thunder to the foreign powers. They will be aware, that I return to the field, to conquer or die: and, to get rid of me, they will grant all you ask. If, on the contrary, you leave me to gnaw my sword here; they will laugh at you, and you will be forced to receive Louis XVIII. *cap in hand*. We must come to a close: if your five Emperors will not have me, to save France, I must dispense with their consent. It will be sufficient for me, to show myself, and Paris and the army will receive me a second time, as their deliverer."—"I do not doubt it, Sire," answered M. de Bassano: "but the chamber will declare against you: perhaps it will even venture, to declare you outlawed. On the other hand, Sire, if fortune should not prove favourable to your efforts; if the army, after performing prodigies of valour, should be overpowered by numbers; what will become of France? what will become of your Majesty? The enemy will be justified in abusing their victory; and perhaps your Majesty would have to reproach yourself with having caused the ruin of France for ever."—"Come, I see, I must always give way." The Emperor remained some minutes, without uttering another word. He then said: "You are right: I ought not to take upon myself the responsibility of so great an event. I ought to wait, till the voice of the people, of the soldiers, of the chambers recall me. But how is it, that Paris does not call for me? Do not the people then perceive, that the allies give you no credit for my abdication?"—"Sire, so much uncertainty pervades their minds, that they cannot come to an understanding with each other. If they were fully convinced, that it is the intention of the allies, to restore Louis XVIII., perhaps they would not hesitate to speak out; but they entertain hopes, that the allies will keep their promises."—"That infamous Fouché deceives you. The committee suffers itself, to be led by him. It will have severe reproaches to make itself. There is nobody in it worth any thing, except Caulincourt and Carnot: and they are badly fitted with associates. What can they do with a traitor, a couple of blockheads[74], and two chambers, that do not know what they would be at? You all believe, like innocents, the fine promises of the foreign powers. You believe, that they will give you a fowl in the pot, and a prince of your own liking, do you not? You deceive yourselves. Alexander, in spite of his magnanimous sentiments, suffers himself to be influenced by the English: he is afraid of them; and the Emperor of Austria will do, as he did in 1814, what others think proper."

This conversation was interrupted by the arrival of Generals P. and Chartran. They had already been refused admittance twice: but this time they declared, that they would not go away, till they had spoken with the Emperor. Their business was, to get money from him. General Chartran, as fatally inspired as Labedoyère, told him, that he had ruined himself in his service; that the Bourbons were on the point of returning; that he should be shot, if he had not money to make his escape; and that money he must have. Napoleon caused a thousand crowns, to be given to each; and they went away. The Princess Hortensia, afraid that these illustrious Cossacks should do the Emperor some ill turn, would generously have given them whatever they asked. I had infinite difficulty in tranquillising her, and making her understand, that they had more design on the purse than the person of Napoleon.

After they were departed, Napoleon gave me some commands for Paris. I returned thither. The moment I entered the Tuileries, the committee had just been informed, that the enemy, after having beaten our troops, was advancing with all speed to Paris. This news rendered the government uneasy; and, as there was no orderly officer then at hand, the Duke of Vicenza requested me, to go and reconnoitre. I set off. On my arrival at the entrance of Bourget, I met General Reille with his army. He informed me, that the enemy was following him; but that there was no reason, to be in fear for the capital. "I know not what is passing there," said he to me; "but this very moment the brother of M. de Talleyrand was brought before me. He had with him a false passport, under the name of Petit. I had an inclination, to send him before the committee of government: but he declared to me, that he was employed by it on a mission as important as it was urgent; and as, at all events, one enemy more can do us no injury, I thought it better to let him pass, than risk the frustrating of his mission by useless delays." I hastened to return, to calm the anxiety of the government.

As soon as I was at liberty, I flew to Malmaison. Napoleon, who felt himself obliged by this continual posting, always condescended to receive me immediately. I gave him an account of every thing, that could be interesting to him. I did not omit to inform him, that the enemy was already master of part of the environs of Paris; and that it was important for him, to be on his guard. "I shall have no fear of them to-morrow," said he to me; "I have promised Decrès to set out, and I will be gone to-night. I am tired of myself, of Paris, of France. Make your preparations, and do not be out of the way."—"Sire," answered I, "when I promised yesterday, to attend your Majesty, I consulted only my attachment; but when I imparted this resolution to my mother, she conjured me by her gray hairs, not to desert her. Sire, she is seventy-four years old[75]: she is blind; my brothers have perished in the field of honour; she has only me, me alone in the world, to protect her: and I confess to your Majesty, that I had not the heart to refuse her."—"You have done well," said Napoleon to me, "you owe yourself to your mother: remain with her. If at some future time you should be master of your own actions, come to me: you will always be well received."—"Your Majesty is resolved, then," I replied, "to depart?"—"What would you have me do here now?"—"Your Majesty is right: but...."—"But what? would you have me remain?"—"Sire, I confess to your Majesty, I cannot look on your departure without alarm."—"In fact the path is difficult; but fortune and a fair wind...."—"Ah, Sire! fortune is no longer in our favour: besides, whither will your Majesty go?"—"I will go to the United States. They will give me land, or I will buy some, and we will cultivate it. I will end, where mankind began: I will live on the produce of my fields and my flock."—"That will be very well, Sire: but do you think, that the English will suffer you, to cultivate your fields in peace?"—"Why not? what harm could I do them?"—"What harm, Sire! Has your Majesty then forgotten, that you have made England tremble? As long as you are alive, Sire, or at least at liberty, she will dread the effects of your hatred and your genius. You were perhaps less dangerous to her on the degraded throne of Louis XVIII., than you would be in the United States. The Americans love and admire you: you have a great influence over them; and you would perhaps excite them to enterprises fatal to England."—"What enterprises? The English well know, that the Americans would lose their lives to a man in defence of their native soil; but they are not fond of making war abroad. They are not yet arrived at a pitch, to give the English any serious uneasiness. Some future day perhaps, they will be the avengers of the seas; but this period, which I might have had it in my power to accelerate, is now at a distance. The Americans advance to greatness but slowly."—"Admitting, that the Americans can give England no serious uneasiness at this moment, your presence in the United States will at least furnish it with an occasion, to stir up Europe against them. The combined powers will consider their work as imperfect, till you are in their possession; and they will compel the Americans, if not to deliver you up, at least to expel you from their territory."—"Well! then I will go to Mexico. I shall there find patriots, and will put myself at their head."—"Your Majesty forgets, that they have leaders already: people bring about revolutions for themselves, not for others; and the chiefs of the independents would be disconcerted by your Majesty's presence, if they did not oblige you, to seek an asylum elsewhere...."—"Well, I will leave them as they are; and go to Caracas; if I do not find myself well received there, I will go to Buenos Ayres; I will go to California; in fine, I will go from shore to shore, till I meet with an asylum against the malignancy and persecutions of men."—"Supposing your Majesty to speak seriously, can you reasonably flatter yourself with continually escaping the snares and fleets of the English?"—"If I cannot escape them, they will take me: their government is good for nothing, but the nation is great, noble, generous; they will treat me as I ought to be treated. After all, what would you have me do? Do you wish, that I should suffer myself to be taken here like a dolt by Wellington, and give him the pleasure of parading me in triumph through the streets of London like King John? Since my services are refused, there is but one step I can take: to depart. The destinies will do the rest."—"There is still another, Sire, if I dared suggest it to you: your Majesty is not a man to run away."—"What do you call running away?" said Napoleon with a proud and angry look: "where do you see me running away?"—"I entreat your Majesty not to dwell on that expression."—"Go on, go on."—"I think then, Sire, that your Majesty ought not thus to quit France, first, for your safety's sake, next for your honour's. The English are informed, that you have the intention of going to the United States; and no doubt our coasts already swarm with their cruisers. This is not all: your Majesty is aware of the hatred and perfidy of the Duke of Otranto: and who can say, whether secret orders have not been issued, to delay your departure, or retard the progress of the vessels, that you may be taken by the English? I consider it impossible, therefore, that your Majesty should escape them; or, if you should escape, but that you must ultimately fall into their hands, sooner or later. In this dilemma, it is right, at least, to endeavour to fall as nobly as possible."—"What are you driving at?" said Napoleon peevishly, thinking I meant to propose suicide to him: "I know, I might say, like Hannibal, 'Let us deliver them from the terror my name inspires:' but suicide is the business only of minds not thoroughly steeled, or of distempered brains. *Whatever my destiny may be, I will never hasten my end a single moment.*"—"Such is not my meaning, Sire; and, since your Majesty condescends to listen to me, were I in your place, I would renounce the chimerical hope of finding an asylum in a foreign country; and I would say to the chambers: I abdicated, in order to disarm our enemies; I learn, that they are not satisfied; if they must have my liberty, or my life, I am ready, to place myself in their hands, happy to be able at this price, to save France and my son. How noble it would be," exclaimed I, "to see Napoleon the Great, after having laid down the crown placed on his head by twenty years of victory, offering himself as a sacrifice to the independence of his country!"—"Yes, yes," said Napoleon, "the sacrifice would be noble; but a nation of thirty millions of souls, that could suffer it, would be dishonoured for ever. Besides, to whom shall I surrender myself? to Blucher? to Wellington? They have not the power necessary, to treat with me on such conditions. They would begin with making me their prisoner; and then would do with me, and with France, whatever they took into their heads."—"I would surrender myself, Sire, to the Emperor Alexander."—"To Alexander! you know nothing of those Russians. It would cost the lives of both of us. However, your idea deserves consideration: I will reflect upon it. Before taking a step, that cannot be retracted, it is proper to look at it twice. The sacrifice of myself would be nothing on my own account; but perhaps it would be lost to France. The faith of an enemy is never to be trusted. See if Maret and Lavalette be here, and send them to me."

Every thing, that bears the stamp of greatness of mind, seduces and transports me. I confess, that my imagination was fired at the idea of Napoleon generously devoting himself for France, and for his son. But this remark of Napoleon's, "A nation of thirty millions of men, that could suffer such a sacrifice, would be for ever dishonoured," a remark that I had not foreseen, dissipated the enchantment. On quitting the closet, I was stopped by the Duke of Rovigo, who said to me: "You have been talking a long while with the Emperor, has any thing new passed?"—"No," answered I; "we have been talking of his departure:" and I gave him an account of our conversation. "Your advice was noble," replied he; "but what I gave him was, I think, preferable. It was, to come and fall with us before the walls of Paris. He will not do so; because, in the first place, Fouché will not leave it in his power; and, in the next, because the fear of endangering every thing has laid hold of him. He will set off to-night. God knows whither we shall go: but no matter, I will follow him. My first object is, to know that he is out of danger. Besides, I would rather ramble at a venture with him, than remain here. Fouché thinks, that he shall get himself out of the scrape: he is mistaken; he will be hanged like the rest, and more richly deserve it. France is sunk, lost! I wish I was dead!"

While I was conversing with the Duke of Rovigo, Napoleon was discussing the proposal, which I had ventured to submit to him. Several times he was on the point of adopting it; but still recurred to his prevailing idea, that such a sacrifice was unworthy a great nation; and that France probably would derive no more advantage from it, than had been derived from his abdication. All things considered, therefore, Napoleon resolved, to entrust his fate "to fortune and the winds." But the committee, advised by a despatch from our plenipotentiaries, which I shall transcribe farther on, "that the escape of Napoleon, before the conclusion of the negotiations, would be considered by the allies as an act of bad faith on our part, and would compromise the safety of France," directed him to be informed, that unforeseen political circumstances compelled it, to subject his departure anew to the arrival of the safeconduct. Thus Napoleon was obliged to remain.

I returned to Paris. Here I learned, that the enemy had made immense progress; and, according to custom, I was desirous of getting off, to acquaint Napoleon with it. The barriers were strictly closed, and no one could go out without permission. I endeavoured to obtain one. The Duke of Otranto answered me, that my presence with the cabinet was necessary; and ordered me to remain. I knew, that one Chauvin, who was to go with the Emperor, was setting out for Malmaison. I ran to acquaint him with what was passing; and directed him, to give the information to Count Bertrand. At the same moment M. G. D.[76], informed, I know not by what means, that the Prussians designed, to carry off the Emperor; that Blucher had said, "If I can catch Bonaparte, I will hang him up at the head of my army;" and that Wellington had strenuously opposed this cowardly and criminal design, M. G. D. hastened, to transmit this information to Napoleon; and soon after found means, by favour of his employment in the national guard, to repair in person to Malmaison. Napoleon made him relate at large all he knew. When he was acquainted with the position of the Prussians, he laid it down on the map[77], and said with a smile: "Aha! so I have suffered myself in fact to be turned." He then sent an orderly officer, to see whether the bridges of Bezons and Peck had been broken down. He found, that the latter was not. "I desired it, however: but I am not surprised at it."

The Emperor then made some arrangements, to secure himself against a surprise: but these precautions were superfluous; he had found, without calling for it, an inviolable rampart against the enterprises of his enemies in the devotion of his old companions in arms. The soldiers, officers, and generals, posted in the direction of Malmaison, sent him assurances, that they would watch over him, and were ready to pour out their blood to the last drop in his defence. One of the commanders of the red lancers of the guard, the young de Brock, rendered himself particularly distinguished by his indefatigable zeal.

The schemes of Blucher, and the proximity of our troops to the place where the Emperor was detained, gave the committee the most serious alarms.

They had at once to fear:

That Napoleon, roused by the sound of arms, and the acclamations of his faithful soldiers, would be unable to repress the desire of coming to fight at their head:

That the army, still idolizing its ancient general, would come to tear him from his state of repose, and oblige him to lead it against the enemy:

Or, lastly, that the enemy would contrive to seize his person by surprise, or by force.

The removal of the Emperor to a distance would quiet at once this state of anxiety: but the despatch of the plenipotentiaries stood in the way; and the committee, restrained by the fear of offending the allies, dared not either oblige, or even authorize Napoleon to remove. Meantime the Duke of Wellington informed M. Bignon, "that he had no authority from his government, to give any answer whatever to the demand of a passport and safeconduct for Napoleon Bonaparte." Having no longer any plausible pretence for detaining him, and unwilling to take on itself the disgrace and responsibility of events, the committee no longer hesitated on the path it had to pursue: it directed the Duke Decrès and Count Boulay, to go immediately to the Emperor (it was half after three in the morning); to inform him, that Lord Wellington had refused the safeconducts; and to notify to him the injunction, to depart immediately.

The Emperor received this communication without any emotion, and promised to be gone in the course of the day.

Orders were immediately given to General Beker, not to allow him to return:

To the prefect of the Lower Charente, to prevent his stay at Rochefort, as far as possible:

To the commandant of the marine, not to suffer him to set foot on shore, from the moment he should embark, &c. &c. &c.

Never was criminal surrounded with precautions more numerous, and at the same time more useless.

If Napoleon, instead of yielding to the fear of compromising the independence and existence of the nation, had wished to revive a second 20th of March, neither the instructions of General Beker, nor the threats of Marshal Davoust, nor the intrigues of M. Fouché, could have prevented him: it would have been sufficient for him to make his appearance. The people, the army, would have received him with enthusiasm and not one of his enemies, the Prince of Eckmuhl at their head, would have dared to lift their eyes, and oppose his triumph.

The moments preceding his departure were exceedingly affecting. He conversed with the few friends, who had not deserted him, on the great vicissitudes of fortune. He deplored the evils, which their devotion to his person, and to his dynasty, would accumulate on their heads; and exhorted them, to oppose their strength of mind, and the purity of their consciences, to the persecutions of their enemies. The fate of France, who can doubt it? was also the object of his anxious and tender solicitude: he put up ardent prayers for its repose, its happiness, and its prosperity.

When information was brought him, that all was ready, he pressed the Princess Hortensia affectionately to his bosom; tenderly embraced his friends, melting into tears; and recommended to them a new unity, courage, and resignation. His demeanour was firm, his voice calm, his countenance serene: not a complaint, not a reproach, escaped his lips.

On the 29th of June, at five in the afternoon, he threw himself into a carriage prepared for his suite; and made General Gourgaud, and his orderly officers, take that intended for himself. His eyes were several times turned towards that last abode, so long the witness of his happiness and his power. He thought, no doubt, that he should see it again no more!

He had demanded, that an advice-boat should be placed under his orders; and that rear-admiral Violette should have the command of his convoy. The committee, which, in all its intercourse with the Emperor, had not ceased to pay him the most respectful attention, readily complied with these demands. Admiral Violette being absent, it was agreed, that the command should be given to the senior captain of the two frigates; and the following are the instructions given him.

"Instructions for Captain Philibert, commanding the Saale, and Poncé, commanding the Medusa.

"Very secret.

"The two frigates are appointed, to carry him, who was lately our Emperor, to the United States of America.

"He will embark in the Saale, with such persons of his suite as he shall choose. The rest will embark in the Medusa.

"The baggage will be distributed between the two frigates agreeably to his directions.

"If, previous to sailing, or on the voyage, the Medusa shall be found to be a swifter sailer than the Saale, he will go on board the Medusa, and captains Philibert and Poncé will exchange their commands.

"The profoundest secrecy is to be kept respecting the embarkation, which will be conducted under the care of the maritime prefect, as well as respecting the person on board.

"Napoleon travels, incognito; and he will make known himself the name and title, by which he chooses to be called.

"Immediately after his embarkation, all communication with the shore must cease.

"The commanders of the frigates, the officers, and the crews, will be informed by their own hearts, that it is their duty, to treat him personally with all the attention and respect due to his situation, and to the crown he has worn.

"When on board, the highest honours will be paid him, unless refused by himself. He will dispose of the interior of the frigates for his own accommodation, in whatever manner he may deem most convenient, without detriment to their means of defence. His table, and the service of his person, will be conducted as he shall direct.

"Every thing that can contribute to his accommodation on the voyage will be prepared, without regard to the expense; and the prefect has received orders for this purpose.

"Such provision for himself and suite will be sent on board by the prefect, as is compatible with the profound secrecy to be observed respecting his abode and his embarkation.

"When Napoleon has embarked, the frigates will put to sea within four-and-twenty hours at farthest, if the wind permit, and the enemy's cruisers do not prevent their sailing.

"They will not remain in the road twenty-four hours after the embarkation of Napoleon, unless he desire it; for it is of importance, to depart as soon as possible.

"The frigates will proceed with all possible speed to the United States of America; and will land Napoleon and his suite either at Philadelphia, or at Boston, or at any other port of the United States, that they can most easily and speedily reach.

"The commanders of the two frigates are forbidden to enter any roadsteads, from which they might find difficulty or delay in departing. They are authorized to do so, only if it should be necessary for the safety of the vessels.

"They will avoid all the ships of war they may fall in with: if they should be obliged to engage a superior force, the frigate, that has not Napoleon on board, will sacrifice herself to detain the enemy; and to give that, on board of which he is, an opportunity of escaping.

"I need not remind you, that the chambers and the government have placed Napoleon under the protection of French loyalty.

"When arrived at the United States, the disembarkation will take place with all possible celerity; and the frigates will not remain there more than four-and-twenty hours, under any pretence whatever, unless they be prevented from sailing by a superior force; and they will return directly to France.

"The laws and regulations respecting the police of vessels at sea, and the military subordination of the persons embarked as passengers to the commanders of the vessels, will be strictly observed.

"I recommend to the captains' own sense of duty, as well as to their delicacy, every circumstance not provided for by these presents.

"I have nothing to add to what I have said already, that the person of Napoleon is placed under the safeguard of the loyalty of the French people; and this trust is confided specially, on the present occasion, to the captains of the Saale and the Medusa, and the officers and crews of these two vessels.

"Such are the orders, which the committee of government has directed me to transmit to captains Philibert and Poncé.

(Signed) "The Duke Decrès."

On the 29th of June, the committee informed the two chambers by a message, that "the approach of the enemy, and the fear of an internal commotion, had imposed on it the sacred duty, of causing Napoleon to depart."

The terms, in which this message was couched, gave reason to suppose, that the Emperor had shown some resistance. M. de Lavalette called on the Duke Decrès to explain the facts; and it was then known, that the Emperor had not hesitated for a moment, to submit to the fate imposed upon him by his abdication; and that, if he did not set out before, it was because the committee had judged it proper to defer his departure, till the arrival of the safeconducts demanded.

The Emperor had at first expressed his intention of not stopping on the road. When he arrived at Rambouillet, he alighted from his carriage, and said, that he would pass the night at the castle. He made the grand marshal write to the keeper of the moveables of the crown, to require him to send to Rochefort, where they would be embarked, the necessary beds and furniture for seven or eight principal apartments. He had previously claimed the library of Petit Trianon, M. de Visconti's Greek Iconography, and a copy of the grand work of the Egyptian Institute. The faculty of associating thoughts the most serious with ideas of the greatest simplicity, occupations the most vast with cares the most minute, was one of the distinguishing features of the character of Napoleon.

At daybreak he received a courier from M. de ****. He read his despatches, and then said to General Beker, casting a sorrowful look toward Heaven: "The business is finished! it is all over with France! let us begone!"

He was received on his journey with the most lively testimonies of interest and attachment: but nothing could equal the transports, which the troops and inhabitants of Niort expressed at seeing him. He recommended to General Beker, to inform the government of this. "Tell them, general, that they knew little of the spirit of France; that they were too hasty in sending me away; that, if they had accepted my proposal, the face of affairs would have been changed; that I might still, in the name of the nation, exert a great influence on the course of political transactions, in backing the negotiations of government by an army, to which my name would serve as a rallying point."

The general was preparing, to forward to the committee the words of the Emperor; and had just finished his despatch, when information was brought that a heavy cannonade had been heard on the 30th. The Emperor immediately made him add the following postscript, which the general wrote from his dictation: "We hope, that the enemy will allow you time, to cover Paris, and to see the issue of the negotiations. If, under these circumstances, the English cruisers should prevent the Emperor's departure, he is at your disposal as a soldier."

The Emperor continued his course; and, his journey from Niort to Rochefort affording no remarkable incident, I resolved, though with regret, to lose sight for a moment of this august victim, and return to the government, that had succeeded him.

The government, impressed with the importance of its functions, had not ceased, since its formation, to use its utmost endeavours, to justify the confidence of the chambers. Its politics, which were perfectly open, were included in these few words: no war, no Bourbons: and its double resolve was, to make every concession to the allies, necessary to obtain a peace conformable to the wishes of the nation; or to oppose to them an inflexible resistance, if they resolved to intrench on the independence of the nation, and impose on it a sovereign not of its own choice.

The Duke of Otranto, president of the committee, appeared in the council, and in public, to approve the principles and determinations of his colleagues. In private, it was a different affair. Devoted in appearance to all parties, he flattered and deceived them in turn, by pretended confidential communications, and chimerical hopes. He spoke of liberty to the republicans, of glory and Napoleon II. to the Bonapartists, of legitimacy to the friends of the King, of guarantees and a general peace to the partizans of the Duke of Orleans; and thus contrived to secure himself on all sides, in case of need, favourable chances and supporters[78]. Men familiar with his practices were not the dupes of his artifices, and endeavoured to unmask them: but his apparent conduct was so irreproachable, that their warnings were considered as the result of personal prejudice, or unjust suspicion.

Besides, it was agreed on all hands, that the fate of France depended on the negotiations with foreign powers: and it was hoped, that the plenipotentiaries, and particularly Messrs. d'Argenson and la Fayette, whose principles were inflexible, would render every kind of surprise or treachery impracticable.

These plenipotentiaries had left Paris on the 25th of June. Their instructions were as follows:

Instructions for Messieurs the Plenipotentiaries of the Committee of Government to the Allied Powers.

"Paris, June the 23d, 1815.

"The object of the mission of messieurs the plenipotentiaries, appointed to repair to the allied powers, has no farther need of being developed. It is in their hearts, as it is in the hearts of all Frenchmen: the business is, to save their country.

"The salvation of the country is connected with two essential subjects: the independence of the nation, and the integrity of its territories.

"The independence of the nation cannot be complete, except the constituent principles of the present organization of France be secure from every foreign attack. One of the principles of this organization is the inheritance of the throne in the imperial family. The Emperor having abdicated, his rights have devolved on his son. The foreign powers cannot make the least attack on this principle of inheritance, established by our constitutions, without violating our independence.

"The declaration of the 13th, and the treaty of the 25th of March, have received an important modification by the explanatory article, which the British cabinet annexed to the ratification of this treaty: an article, by which this cabinet announces, *that it has no intention of pursuing the war for the purpose of imposing a particular government on France*. This modification has been adopted by the allies; it has been sanctioned by Lord Clancarty's letter of the 6th of May, to the drawing up of which all the other plenipotentiaries gave their assent; it has been sanctioned by a note of Prince Metternich's, dated the 9th; and finally by the declaration of the combined powers dated the 12th of the same month.

"It is this grand principle, acknowledged by the combined powers, to which messieurs the plenipotentiaries ought particularly to appeal.

"We cannot conceal, that it is much to be feared, that the combined powers will think themselves at present bound more by the declarations, which they made before the commencement of hostilities. They will not fail to object,

"That, if, previous to the war, they set up a distinction between the nation and the Emperor, this distinction no longer exists, when the nation, by uniting all its forces in the hands of this prince, has in fact united his fate with its own:

"That, though, previous to the war, they were sincere in their intention of not interfering in the internal concerns of France, they are compelled to interfere in them now, precisely for the prevention of any similar recurrence of war, and for ensuring tranquillity for the future.

"It would be superfluous, to point out to messieurs the plenipotentiaries the answers they may make to these objections. They will find their best refutation in the sentiments of national honour, which, after the whole nation had joined the Emperor, could not but fight with him and for him; and could not separate from him, till some act, such as that of an abdication, dissolved the ties between the nation and its sovereign. It will be easy to them to demonstrate, that, if this sacred duty of honour compelled the French nation, to make war for its own defence, as well as that of the head, that was attempted to be taken from it; the abdication of this head replaces the nation in a state of peace with all the powers, since it was this head alone, that they wished to remove: and that, if the declaration made by the combined powers, of having no intention to impose on France a particular government, were frank and sincere, this sincerity, and this frankness, ought now to be manifested by their respect for the national independence, when recent circumstances have removed the only grievance, of which they thought themselves authorised to complain.

"There is an objection of a more serious nature, which the combined powers might bring forward first, if they be determined to avail themselves of all the advantages, which their military position seems to offer them. This objection would be that of an inclination to refuse to acknowledge the committee of government, and the plenipotentiaries, and the acts of the national representatives, as proceeding from a state of things illegal in their eyes, because they have constantly refused, to admit the principle, on which it is founded. This objection, if it be strongly urged, and the combined powers will not wave it, will leave little prospect of the possibility of an accommodation. However messieurs the plenipotentiaries will assuredly neglect no endeavour, to combat such objections; and they will be in no want of arguments, to combat them with success, particularly with respect to the British government, the present dynasty of which reigns solely in virtue of those principles, the application of which we in our turn have occasion to claim.

"Perhaps, too, without disavowing the independence of the French nation, the allied sovereigns will persist in declaring, that they have no proof, that the wishes of the nation are the wishes expressed by the government, or even by the chambers; and that thus, in order to know the real wishes of the nation, they must begin by restoring things to the state in which they were before the month of March, 1815; leaving to the nation afterwards to decide, whether it ought to retain its old government, or give itself a new one.

"The answer to these objections also will be found in that which England itself formerly gave to the enemies, who were for disputing its right of changing its government and its dynasty. England then answered, that the simple fact of the possession of the sovereign authority authorised foreign powers, to treat with him, who was invested with it. Thus, in case the authorities actually existing in France were not, what in fact they are, clothed in the most perfect legality, the refusal to treat with them can be supported by no solid argument. It would be declaring, that they are resolved to try, how far they can carry the claims of force; and announcing to France, that there is no security for her but in the resources of desperation.

"In fine, there is one less obnoxious chance, against which also we ought to be provided. It is, that the combined powers, faithful at least in part to their declaration, do not absolutely insist on imposing the Bourbon family on France; but that, on the other hand, they require the exclusion of the son of the Emperor Napoleon, under pretence, that a long minority might give rise either to a dangerous display of ambitious views on the part of the principal members possessing the authority in France, or to internal commotions, the shock of which would be felt abroad. Were the question brought to this point, messieurs the plenipotentiaries would find in the principles of the objection itself the principle of its answer; since the division of power in the hands of a council commonly renders its authority weaker, and the minority of a prince is always a period of slackness and languor in the government. They would find it particularly in the present temper of the French nation, in the want it feels of a long peace, in the fears which the idea of a continuation or renewal of war must inspire, and in the shackles imposed by the laws of the constitution on the passions of the members of the government. Besides, whatever its construction may be, they will find in all its circumstances, and in a thousand others besides, very valid arguments, to oppose to those, that may be alleged against the maintenance of hereditary principles in the dynasty of the Emperor Napoleon.

"The first and most solid pledge, that the allies can give the French nation of their intention to respect its independence, is to renounce without reserve all design of subjecting it anew to the government of the Bourbon family. The allied powers must now be well convinced themselves, that the re-establishment of this family is incompatible with the general tranquillity of France, and consequently with the repose of Europe. If it be their wish, as they declare, to produce a stable order of things in France and other nations, the purpose would be completely defeated. The return of a family, strangers to our manners, and continually surrounded by men, who have ceased to be French, would rekindle a second time among us every kind of animosity, and every passion; and it would be an illusion, to expect a stable order to arise from the midst of so many elements of discord and trouble. Thus the exclusion of the Bourbon family is an absolute condition of the maintenance of the general tranquillity; and for the general interest of Europe, as well as for the particular interest of France, it is one of the points, to which messieurs the plenipotentiaries must most strongly adhere.

"The question of the integrity of the territory of France is intimately connected with that of its independence. If the war, declared by the allied powers against the Emperor Napoleon, were in fact declared against him alone, the integrity of our territory is not threatened. It is of importance to the general balance of power, that France should retain at least the limits assigned it by the treaty of Paris. What the foreign cabinets themselves considered as proper and necessary in 1814, they cannot look upon with other eyes in 1815. What pretence can justify now a dismemberment of the French territory by the foreign powers? Every thing in the system of Europe is altered; all to the advantage of England, Russia, Austria, and Prussia; all to the detriment of France. The French nation is not jealous; but it will not be subjugated, or dismembered.

"Thus the efforts of messieurs the plenipotentiaries will have two leading objects; the maintenance of the national independence, and the preservation of the integrity of the French territories.

"These two objects are linked together, and mutually dependent on each other: they cannot be separated, and no modification of either of them can be admitted, without endangering the safety of the country.

"But if the foreign powers should make any proposals, capable of being reconciled with our dearest interests; and they should be offered to us as the ultimatum of our safety; messieurs the plenipotentiaries, refraining from the expression of a premature opinion, will hasten *to give an account of them, and to demand the orders of government.*

"Whatever may be the dispositions of the foreign powers; whether they acknowledge the two principles, that are pointed out to messieurs the plenipotentiaries as the bases of their mission; or the negotiations lead to other discussions, of a nature to require enlarging upon; it is highly important, on either supposition, that a general armistice should be previously agreed on. The first care of messieurs the plenipotentiaries must consequently be, to demand an armistice, and insist on its being promptly concluded upon.

"There is one sacred duty, that the French nation cannot forget; which is, *to stipulate the safety and inviolability of the Emperor Napoleon out of its territory*. This is a debt of honour, which the nation feels the necessity of acquitting toward a prince, who long covered it with glory; and who in his misfortunes renounces the throne, that the nation may be saved without him, since it appears, that with him it cannot be saved.

"The choice of the place, to which the Emperor will have to retire, may be a subject of discussion. Messieurs the plenipotentiaries will appeal to the personal generosity of the sovereigns, to obtain a residence to be fixed upon, with which the Emperor will have reason to, be satisfied.

"Independently of the general considerations, which messieurs the plenipotentiaries will have to urge to the allied sovereigns indiscriminately, they will themselves judge of the various arguments, which they will have to employ with respect to the different cabinets separately.

"The interests of England, Austria, Russia, and Prussia, not being the same; it will be proper, to exhibit under different points of view to each of these cabinets the advantages, that the new order of things, recently established in France, may offer them respectively. All the powers will find in it a guarantee of the preservation of whatever they possess, either of territory, or of influence: but, with these general advantages, some of them must find themselves separately benefited.

"Austria may well be supposed, not to see with pleasure the re-establishment of one branch of the Bourbon dynasty on the throne of Fiance, while another branch of the same house reascends the throne of Naples.

"This circumstance, which belongs to the policy of the cabinet, may also receive some support from family affection: the regard of his Majesty the Emperor of Austria for his grandson may induce him, not to oppose the high destiny offered to him. It may be, that the Austrian cabinet may perceive in this bond of relationship a means of strengthening its cause by the support of the French nation; and that, alarmed at the aggrandisement of Russia and of Prussia, whose alliance no doubt is a grievance to it, it may lay hold of the opportunity of an advantageous reconciliation with France, so as in case of need to find in it a powerful auxiliary against those two governments.

"Other reasons offer themselves, to incline the cabinet of Petersburg toward us. The liberal opinions professed by the Emperor of Russia authorize a language to be held to his minister, and even to this potentate himself, to which few other sovereigns would be capable of listening. There is room for thinking also, that this monarch takes but little interest personally in the welfare of the Bourbon family, whose conduct in general has not been pleasing to him. He had not much reason to be satisfied with it, when he found it express its gratitude almost exclusively to the Prince Regent of England. Besides, the object of Russia is attained all its thirst of power, and its self-love, are equally satisfied. Tranquil for a long time to come, and victor without having fought, the Emperor Alexander may proudly return to his dominions, and enjoy a success, that will not have cost him a single man. The continuance of the war with France would now be to him a war without an object. It would be repugnant to all the calculations of good policy, and to the interests of his people. Messieurs the plenipotentiaries will avail themselves of these circumstances, and of many others also, to endeavour to neutralize a power so formidable as Russia.

"That continental power, from which France has the least favour to expect, is the court of Berlin: but this court is that of which the forces have received the most violent check; and if Russia and Austria be ever so little disposed; to enter into negotiations, Prussia will be inevitably compelled to accede to them. Besides, even with this court, arguments of great weight will not be wanting, to render it more amicably disposed, if it will listen only to its real and permanent interests.

"Messieurs the plenipotentiaries will find with the allied sovereigns the British plenipotentiaries and it will be with these, perhaps, that the negotiation will present most difficulties. The question with respect to the allies is scarcely a matter of discussion: with this power, every argument and every principle are in our favour; but it remains to be seen, whether its will be not independent of all principles, and of all arguments.

"The particulars noticed above were no doubt unnecessary; as every thing there mentioned would have suggested itself to messieurs the plenipotentiaries themselves. But these hints may not be without their use, since their natural effect will be, to lead the minds of messieurs the plenipotentiaries to more weighty considerations, and more powerful motives, which they will know how to employ seasonably for the grand purpose of the important and difficult mission with which they are charged.

"Messieurs the plenipotentiaries will find in the reports made to the Emperor by the Duke of Vicenza on the 12th of April and 7th of June last, as well as in the justificatory pieces, that accompany these reports, all the data they can require, to form a just estimate of our situation with regard to the foreign powers, and to regulate their conduct toward the ministers of these different powers."

On the 26th of June the plenipotentiaries had their first interview with two Prussian officers delegated by Marshal Blucher. They gave an account of it to the committee by the following despatch, addressed to M. Bignon, who had the portfolio of foreign affairs.

"Laon, June the 26th, 1815,
"Ten o'clock in the evening.

"Monsieur le Baron Bignon,

"We have received the letter, which you did us the honour to write to us yesterday the 25th, respecting the Emperor's intention of repairing to the United States of America with his brothers.

"We have at length just received our passports, to proceed to the head-quarters of the allied sovereigns, which we shall find at Heidelberg or at Manheim. The Prince of Schoenburgh, aide-de-camp of Marshal Blucher, accompanies us. We shall take the road through Metz; and set off in an hour.

"Marshal Blucher has declared to us, by the Prince of Schoenburgh and Count Noslitz, who was more particularly empowered by him, that France will be in no degree restricted in the choice of a government: but in the armistice he proposed, *he required for the security of his army the fortified towns of Metz, Thionville, Mézières, Maubeuge, Sarrelouis, and others*. He sets out with the principle, that he ought to be secured against any attempts, which the party, that he supposes the Emperor to have, may make. We combated this argument by irrefragable reasons, without gaining any ground. You are sensible, sir, that it was impossible for us, to accede to such demands.

"We did all in our power, to obtain the armistice on moderate terms; but it was impossible for us, to come to any conclusion, 'because,' said the prince, 'he is not authorized to grant one, and immense advantages alone could induce him, to take such a step, as long as the principal object is unattained.'

"We offered a suspension of hostilities, at least for five days. The refusal was equally positive, and for the same motives. Count de Noslitz has offered in the name of Prince Blucher, to receive at his head-quarters, *and at those of the Duke of Wellington, any commissioners you may send, who shall be exclusively employed in the negotiations necessary to stay the march of the armies, and prevent the effusion of blood*. It is a matter of urgency, that these commissioners set out to-morrow even, and that they take the road to Noyon, where orders will be given by Marshal Blucher to receive them. Noyon will be his head-quarters.

They cannot too often repeat, that the Emperor has no great party in France; that he availed himself rather of the faults of the Bourbons, than of any dispositions existing in his favour; and that he could not fix the attention of the nation, but for the allies failing to adhere to their declaration.

"We have hopes of seeing our negotiations take a successful turn, though we cannot be insensible to their difficulties. The only means of preventing the events of the war from occasioning their failure absolutely consist in granting a truce of a few days. The choice of negotiators may have some influence on this; and we repeat, there is not a moment to be lost in sending them to the English and Prussian armies.

"The two aides-de-camp of Prince Blucher declared repeatedly, that the allies are in no respect tenacious of the restoration of the Bourbons: but we have proofs, that they are inclined to approach as near as possible to Paris, and then they may frame some pretence, to change their language.

"All these things should only hasten still more the measures, to be taken for re-organizing the army, and particularly for the defence of Paris; an object to which their thoughts appear essentially turned.

"From the conversations we have had with the two aides-de-camp, it follows definitively, and we repeat it with regret, that the person of the Emperor will be one of the greatest difficulties. They think, that the combined powers will require guarantees and precautions, that he may never re-appear on the stage of the world. They assert, that their people themselves demand security against his enterprises. *It is our duty to observe, that his escape before the conclusion of our negotiations would be considered as an act of bad faith on our part, and might essentially involve the safety of France.* We have hopes, however, that this affair also may be terminated to the Emperor's satisfaction; since they have made few objections to his residence, and that of his brothers, in England; which they appeared to prefer to the scheme of a retreat in America.

"*The imperial prince has not been mentioned in any of our conversations.* It was not our business, to start this subject, on which they did not enter.

(Signed) "H. Sébastiani.
Count de Pontécoulant.
Count de Pontécoulant.
La Fayette.
D'Argenson.
Count de la Forêt.
Benjamin Constant."

The committee, immediately on the receipt of this despatch, appointed Messieurs Andréossy, de Valence, Flaugergues, Boissy d'Anglas, and Labenardiere, to repair in quality of commissioners to the head-quarters of the allied armies, to demand a suspension of hostilities, and negotiate an armistice.

The Duke of Otranto, ever eager to open an ostensible correspondence, under cover of which he might carry on secret communications if necessary, persuaded the government, that it would be proper to pave the way for the commissioners by a previous step; and in consequence he addressed a letter of congratulation to the Duke of Wellington, in which he entreated him with pompous meanness, to bestow on France his suffrage and protection.

Copies of the former instructions were delivered to the commissioners; and to these were added the following:

"*Instructions for Messieurs the Commissioners appointed to treat for an Armistice.*

"Paris, June the 27th, 1815.

"The first overtures made to our plenipotentiaries on the conditions, at the price of which the commander in chief of one of the enemy's armies would consent to an armistice, are of a nature to alarm us respecting those, which the commanders of the armies of the other powers might also demand, and to render the possibility of an arrangement very problematical. However unfavourable our military situation at the present moment may be, there are sacrifices, to which the interest of the nation will not allow us to submit.

"It is evident, that the motive, on which Prince Blucher founded his demand of six of our fortified towns, which were named, and some others besides, which were not named, *the security of his army*, is one of those allegations brought forward by force, to carry as far as possible the advantages arising from the success of the moment. This allegation is very easily refuted: since it may be termed an act of derision, to demand pledges for the security of an army already master of a considerable portion of our territory, and which is marching without obstacle almost alone in the heart of France. There is another declaration made on the part of Prince Blucher, calculated still more to disquiet us: which is, that he can be induced only by immense advantages, to take upon himself to conclude an armistice, for which he has no authority. In this declaration there is a frankness of exaction, that offers many difficulties in the way of accommodation. However, though the committee of government is far from being inclined to favour the cessions required, it does not tie itself up, by a peremptory refusal, from entering into discussions of an arrangement, the conditions of which are not carried beyond the bounds traced by the true interests of the public.

"If, to arrive at a conclusion, we must submit to the cession of some fortified town, it is thoroughly to be understood, that such a cession ought not to take place, unless it were the guarantee of an armistice, to be prolonged till peace is concluded. It is unnecessary to add, that the delivery of such a town is not to take place; till the armistice has been ratified by the respective governments.

"One of the points, that demands all the zeal of messieurs the commissioners, is that of fixing the line, where the occupation of the French territory by the enemy's armies is to stop.

"It would be of great importance, to obtain the line of the Somme; which would place the foreign troops nearly thirty leagues from Paris, messieurs the commissioners ought strongly to insist on keeping them at least at this distance.

"If the enemy were yet more exacting, and we should be finally compelled to greater condescension, a line traced between the Somme and the Oise should not let them approach within twenty leagues of Paris. The line, that separates the department of the Somme from that of the Oise, might be taken, detaching from the latter the northern part of the department of the Aisne, and thence a straight line through the department of the Ardennes, which should be continued till it reached the Meuse near Mézières.

"However, in fixing the line of the armistice, we must rely on the ability of messieurs the commissioners, to endeavour to obtain the most favourable arrangement.

"Their mission being to the English and Prussian armies in common, there is no occasion to inform them, that it is indispensable for the armistice to be common to both armies.

"It would be very important likewise, to introduce into the armistice, as one of its clauses, that it should extend to the armies of all the other enemies, taking for its basis the *status quo* of the respective armies, at the moment when information of the armistice should reach them. If this stipulation be rejected, under pretence, that the commanders of the English and Russian armies have no right, to make arrangements in the names of the commanders of the armies of the other powers; they may at least consent, to invite the others to accede to it on the basis above mentioned.

"As even the negotiations for the armistice, from the nature of the conditions already placed foremost, which must be the subject of more serious debate, will inevitably occasion some delay, it is a precaution rigidly necessary to be obtained, that, in order to treat of an armistice, all movements should be stopped for a few days, or at least for eight and forty hours.

"There is one precautionary arrangement, which messieurs the commissioners must not neglect. This is, to stipulate, that the enemy's armies shall levy no extraordinary contributions.

"Though the particular object of their mission is the conclusion of an armistice, as it is scarcely to be imagined, that messieurs the commissioners, in their intercourse with the Duke of Wellington and Prince Blucher, will not hear from these generals either proposals, or suggestions, or at least simple conjectures, respecting the views the allied sovereigns may adopt with respect to the form of government in France; messieurs the commissioners undoubtedly will not fail, carefully to collect every thing, that may appear to them capable of having any influence on the part to be taken definitively by the government.

"The copy of the instructions given to messieurs the plenipotentiaries appointed to repair to the allied sovereigns, which has been delivered to them, will make them acquainted with the bases, on which the government has been desirous hitherto of founding its negotiations. It is possible, that the course of events may oblige it, to *extend these bases*: but messieurs the commissioners will judge, that, if absolute necessity compel it, to assent to arrangements *of a different nature*, so that we cannot preserve *the principle of our independence in all its plenitude*, it is a sacred duty, to endeavour to emancipate ourselves from the greater part of the inconveniences, that are attached to the bare misfortune of its being modified.

"A copy of the letter, written from Laon by messieurs the plenipotentiaries, and dated yesterday, the 26th, is also delivered to messieurs the commissioners. The resolutions[79], which have been taken to-day by the government, will furnish them with the means of answering all the objections, that may be made to them on the danger and possibility of the return of the Emperor Napoleon.

"That the language of messieurs the commissioners may perfectly accord with all that has been done by the committee of government, copies of the letters, that have been written to Lord Castlereagh and the Duke of Wellington, respecting the approaching departure of Napoleon and his brothers, are hereto annexed.

"On the questions relative to the form of government of France, provisionally, messieurs the commissioners will confine themselves to hearing the overtures, that may be made to them; and they will take care, to transmit an account of them, in order that, according to the nature of their reports, government may come to such a determination, as the safety of our country may prescribe."

From this document it appears, that the committee, already foreseeing the impossibility of preserving the throne to Napoleon II., was disposed to enter into a discussion with the allies on the choice of a sovereign. Bound by its mandate, it would never have consented willingly, to covenant with the Bourbons; but it would have had no repugnance, at least as I conjecture, to allow the crown to be placed on the head of the King of Saxony, or of the Duke of Orleans.

The party of the latter prince, for which M. Fouché had collected recruits, was reinforced by a great number of deputies and generals. "The qualities of the duke; the remembrance of Jemappes, and of some other victories under the republic, in which he was not unconcerned; the possibility of forming a treaty, that should reconcile the interests of all parties; the name of Bourbon, which might have been employed abroad, without uttering it at home: all these motives, and others besides, afforded in this choice a prospect of repose and security even to those, who could not see in it the presage of happiness."

The King of Saxony had no other title to the suffrages of France, than the heroic fidelity, which he had maintained toward it in 1814. But after him the empire might have returned to Napoleon II.: and as a prince, possessed of experience, wisdom, and virtue, may reign indifferently over any people, and render them happy, the French nation would have resigned itself to the government of a foreign monarch, till the day when his death would have restored the sceptre to the hands of its legitimate possessor.

The deference which the committee was prepared to pay to the will of the allied powers, was not the effect of its own weakness. It was enjoined it by the alarming reports, which Marshal Grouchy sent it daily, of the defection and dejected state of the army.

The soldiers, it is true, discouraged by the abdication of the Emperor, and the reports of the return of the Bourbons, appeared irresolute. "Our wounds," said they, "will no longer entitle us to any thing but proscription." The generals themselves, rendered timid by their uncertainty of the future, spoke with circumspection: but all, generals and soldiers, maintained the same sentiments in the bottom of their hearts; and their hesitation, their lukewarmness, were the work of their leader; who, in France as on the banks of the Dyle, wanting resolution and strength of mind, did not take the trouble to conceal, that he considered the national cause as lost, and awaited only a favourable opportunity, to pacify the Bourbons and their allies by a prompt and complete submission.

The committee, however, having their eyes opened by private letters, conceived suspicions of the veracity of the marshal's reports. It commissioned

General Corbineau, to give it an account of the state of the army. Informed of the truth, it was no longer afraid of being obliged to submit humbly to the law of the victor: and, desirous of preventing Marshal Grouchy, whose intentions had ceased to be a mystery, from endangering the independence of the nation by an inconsiderate act, it prohibited him from negotiating any armistice, or commencing any negotiation; and ordered him, to lead his army to Paris.

The Prince of Eckmuhl, whose want of firmness was so wretchedly displayed in the retreat from Moscow, could not resist this fresh blow: the example of Marshal Grouchy led him away; and, persuaded like him, that it was necessary to submit without delay, he declared to the government, that there was not a moment to be lost in recalling the Bourbons, and proposed to it, to send to the king the following offers:

1st, To enter Paris without a foreign guard:

2d, To take the tri-coloured cockade:

3d, To guaranty security of person and property to all, whatever may have been their functions, offices, votes, or opinions:

4th, To retain the two chambers:

5th, To ensure to persons in office the retention of their places, and to the army that of their ranks, pensions, honours, and prerogatives:

6th, To retain the legion of honour, and its institution, as the first order in the state.

The committee, too *clear-sighted* to be caught by this proposal, was eager to reject it; and, faithful to its system of concealing nothing from the two chambers, acquainted the principal members with it; repeating to: them, that, be the event what it might, "it would never propose to them any thing pusillanimous, or contrary to its duty; and that it would defend to the last extremity the independence of the nation, the inviolability of the chambers, and the liberty and security of the citizens."

The representatives answered this declaration by placing Paris in a state of siege, and voting an address to the army[80]. "Brave soldiers," such were its words; "a great reverse must have astonished, but not dejected you. Your country has need of your constancy and courage. To you it has confided the care of the national glory; and you will answer its expectations.

"Plenipotentiaries have been sent to the allied powers ... the success of the negotiations depends on you. Close round the tri-coloured flag, consecrated by glory and the wishes of the nation. You will see us, if necessary, in your ranks; and we will convince the world, that twenty-five years of glory and sacrifices will never be effaced, and that a people, who wills to be free, must ever remain so."

The attitude of the chamber and of the government did not remove the apprehensions of the Prince of Eckmuhl. He returned to the charge; and wrote to the president of the committee, in the night of the 29th, "that he had vanquished his prejudices and opinions, and found, that no means of safety existed but in concluding an armistice, and immediately proclaiming Louis XVIII."

The president answered him:

"I am as well persuaded as you, M. marshal, that nothing better can be done, than to treat with promptitude of an armistice: but we must know, what the enemy wants. An injudicious conduct would produce three evils:

"1st, That of having acknowledged Louis XVIII. previous to any engagement on his side:

"2d, That of being equally compelled, to admit the enemy into Paris:

"3d, That of obtaining no conditions from Louis XVIII.

"I take upon myself, to authorize you, to send to the advanced posts of the enemy, and to conclude an armistice, making every sacrifice, that is compatible with our duties, and with our dignity. It is better to give up fortified towns, than to sacrifice Paris."

The Duke of Otranto having laid this letter before the committee, it thought, that the answer of its president *decided implicitly the question of the recall of Louis XVIII.*, and allowed the Prince of Eckmuhl too great latitude. It made him write immediately a supplementary letter, saying: "It is unnecessary to remind you, M. marshal, that your armistice must be purely military, and must contain no political question. It would be proper, that this demand of an armistice should be made by a general of the line, and a major-general of the national guard."

Thus in the space of the twenty-four hours, that preceded and followed the Emperor's departure, the committee had to repel, and did repel, the instigations more or less culpable of the minister at war, the general in chief of the army, and the president of the government[81].

The army, however, had arrived step by step at the gates of Paris.

Marshal Grouchy, dissatisfied and disconcerted, gave in his resignation on the score of his health.

The Prince of Eckmuhl, who, by an air of sincerity, and reiterated protestations of devotion and fidelity, had regained, thanks to the Duke of Otranto, the confidence of the majority of the members of the committee, was invested with the command in chief of the army.

On the 30th of June a message informed the chambers, that the enemies were within sight of the capital; that the army, re-organized, occupied a line of defence, by which Paris was protected; that it was animated with the best disposition; and that its devotion equalled its valour.

Deputations from the two chambers immediately set out, to carry to the defenders of their country the expression of the principles, the sentiments, and the hopes of the national representation. Their patriotic language, their tri-coloured scarfs, and the name of Napoleon II., which they took care to employ, electrified the soldiery; and completely restored to them that confidence in themselves, and that resolution to conquer or die, which are the infallible presages of victory.

The moment for marching to battle was propitious. The Prince of Eckmuhl solicited peace.

The Duke of Albuféra had just concluded an armistice with Marshal Frimont, commander of the Austrian forces. The prince informed the Duke of Wellington of it; and demanded of him, to cause a cessation of hostilities, *till a decision of congress should take place.* "If I appear on the field of battle with the idea of your talents," he added, "I shall carry with me the conviction, that I am fighting for the most sacred of causes, that of the defence and independence of my country; and, whatever may be the result, my lord, I will merit your esteem."

If, instead of holding a language more suitable to a man half vanquished, than to a French general accustomed to conquer, another chief, differently inspired, had declared with noble firmness, that he was ready, if a stop were not put to unjust aggressions, to give to his eighty thousand brave soldiers the signal of victory or death; the enemy would unquestionably have desisted from pursuing a war, now become without object, without utility, and without glory. But the Duke of Wellington, faithfully informed of the true state of things, knew that the Prince of Eckmuhl, satisfied with having surmounted his prejudices and opinions, appeared more disposed to neutralize the courage of his troops, than to put it to the proof; and Wellington refused the suspension of hostilities proposed. It entered into the policy of the princes, who had taken up arms for legitimacy, to compel us to receive Louis XVIII. *cap in hand*: and the consequence of this was, that the allied generals avoided treating; as the sentiments of the president of the committee, and of the general of the French army, fully satisfied them, that they might wait without any risk, till circumstances or treachery compelled us, to submit to the law of necessity.

Wellington had rejected the proposal of Marshal Davoust, under the frivolous pretence, that the Emperor had resumed the command of the army. It is naturally to be presumed, that the committee had not neglected, to give the commissioners immediate information of the departure of Napoleon, and of the circumstances, that had preceded it. But it had hitherto received no communication from them. Their correspondence, intentionally fettered by the allies, had been farther prevented by our advanced posts; who, considering the persons appointed to hold a parley as machinators of treason, stopped their way with their muskets. The committee resolved, therefore, to obtain news of them at any price: and, on the recommendation of the Duke of Otranto, it despatched to them M. de Tromeling. It was not ignorant, that this emigrant officer, a Vendean, and long detained in the Temple as the companion of Sir Sidney Smith and Captain Wright, little merited the confidence of the patriots. But the double-faced agents of M. Fouché alone could open the enemy's lines; and it was obliged, in spite of itself, to make use of them.

M. de Tromeling set out. Instead of delivering his despatches to the commissioners, he was afraid of their being taken from him by the enemy, and he destroyed them. The committee thought, that he had rather deceived himself by his cunning; but it readily excused this error, to attend wholly to the news he had brought.

Our commissioners arrived at the English head-quarters on the 28th, and were eager to solicit a suspension of arms.

Lord Wellington informed them, that he wished to consult with Prince Blucher on this point; and on the 29th of June, at half after eleven in the evening, he sent them the following answer.

Head quarters of Prince Blucher,
June the 29th, 1815, 11-½ at night.

"Gentlemen,

"I have the honour to acquaint you, that having consulted Marshal Prince Blucher on your proposal for an armistice, his highness has agreed with me, that, under present circumstances, no armistice can take place, while Napoleon Bonaparte is in Paris, and at *liberty*; and that the operations are in such a state, that he cannot stop them.

"I have the honour, &c.

"Wellington."

On the 1st of July in the morning, they had a conference, of which they gave an account to the government by the following despatch, addressed to Baron Bignon, secretary of state, assistant to the minister of foreign affairs.

"Louvres, July the 1st, 1815, forenoon.

"Monsieur le Baron,

"The despatches, Nos. 1, 2, and 3, which we have had the honour to address to you, remain unanswered[82]. We are absolutely deprived of the knowledge of what is passing at Paris, and in the rest of France. To whatever cause this want of communication is to be ascribed, it renders our situation painful, and is detrimental to the activity of our proceedings. It may render them useless: we request you, to remedy this as speedily as possible.

"At present we are authorized to think, that, as soon as you have made known, that Napoleon Bonaparte is at a distance, a suspension of hostilities for three days may be signed, in order to adjust an armistice, during which a treaty for peace may take place.

"Directed by the instructions given us, to listen to what may be said to us, and make you acquainted with it, we have to inform you, the Duke of Wellington has repeated to us several times, that as soon as our government has a head, peace will speedily be concluded.

"Speaking, as he says, merely as a private individual, but supposing however, that his opinion may be taken into consideration, he more than objects to the government of Napoleon II.; and thinks, that, under such a reign, Europe could enjoy no security, and France no repose.

"They say, that they do not pretend to oppose the choice of any other head to the government. They repeat on every occasion, that the powers of Europe do not pretend, to interfere in this choice: but they add, that, if the prince chosen were such, as by the nature of his situation to excite apprehensions for the tranquillity of Europe, by rendering that of France problematical, it would be necessary for the allied powers to have guarantees; and we have reason to believe, that these guarantees would be cessions of territory.

"One person alone, Louis XVIII. seems to unite all the conditions, that could prevent Europe from demanding guarantees for its security.

"Already, they say, he resides at Cambray. Quesney has opened its gates to him. These places, and other towns, are in his power; either by having delivered themselves up, or having been put into his hands by the allies.

"The Duke of Wellington admits and enumerates a considerable part of the faults committed by Louis XVIII. during his government of a few months. He puts in the first rank his having given to the princes of his family entrance into his council; his having had a ministry without union, and without responsibility; his having created a military household, not chosen from the soldiers of the army; and his not having placed about him persons, who were truly interested in the maintenance of the charter.

"It seems to him, that, by making known our grievances, *without settling conditions*, engagements might be formed with the public, which would remove its apprehensions for the future, by giving France the guarantee, it might desire.

"If a discussion of conditions take place, others beside the actual authorities might deliberate, resumed the Duke.

"If any time be lost, generals of other armies might interfere in the negotiations; and they would be rendered more complicated by additional interests.

"We add two proclamations of Louis XVIII. &c.

(Signed)   "Andréossy,
                         "Count Boissy d'Anglas,
                         "Flaugergues,
                         "Valence,
                         "Labesnardier."

M. Bignon's despatch, announcing the departure of Napoleon, having reached them after the conclusion of this first conference, they hastened to communicate it to Lord Wellington; and to claim a suspension of hostilities, in order to conclude an armistice, to which the presence of Napoleon had hitherto been the only obstacle.

Lord Wellington answered them: "that it was necessary for him, to confer with Prince Blucher, and that he would give them an answer in the course of the day."

In the evening they had a fresh conference with this general, which gave occasion to the following despatch:

"Louvres, July the 1st, half after 8 in the evening.

"Lord Wellington has communicated to us a letter from Manheim, written in the names of the Emperors of Russia and Austria by MM. de Nesselrode and de Metternich. This letter strongly urged the continuance of operations; and declares, that, if any armistice be entered into by the generals, who are at this moment near Paris, their majesties will not consider it as putting any stop to their march, but will order their troops, to approach Paris.

"The Count d'Artois has just arrived at the head-quarters of the Duke of Wellington, who received us alone in his saloon. We did not perceive the prince; he was in a separate apartment.

"We insisted on the execution of the promise given us. The Duke of Wellington answered, that he had always declared to us, he could enter into no definitive engagements, till he had conferred with Marshal Prince Blucher; to whom he would go, to prevail on him to join with him in agreeing on an armistice.

"He added, he would not conceal from us, that the Field Marshal had an extreme aversion to every thing, that would stay his operations, which extended already to the left bank of the Seine; and that he could not avoid supporting his movements, if he could not bring him to agree in his opinion.

"He communicated to us a proposal for an armistice, made by the Prince of Eckmuhl, which he had just received.

"He assured us, that, as soon as he had seen Prince Blucher, he would return, and join us at Louvres; and sent to request us, to repair to Gonesse.

"In talking on the possible conditions of an armistice, he insinuated, that he should require the army to quit Paris; which we declined, objecting, that on the contrary it was proper for the army of the allies, to take remote positions; otherwise it would be impossible, to deliberate freely on the important interests of our country, the influence of which on those of Europe he appeared to acknowledge.

"The conference thus terminating, we have some reason to think, that Lord Wellington will give the Count d'Artois to understand, that he ought to remain at a much more considerable distance from Paris."

To this Baron Bignon immediately sent the following answer:

"*To Messieurs the Commissioners charged with the Armistice.*

July the 1st.

"You announced to us, gentlemen, that you were authorized to believe, that, if Napoleon Bonaparte were away, a suspension of hostilities might be signed, during which a treaty for peace might be entered into. *The desired condition being fulfilled*, there is at the present moment no motive, that can oppose a suspension of hostilities, and an armistice. It is strongly to be desired, that the suspension of hostilities, instead of being for three days only, should be at least for five.

"We do not think, that the English and Prussians alone will attempt to force our lines. It would be gratuitously incurring useless losses. According to their own account, they can be joined by the Bavarians only in the first fortnight of this month: so that it may be convenient to them to wait for this reinforcement, which is an additional reason for their not refusing an armistice, that will be attended with as much or more advantage to themselves than to us. In fine, if the allies do not choose, to forget altogether their solemn declarations, what do they now require? The only obstacle, that, according to them, opposed the conclusion of peace, is irrevocably removed: thus nothing any longer opposes its re-establishment; and, to arrive at peace, nothing is more urgent than an armistice.

"The committee of government has had laid before it all the particulars, that you have transmitted, of the language held to you by the Duke of Wellington. It desires, gentlemen, that you will persist in distinguishing the political question of the form of government of France from the actual question, the conclusion of an armistice. Without repelling any of the overtures made you, it is easy, to give the Duke of Wellington to understand, that, if, in the present state of affairs, the political question of the government of France *must inevitably become the subject of a sort of discussion between France and the allied powers*, the general interest of France, and of the powers themselves, is to do nothing precipitately; and not to decide on a definitive part, till after having maturely weighed what will offer real guarantees for the future. It is possible, that the allied powers themselves, when better informed of the sentiments of the French nation, will not persevere in the resolutions they may have formed from different data. Napoleon is no longer at Paris, and has not been for nearly a week. His political career is at an end. If any national disposition in favour of the Bourbons existed, this disposition would have been loudly manifested, and their recall would have been already consummated. It is evident, therefore, that the re-establishment of this family is not the will of the nation. It remains for the allied sovereigns to examine, whether, in wishing to impose it on the nation in despite of its will, they do not themselves act contrary to their own intentions; since, instead of securing the internal peace of France, they would only be sowing in it the seeds of fresh discord.

"The proclamations of Louis XVIII. are known here: and the nature of these proclamations already destroys all the hopes, that the language of the Duke of Wellington might give. It may be judged from the spirit that breathes in these pieces recently published, that the present royal ministry either could not, or would not prevent, what the French nation might expect from that government.

"For the rest, gentlemen, you should confine yourselves to hearing every thing: you ought to affirm, that France itself desires nothing, but what will be of the greatest benefit to the general interest: and that, if it would prefer any plan to the re-establishment of the Bourbons, it is because there is none, that offers it so many inconveniences, and so few advantages.

"You must strongly repeat, gentlemen, to the Duke of Wellington and Prince Blucher, that, if the French government warmly insist on an armistice, it is because it perceives the possibility of coming to a good understanding on points, on which opinions appear to be farthest divided. It is because the communications and connexions, established between their head-quarters and us, enable us thoroughly to appreciate the true spirit of France. We think in particular, that the nobleness of the Duke of Wellington's character, and the wisdom of the allied sovereigns, cannot lead them to a desire, to force the French nation to submit to a government, that is repugnant to the real wishes of the great majority of the population."

This language, so remarkable for its moderation, was corroborated by the *ostensible* letter below, which the Duke of Otranto thought proper to address to each of the generals in chief of the besieging armies.

"My Lord (or Prince),

"Independently of the course of our negotiations, I make it my duty, to write personally to your lordship on the subject of an armistice, the refusal of which, I confess, seems to me inexplicable. Our plenipotentiaries have been at head-quarters ever since the 28th of June, and we have not yet a positive answer.

"Peace already exists, since the war has no longer an object. Our right to independence, and the engagement taken by the sovereigns to respect it, would not the less subsist after the taking of Paris. It would be inhuman, therefore, it would be atrocious, to engage in sanguinary battles, that would make no alteration in the questions to be decided.

"I must speak candidly to your lordship; our state of possession, our legal state, *which has the double sanction of the people and of the chambers, is that of a government, where the grandson of the Emperor of Austria is the head of the state. We cannot think of altering this state of things, unless the nation acquires a certainty, that the powers revoke their promises, and that the preservation of our present government is in opposition to their common wishes.*

"What then can be more just, than to conclude an armistice? Are there any other means of allowing the combined powers time to explain themselves, and France time to be acquainted with their wishes?

"It will not escape your lordship, that already one great power finds in our state of possession a personal right to interest itself in our interior concerns. As long as this state remains unaltered, the two chambers have hence an additional obligation, not to consent at present to any measure capable of altering our possession.

"Is not the step, that has been adopted on our eastern frontier, the most natural to follow? It was not confined to an armistice between General Bubna and Marshal Suchet: it was stipulated, that we should return to our limits according to the treaty of Paris; because, in fact, the war ought to be considered as ended by the simple fact of the abdication of Napoleon.

"Field-marshal Frimont, on his part, has agreed to the armistice, to meet by preliminary arrangements those, that may take place between the allies. We do not even know, whether England and Prussia have changed their minds on the subject of our independence; for the march of the armies cannot be any certain indication of the minds of the cabinets. Neither can the will of two powers suffice us; it is their general agreement we want to know. Would you anticipate this agreement? Would you oppose an obstacle to it, in order to give rise to a new political tempest from a state of things so near to peace?

"I am not afraid, for my own part, to anticipate all objections. Perhaps you suppose, that the occupation of Paris by two of the allied armies will second the views you may entertain of restoring Louis XVIII. to the throne. But can an augmentation of the evils of war, which can be ascribed to this motive alone, be a means of reconciliation?

"I must declare to your lordship, that every sinister attempt to impose on us a government, before the allied powers have explained themselves, would immediately oblige the chambers to take measures, that would not leave the possibility of a reconciliation in any case. It is even the interest of the King, that every thing should remain in a state of suspension: force may replace him on the throne, but cannot keep him there. It is neither by force, nor by surprise, nor by the wishes of one party, that the national will can be brought to change its government. It would even be in vain, at the present moment, to offer us conditions, to render a new government more supportable. There are no conditions that can be examined, as long as the necessity of bending our necks to the yoke, of renouncing our independence, is not proved to us. Now, my lord, this necessity cannot even be suspected, before the allied powers are in accord. None of their engagements have been revoked: our independence is under their protection: it is we, who enter into their views; and, according to the sense of their declaration, it is the besieging armies, that deviate from them.

"According to these declarations, and never were there any more solemn, every employment of force, in favour of the King, by these armies, on that part of our territory, which is solely in their power, will be considered by France as an avowal of the formal design of imposing on us a government against our will. We may be allowed to ask your lordship, whether you have received any such authority. Besides, force is not a pacificator: a moral resistance repelled the late government, that the King had been made to adopt: the more violence is employed toward the nation, the more invincible would this resistance be rendered. It cannot be the intention of the generals of the besieging armies, to compromise their own governments; and to revoke in fact the law, that the allied powers have imposed on themselves.

"My lord, the whole question lies in the compass of these few words.

"Napoleon has abdicated, as the allied powers desired: peace is therefore restored: who the prince shall be, that is to reap the fruit of this abdication, ought not even to be brought into the question.

"Is our state of possession to be altered by force? The allied powers would not only violate their promises, promises made in the face of the whole world, but they would not obtain their end. Is the change to come from the will of the nation? Then it is necessary, in order to lead this will to declare itself, for the allied powers first to make known their formal refusal, to let our present government subsist. An armistice, therefore, is indispensable.

"The full force of these considerations, my lord, it is impossible not to perceive. Even in Paris, should the event of a battle open its gates to you, I should still hold to your lordship the same language. It is the language of all France. Were rivers of blood made causelessly to flow, would the pretensions, that gave rise to them, be more secure, or less odious?

"I hope soon to have an intercourse with your lordship, that will lead us both to the work of peace, by means more conformable to reason and justice. An armistice would allow us, to treat in Paris: and it will be easy for us to come to an understanding on the great principle, that the tranquillity of France is a condition inseparable from the tranquillity of Europe. It is only from a close inspection of the nation and of the army, that you can judge, on what the quietness and stability of our future condition depend.

"I beg, &c. &c."

Though in this letter the Duke of Otranto pleaded the cause of Napoleon II., and pretended to be ignorant of the dispositions of the allies, it was nevertheless very easy to perceive, that he considered the question as irrevocably decided in favour of the Bourbons. Their name, which he had long avoided mentioning, was incessantly on his lips: but always the same, always inclined naturally and systematically, to have more strings than one to his bow, he appeared to incline alternately *for the younger branch, and for the reigning branch.* At one time the former seemed to him to offer preferably, and in a higher degree, all the guarantees the nation could desire: at another he insinuated, that it would be possible, to come to an accommodation with the King, if he would consent, to dismiss certain dangerous persons, and make fresh concessions to France.

This change, too sudden not to be noticed, drew on his conduct more than ever the scrutinizing eyes and reproaches of the antagonists of the Bourbons.

He was accused of encouraging by impunity the newspaper writers and pamphleteers, who openly advocated the recall of the ancient dynasty of protecting the royalist party; and of having restored to liberty one of its most subtle agents, Baron de Vitrolles.

He was charged with holding nocturnal conferences with this same M. de Vitrolles, and several eminent royalists; and with daily sending emissaries, unknown to his colleagues, to the King, to M. de Talleyrand, and to the Duke of Wellington.

Two of the deputies, M. Durbach and General Solignac, went to him, and declared, that they were acquainted with his manœuvres; that his ambition blinded him; that no compact could ever subsist between Louis XVIII. and the murderer of his brother; and that sooner or later France would take vengeance on this treason.

An old minister of state, M. Deferment, reproached him to his teeth with privately selling the lives and liberties of the French.

Other accusations, not less serious, or less virulent, were addressed to him by M. Carnot, and by General Grenier. "If he betray us," said the latter, "I will blow his brains out."

The Duke of Otranto, accustomed to brave political storms, coolly repelled these imputations. He reminded his accusers of the numerous pledges he had given to the revolution. He offered his head as the guarantee of his fidelity. His protestations, his oaths, and the imperturbable assurance, with which he answered for the safety and independence of the nation, if he were suffered to go on his own way, allayed the storms: but he had too much penetration, not to be aware of the ground on which he stood; he could not but feel, that he was lost, if he did not hasten to a conclusion; and there is every reason to believe, that he rejected *no means* of arriving speedily at a decisive result[83].

Blucher, however, to whom only a shadow of defence was opposed, had crossed the Seine at the bridge of Pecq, which had been preserved by the care of a journalist named Martainville, and appeared to intend, to spread his troops round the south-west of Paris[84]. Our generals, witnessing this adventurous march, were unanimously of opinion, that the Prussians had compromised themselves. They summoned the Prince of Eckmuhl to attack them; and he could not avoid assenting to it.

The whole army, generals, officers, soldiers, were still animated with a devotion, that nothing could rebut. Proud of the confidence placed in them by the national representatives, they had answered their appeal by an address full of spirit and patriotism; they had sworn to each other, to die in defence of the honour and independence of the nation; and they were impatient, to fulfil their oaths.

General Excelmans was sent after the Prussians with six thousand men. A corps of fifteen thousand infantry, under the command of General Vichery, was to follow him by the bridge of Sevres, and connect its movements with six thousand foot of the 1st corps, and ten thousand chosen horse, who were to march by the bridge of Neuilly. But at the moment of executing these movements, the success of which would unquestionably have ensured the destruction of the Prussian army, counter-orders were issued by the Prince of Eckmuhl, from what motives I know not. General Excelmans alone maintained the battle. He attacked the enemy in advance of Versailles, drove them into an ambuscade, cut them to pieces, and took from them their arms, baggage, and horses. Generals Strulz, Piré, Barthe, and Vincent, colonels Briqueville, Faudoas, St. Amand, Chaillou, Simonnet, Schmid, Paolini, and their brave regiments, performed prodigies of valour, and were intrepidly seconded by the citizens of the neighbouring communes, who had preceded as sharpshooters the arrival of our troops on the field of battle, and during the battle proved themselves worthy, to fight by their side.

This victory filled the Parisian patriots with hope and joy. It inspired them with the noble desire of imitating the fine example, that had just been set them. But when it was known, that a general engagement had been unanimously desired and agreed upon; and that the enemy, had it not been for counter-orders, surprised and cut off, would have been annihilated, this intoxication was changed into depression, and a cry was raised on all hands of infamy and treason.

Excelmans and his brave men, not being supported, were obliged to retreat. The Prussians advanced, the English moved out to support them; they formed a junction, and came and encamped together on the heights of Meudon.

The committee hastened to inform the commissioners of the critical situation of Paris, and desired them, as the Duke of Wellington was incessantly sending them from Caiphas to Pilate, to endeavour to see Prince Blucher. They answered, "that they had never been able to have any communication with the marshal; and that they could not establish a conference with him, unless through the intervention of Lord Wellington, without the risk of occasioning a rupture."

They added to their despatch a fresh letter, by which his lordship announced to them, that "Prince Blucher continued to express to him the greatest repugnance to the conclusion of an armistice," &c. &c.

The government no longer doubted the ill will of the English general. Count Carnot said, "that they must address themselves definitively to the brutal frankness of Blucher, rather than live in the uncertainty, in which they were kept by the civilities of Wellington."

The Duke of Vicenza thought the same, that the only way of coming to a conclusion was by bluntly making a proposal without the knowledge of the English. He remarked to the committee, that the great repugnance shown by Marshal Blucher to concluding an armistice, no doubt, arose from his being probably unwilling, to negotiate under the direction and influence of Wellington, to whose head-quarters he apparently avoided paying a visit. That he would be much more tractable, if he were addressed directly. That, by taking this step, they would also have the advantage of removing the negotiations from the place, where the Bourbons were; and of being able more easily to avoid the political question, on which Wellington seemed far more decided than Blucher. The commission, influenced by these observations, adopted the advice of M. Carnot; and the Prince of Eckmuhl was ordered, to address to Marshal Blucher direct proposals, founded principally on the armistice concluded with the chiefs of the Austrian forces.

The prince immediately answered:

"If Marshal Frimont have thought himself authorised, to conclude an armistice, this is no reason for our doing the same. We shall follow up our victory: God has given us the means, and the will.

"Consider what you have to do. Do not precipitate a city anew into calamities; for you are aware to what lengths an enraged soldiery may go, if your capital be taken by assault. Would you draw down on your head the curses of Paris, as you have those of Hamburgh?

"*We are resolved to enter Paris, to secure the honest people there from the plunder; with which they are threatened by the populace* [85]. It is only in Paris, that we can conclude a secure armistice."

This letter was revolting to the committee; but however great its just indignation, there was now no middle path: *the commander in chief had refused, to avail himself of a palpable fault of the enemy: the opportunity of victory had been let slip: it was necessary, to sustain a siege, or capitulate.*

The committee, sensible of all the importance of the part it should take, was desirous of having recourse to the skill, the councils, and the responsibility of the most experienced men. It sent for the immortal defenders of Genoa and Toulouse, the conqueror of Dantzic, Generals Gazan, Duverney, and Evain, Major-General Ponton of the engineers, who had distinguished himself at the siege of Hamburgh, and in fine the presidents and committees (*bureaux*) of the two chambers.

Count Carnot, who had been to examine our positions and those of the enemy in company with General Grenier, made a report on the situation of Paris to the assembly.

He stated:

That the fortifications erected on the right bank of the Seine appeared sufficient, to secure Paris against any assault on that side. But that the left bank was entirely open, and presented a spacious field to the enemy's attempts.

That the English and Prussian generals had moved the greater part of their armies to this vulnerable point *with impunity*: and appeared disposed, to attempt an attack with open force. That, if they failed the first time, they might return to the charge a second; and renew their attempts, till they rendered themselves masters of the capital. That they would have fresh troops, to oppose to us continually; while ours, obliged to be constantly on their guard, would soon be exhausted with fatigue.

That the arrival of subsistence was becoming difficult; and that a corps of sixty thousand Bavarians would apparently block up the way between the Seine and Marne in the course of a few days.

That the enemy, already masters of the heights of Meudon, and the best surrounding positions, might entrench themselves there, cut off our retreat, and reduce Paris and the army, to surrender at discretion.

The president of the committee, after having called the attention of the members of the assembly to these serious considerations, requested them to give their opinions.

It was observed to him, that it appeared necessary, previously to make known the present state of the negotiations. This the committee did not refuse: but the communication having brought on a discussion respecting the Bourbons, the committee reminded them, that they ought to confine themselves to the military question; and that the point was, purely and simply to decide, whether it were advisable or possible, to defend Paris.

The Prince of Essling, being called upon, said, that this city would be impregnable, if the inhabitants would make of it a second Saragossa: but there was not sufficient harmony in their sentiments, to think of a resolute resistance and the most prudent part would be, to obtain a suspension of hostilities at any price.

The Duke of Dantzic declared, that he did not think it impossible, to prolong their defence, by rapidly accelerating the works begun in the plains of Montrouge.

The Duke of Dalmatia maintained, that the left bank of the Seine was not tenable: that it was even very hazardous, since the occupation of Aubervilliers, to remain on the right side: that if the line of the canal, that joins St. Denis to Lavillette, should be forced, the enemy might enter by the barrier of St. Denis pell-mell with our troops.

Some of the members, agreeing in opinion with the Duke of Dantzic, demanded, that positive information should be procured respecting the possibility of putting the left bank into a state of defence, previous to coming to a decision. In fine, after some debate, it was decided, that the assembly was not competent, to determine such a question: and that it should be submitted to the examination and decision of a council of war, which the Prince of Eckmuhl should convene for the night following.

The occupation of Paris by the foreigners was the object of the impatient wishes of the royalists, and of the men who had sold or devoted themselves from policy, ambition, or fear, to the party of the Bourbons. Persuaded, that it would decide the fate of France in 1815, as it had done in 1814, they had omitted beforehand no step, no promise, no threatening insinuation, that could tend to accomplish their wishes and their triumph by the surrender of the city.

The Duke of Otranto, whether he were in concert with the royalists, or considered the speedy capitulation of Paris necessary to his own security; or were desirous of making a merit, at some future day, of having brought France under the sway of its legitimate sovereign without effusion of blood; appeared to consider it of great importance that the defence of Paris should not be prolonged. "Every thing is on the point of being settled," said he to the members, who had most influence in the chambers and in the army: "let us be very careful not to sacrifice a secure present to an uncertain future. The allies are agreed, that we shall have *a* Bourbon; but it is necessary, that he submit to the conditions imposed on him by the nation. The chamber will be retained, the generals will remain at the head of the army: all will go well. Is it not better to submit, than to expose France to be partitioned, or delivered over to the Bourbons bound hand and foot? A prolonged resistance would have no other result, than to retard our fall. It would rob us of the price of a voluntary submission, and authorise the Bourbons to be implacable." If little disposition were shown, to share his confidence and his sentiments; he imposed silence on the refractory by all the forms of the most lively interest. "Your opposition," he said to them, "astonishes and grieves me:

would you pass for an incendiary, and incur the penalty of being exiled? Let us go on our own way, I conjure you: I will answer for the future."…. An internal presentiment warned the hearers, that this future would be far from answering the expectations of M. Fouché: but his political life, his great talents, his connexions with the foreign ministers, the attention paid him in 1814 by the Emperor Alexander and the king of Prussia, gave such weight, such an ascendancy, to his words, that they ultimately did violence to their own reason, and gave themselves up, though not without murmuring, to confidence and hope.

The council of war assembled on the night of the 1st of July at the headquarters at Lavillette, under the presidentship of the Prince of Eckmuhl. Care was taken, it appeared, to keep away some suspected generals; and not to neglect calling those officers, whose principles, moderation, or weakness, was known. All the marshals present in the capital were admitted; and they, who had lately refused to fight, did not refuse to come to capitulate.

The committee, in order to prevent all political discussion, had stated the questions, to which the members of the council were to confine their deliberations: but this precaution, as might be supposed, did not prevent their entering familiarly into the moral and political considerations, that might influence the defence or surrender of the place besieged. Marshal Soult pleaded the cause of Louis XVIII.; and was eagerly seconded by other marshals, and several generals, who, though they entered into the council under the national colours, would willingly have gone out of it with the white cockade.

It is impossible, to recapitulate the opinions, given in turn or confusedly by the fifty persons, who were called to take a share in this great and important deliberation. Their speeches, or rather their conversation, turned alternately on Paris and on the Bourbons.

"We are told," said the partisans of Louis XVIII. and the capitulation, "that Paris, covered without by an army of eighty thousand men; and defended within by the federates, the sharpshooters, the national guard, and an immense population; might resist the efforts of the allies for twenty days at least. We are told, that its immense extent will render the arrival of provision easy. We admit the possibility of all this: but what will be the ultimate effect of this resistance? To allow the Emperor Alexander, and the Emperor of Austria, time to arrive…. The allies, we know perfectly well, promise to leave us the power of choosing our sovereign: but will they keep their promises? and what conditions will they annex to them? Already Wellington and Blucher have announced, that they will require guarantees, and fortified towns, if Louis XVIII. be rejected. Is not this equivalent to a formal declaration, that the allies are resolved, to retain that sovereign on the throne? Let us voluntarily rally round him, therefore, while we still can. His ministers led him astray, but his intentions were always pure: he knows the faults he has committed; he will be eager to repair them, and to give us the institutions yet necessary, to consolidate the rights and liberties of the people on bases not to be shaken."

"This reasoning may be just," answered their opponents; "but experience, of more weight than any reasoning, has convinced us, that we must not rely on empty promises. The hopes you have conceived rest on conjecture, or on the word of the agents of the Bourbons. Before we surrender ourselves into the hands of the King, he must make known to us the guarantees, by which we are to be secured. If they be agreeable to us, then we may deliberate but if we open our gates without conditions, and previous to the arrival of Alexander, Wellington and the Bourbons will make a jest of their promises, and oblige us to submit to the will of the conqueror without pity. Besides, why should we despair of the safety of France? Is the loss of a single battle, then, to decide the fate of a great nation? Have we not still immense resources, to oppose to the enemy? Have the federates, the national guard, and all true Frenchmen, refused to shed their blood in defence of the glory, the honour, and the independence of their country? While we are fighting under the walls of the capital, the levy in mass of the patriots will be arranged in the departments: and when our enemies see, that we are determined to defend our independence, they will rather respect it, than expose themselves to a patriotic and national war for interests not their own. We must refuse, therefore, to surrender; and place ourselves in a situation, by a vigorous defence, to give the law, instead of receiving it."

"You maintain," it was replied, "that we may raise in mass the federates and the patriots. But how will you arm them? we have no muskets. Besides, can a levy in mass be organised on a sudden? Before you could have a single battalion at your disposal, Paris would have under its feeble ramparts sixty thousand Bavarians, and a hundred and forty thousand Austrians more to fight. What will you do then? You must ultimately surrender: and the blood you will have shed will be lost without return, and without utility. But will not that we shall have spilt of the enemy fall on our own heads? Will they not make us expiate our mad and cruel resistance by a disgraceful capitulation? If the allies, at the present moment, think themselves strong enough to refuse you a suspension of hostilities, what will they do, when they have their twelve hundred thousand soldiers on our territory? The dismemberment of France, the pillage and devastation of the capital, will be, perhaps, the fruit of the rash defence you propose to us."

These considerations, the force of which was generally felt, were unanimously approved. It was acknowledged, that it would be unquestionably most prudent, not to expose the capital to the consequences and dangers of a siege, or of being taken by assault. It was acknowledged, too, at least by implication, that, the return of the Bourbons being inevitable, it was better to recall them voluntarily, under good conditions, than to leave to the allies the act of restoring them. But the members did not think proper, to explain themselves on this delicate subject; and accordingly confined themselves to laconic answers of the questions proposed by the committee.

Questions proposed by the Committee of Government to the Council of War, assembled at la Villette, July the 1st, 1815.

"1st. What is the state of the intrenchments raised for the defence of Paris?—*Answer.* The state of the intrenchments, and their supply of ordnance, on the right bank of the Seine, though incomplete, is in general satisfactory enough. On the left bank the intrenchments may be considered as null.

"2d. The army, can it cover and defend Paris?—*Ans.* It may: but not indefinitely. It ought not to expose itself to a want of provision, or to have its retreat cut off.

"3d. If the army were attacked on all points, could it prevent the enemy from penetrating into Paris on one side or the other?—*Ans.* It would be difficult for the army to be attacked on all points at once: but should this happen, there would be little hope of resistance.

"4th. In case of a defeat, could the commander in chief reserve, or collect, sufficient means, to oppose a forcible entry?—*Ans.* No general can answer for the consequences of a battle.

"5th. Is there sufficient ammunition for several battles?—*Ans.* Yes.

"6th. In fine, can you answer for the fate of the capital? and for how long a time?—*Ans.* We can warrant nothing on this head.

(Signed)   "The Marshal Minister at War,
"The Prince of Eckmuhl.

"July the 2d, 3 o'clock in the morning."

The answer of the council of war was transmitted immediately to the Tuileries, and there became the subject of a long and profound deliberation.

In fine, after having weighed the advantages and dangers of a protracted defence; after having considered, that Paris, without hope of succour, and surrounded on all sides, would either be taken by assault, or forced to surrender at discretion that the army, without any means of retreat, would find themselves perhaps reduced to choose between the disgrace of surrendering themselves prisoners, and the necessity of burying themselves under the ruins of the capital; the committee decided unanimously, that Paris should not be defended, and that they would submit to deliver it into the hands of the allies, since the allies would not suspend hostilities at any other price.

General Ziethen, who commanded Prince Blucher's advanced guard, was informed of this determination by the Prince of Eckmuhl. He returned him the following answer:

"To the Prince of Eckmuhl.

"July the 2d.

"Monsieur General,

"General Revest has communicated to me verbally, that you demand an armistice, to treat of the surrender of Paris.

"In consequence, M. General, I have to inform you, that I am in no way authorized to accept an armistice. I dare not even announce this demand to his Highness Marshal Prince Blucher: but however, if the deputies of the government declare to my aide-de-camp, Count Westphalen, that they will surrender the city, *and that the French army will surrender itself also*, I will accept a suspension of hostilities.

"I will then communicate it to his highness Prince Blucher, to treat of the other articles.

(Signed) "Ziethen."

When Brennus, abusing his victory, offered an insult to the vanquished, the Romans ran to arms. We, less sensible, and less proud, heard, without shuddering, the insult offered to our eighty thousand brave soldiers, and accepted, without blushing, the disgrace thus inflicted upon them and us!

Our only revenge was to despatch MM. de Tromeling and Macirone, the former to Prince Blucher, the latter to Lord Wellington.

The Duke of Otranto, without the knowledge of the committee, delivered to M. Macirone a confidential note in the following terms:

"The army is dissatisfied, because it is unhappy; encourage it: it will become faithful and devoted.

"The chambers are indocile for the same reason; encourage every body, and every body will be on your side.

"Let the army be sent away: the chambers will consent to it, on a promise to add to the charter the guarantees specified by the King. In order to come to a good understanding, it is necessary, that explanations should take place: do not enter Paris, therefore, in less than three days; in this interval every thing will be settled. *The chambers will be gained; they will fancy themselves independent, and will sanction every thing.* It is not force that must be employed with them, but persuasion."

I know not whether M. de Tromeling were also furnished with a similar note, or whether Lord Wellington interposed his authority; but Prince Blucher, become on a sudden more tractable, consented to treat of the surrender of Paris.

On the 3d of July, General Ziethen announced on his part to the Prince of Eckmuhl, "that the deputies of the government might present themselves: that they would be conducted to St. Cloud, where they would find deputies from the English and Prussian generals."

Baron Bignon, Count de Bondy, and General Guilleminot, provided with powers from the Prince of Eckmuhl (Blucher having declared, that he would have nothing to do with any person but the chief of the French army), repaired to the Prussian advanced posts, and were conducted to St. Cloud; *where, without any regard to the laws of nations, they were deprived of all means of communicating with the government, and kept in a private prison, during the whole continuance of the negotiations.*

Baron Bignon, the principal negotiator, and his two colleagues, defended the political rights, the private interests, the inviolability of persons and property, national and individual, with inestimable firmness and zeal. They were far from foreseeing, that the following convention, which they considered as sacred, would subsequently open such a fatal!! door to the interpretations of vengeance and bad faith.

Convention.

This day, July the 3d, 1815, the commissioners named by the commanders in chief of the respective armies, namely:

M. Baron Bignon, having in charge the portfolio of foreign affairs; M. Count Guilleminot, chief of the staff of the French army; M. Count de Bondy, prefect of the department of the Seine; furnished with full powers by Marshal the Prince of Eckmuhl, commander in chief of the French army, on the one part;

And M. Major-General Baron de Muffling, furnished with powers by his Highness Marshal Prince Blucher, commander-in-chief of the Prussian army; and M. Colonel Hervey, furnished with full powers by his excellency the Duke of Wellington, commander-in-chief of the English army, on the other;

Have agreed on the following articles:

Art. I.

There shall be a suspension of hostilities between the allied armies commanded by his highness Prince Blucher, his excellency the Duke of Wellington, and the French army, under the walls of Paris.

Art. II.

To-morrow the French army shall commence its march, to retire behind the Loire. The total evacuation of Paris shall be effected in three days, and its movement of retiring behind the Loire shall be finished in eight days.

Art. III.

The French army shall take with it its stores, field artillery, military convoys, horses, and property of the regiments, without any exception. This shall equally apply to what belongs to (*le personnel des*) the dépôts, and the different branches of administration, belonging to the army.

Art. IV.

The sick and wounded, as well as the medical officers, whom it may be necessary to leave with them, are under the particular protection of MM. the commissaries in chief of the English and Prussian armies.

Art. V.

The military and non-military persons, mentioned in the preceding article, may rejoin the corps to which they belong, as soon as they are recovered.

Art. VI.

The women and children of all persons belonging to the French army shall be at liberty to remain in Paris.

These women shall meet with no obstruction to their quitting Paris, to rejoin the army, or to taking with them their own property or that of their husbands.

Art. VII.

The officers of the line employed with the federates, or with the sharpshooters of the national guard, may either rejoin the army, or return to their place of residence, or to the place where they were born.

Art. VIII.

To-morrow, July the 4th, at noon, St. Denis, St. Ouen, Clichy, and Neuilly, shall be delivered up; the next day, July the 5th, at the same hour,

Montmartre shall be delivered; and on the 3d day, July 6, all the barriers shall be delivered.

Art. IX.

The interior duty of Paris shall continue to be performed by the national guard, and by the corps of municipal gendarmerie.

Art. X.

The commanders in chief of the English and Prussian armies *engage to respect, and to make those under them respect, the present authorities, as long as they subsist.*

Art. XI.

Public property, except what relates to war, whether it belong to the government, or depend on the municipal authority, *shall be respected*, and the allied powers will not interfere in any manner in its management, or in its conduct.

Art. XII.

The persons and property of individuals shall be equally respected: the inhabitants, and all persons in general, who happen to be in the capital, shall continue to enjoy their rights and liberties, *without being molested, or any inquiry being made into the functions they occupy or may have occupied, their conduct, or their political opinions.*

Art. XIII.

The foreign troops shall oppose no obstacle to the supply of the capital with provision; and on the contrary shall protect the arrival and free circulation of articles intended for it.

Art. XIV.

The present convention shall be observed, and serve as a rule for the mutual conduct of the parties, till a peace is concluded.

In case of a rupture, it shall be announced in the usual forms at least ten days beforehand.

Art. XV.

If any difficulties arise, respecting the execution of some of the articles of the present convention, *the interpretation shall be in favour of the French army,* and of the city of Paris.

Art. XVI.

The present convention is declared common to all the allied armies, saving the ratification of the powers, to which those armies belong.

Art. XVII.

The ratifications shall be exchanged to-morrow, at six o'clock in the morning, at the bridge of Neuilly.

Art. XVIII.

Commissioners shall be named by the respective parties, to superintend the execution of the present convention.

Done and signed at St. Cloud, in triplicate, by the commissioners undernamed, the day and year above mentioned,

(Signed) Baron Bignon.
Count Guillemenot.
Count de Bondy.
Baron de Muffling.
B. Hervey, Colonel.

Approved and ratified,
(Signed) Marshal Prince Eckmuhl.

The title of capitulation was originally given to this treaty: but the Duke of Otranto, aware of the power of words, and dreading the impression this would produce, hastened to recall the copies already distributed, and to substitute the milder title of convention. This precaution, however, fascinated the eyes only of a few friendly deputies. Numerous groups were formed: the government and Prince Eckmuhl were openly charged with having a second time delivered up and sold Paris to the allies and the Bourbons. The patriots, the sharpshooters, the federates, who had offered to defend the city with their lives, were equally indignant, that the city had been given up without firing a single shot. They resolved, to seize on the heights of Montmartre, join the army, and sell dearly to the enemy the last sighs of liberty and of France. But their threatening clamours were not unheard by the government. It called out the national guards; and these at length appeased the malecontents, by opposing to them the example of their own resignation.

The publication of the convention produced an effervescence not less formidable in the camps. The generals assembled, to protest against this impious act, and oppose its accomplishment. They declared, that the Prince of Eckmuhl, *in whose house they had frequently caught M. de Vitrolles*, had forfeited the esteem of the army, and was no longer worthy to command it. They repaired to General Vandamme, and offered him the command. But this officer, who had made one of the council of war, which they did not know, and approved its sentiments, refused his consent to their wishes.

The soldiers, who had been made to swear by the representatives of the people, that they would never suffer the enemy to penetrate into the capital, spontaneously shared the indignation of their leaders; and declared, like them, that they would never consent, to surrender Paris. Some broke their arms, others brandished them in the air with curses and threats; all swore, to die on the spot, rather than desert it. A general insurrection appeared inevitable and at hand; when the General, alarmed at the calamities it might occasion, harangued the soldiers, and at length calmed their irritation. The imperial guard, yielding to the ascendancy the brave and loyal Drouot possessed over it, gave the first example of submission, and every thing was restored to order.

The government, to justify its conduct, and prevent similar insurrections in the other armies, and in the departments, published the following proclamation, a pompous tissue of eloquent impostures, and of fallacious promises[86].

"*The Committee of Government to the French.*

"Frenchmen,

"Under the difficult circumstances, in which the reins of government were entrusted to us, it was not in our power, to master the course of events, and repel every danger: but it was our duty, to protect the interests of the people, and of the army, equally compromised in the cause of a prince, abandoned by fortune and by the national will.

"It was our duty, *to preserve* to our country the precious remains of those brave legions, whose courage is superior to misfortune, and who have been the victims of a devotion, which their country now claims.

"It was our duty, to save the capital from the horrors of a siege, or the chances of a battle to maintain the public tranquillity amid the tumults and agitations of war, *to support the hopes of the friends of liberty*, amid the fears and anxieties of a suspicious foresight. It was above all our duty, to stop the useless effusion of blood. We had to choose *between a secure national existence*, or run the risk of exposing our country and its citizens to a general convulsion, that would leave behind it neither hope, nor a future.

"*None of the means of defence*, that time and our resources permitted, nothing that the service of the camps or of the city required, have we neglected.

"While the pacification of the West was concluding, plenipotentiaries went to meet the allied powers; and all the papers relative to this negotiation have been laid before our representatives.

"The fate of the capital is regulated by a convention: its inhabitants, whose firmness, courage, and perseverance, are above all praise, will retain the guarding of it. *The declarations of the sovereigns of Europe must inspire too great confidence, their promises have been too solemn, for us to entertain any fears of our liberties, and of our dearest interests, being sacrificed to victory.*

"*At length we shall receive guarantees,* that will prevent the alternate and transient triumphs of the factions, by which we have been agitated these five and twenty years; that will terminate our revolutions, and *melt down under one common protection* all the parties, to which they have given rise, and all those, against which they have contended.

"Those guarantees, which have hitherto existed only in our principles and in our courage, *we shall find* in our laws, in our constitution, in our representative system. For whatever may be the intelligence, the virtues, the personal qualities of a monarch, these can never suffice, to render the people secure against the oppressions of power, the prejudices of pride, the injustice of courts, and the ambition of courtiers.

"Frenchmen, peace is necessary to your commerce, to your arts, to the improvement of your morals, to the development of the resources remaining to you: be united, *and you are at the end of your calamities.* The repose of Europe is inseparable from yours. Europe is interested in your tranquillity, and in your happiness.

"Given at Paris, July the 5th, 1815.

(Signed) "The president of the committee,

"The Duke of Otranto."

By the terms of the convention, the first column of the French was to commence its march on the 4th. The soldiers, still irritated, declared they would not set out, till they received their arrears of pay. The treasury was empty, credit extinguished, the government at bay. The Prince of Eckmuhl proposed, to seize the funds of the bank: but this attempt struck the committee with horror. One resource alone, one only hope, remained: this was to invoke the support of a banker, at that time celebrated for his wealth, now celebrated for his public virtues. M. Lafitte was applied to: the chances of the future did not deter him; he listened only to the interest of his country; and several millions, distributed by his assistance through the ranks of the army, disarmed the mutineers, and crushed the seeds of a civil war.

The army began its march. Amid the despair, into which it had been plunged by the capitulation, it had frequently called on Napoleon! The committee, apprehensive that the Emperor, having no longer any measures to keep, would come and put himself in a state of desperation at the head of the patriots and soldiers, sent orders by a courier to General Beker, "to effect the arrival of Napoleon at Rochefort without delay; *and, without departing from the respect due to him, to employ all the means necessary, to get him embarked*; as his stay in France compromised the safety of the state, and was detrimental to the negotiations."

The retreat of the army, the occupation of Paris by the foreigners, and the presence of the King at Arnouville, unveiled the future; and those men who were not blinded by incurable illusions, prepared to fall again under the sway of the Bourbons.

Their partisans, their emissaries, their known agents (M. de Vitrolles and others) had asserted, that the King, ascribing the revolution of the 20th of March to the faults of his ministry, would shut his eyes to all that had passed; and that a general absolution would be the pledge of his return, and of his reconciliation with the French. This consolatory assertion had already surmounted the repugnance of many; when the proclamations of the 25th and 28th of June, issued at Cambray, made their appearance[87]. These in fact acknowledged, that the ministers of the King had committed faults; but, far from promising a complete oblivion of those committed by his subjects, one of them, the work of the Duke of Feltre, on the contrary announced, "that the King, whose potent allies had cleared the way for him to his dominions, by dispersing *the satellites of the tyrant*, was hastening to return to them, to carry the existing laws into execution against the guilty."

Information was soon brought by the commissioners, returned from the head quarters of the allies, and confirmed by the reports of MM. Tromeling and Macirone, that Blucher and Wellington, already taking advantage of our weakness, openly declared, that the authority of the chambers and of the committee was illegal; and that the best thing they could do would be, to give in their resignations, and proclaim Louis XVIII.

All the good effected by the cajolery of M. Fouché, and the hope of a happy reconciliation, now disappeared. Consternation seized the weak-minded; indignation, men of a generous spirit. The committee, disappointed of the hope of obtaining Napoleon II., or the Duke of Orleans; who, according to the expression of the Duke of Wellington, would have been only an usurper of a good family; could no longer disguise from itself, that it was the intention of the foreign powers, to restore Louis XVIII. to the throne; but it had imagined, that his re-establishment would be the subject of an agreement between the nation, the allied monarchs, and Louis.

When it was acquainted with the language held by the enemy's generals, it foresaw, that the independence of the powers of the state, stipulated by the convention, would not be respected; and it deliberated, whether it would not be proper for it and the chambers, to retire behind the Loire with the army. This measure, worthy of the firmness of M. Carnot, who proposed it, was strongly combated by the Duke of Otranto. He declared, that this step would ruin France; "that the greater part of the generals would not assent to it, and that he himself would be the first, to refuse to quit Paris. That it was at Paris the whole must be decided: and that it was the duty of the committee to remain there, to protect the high interests confided to it, and contend for them to the last extremity."

The committee gave up the idea; not out of deference to the observations of M. Fouché, for he had lost all his empire over it; but because it was convinced on reflection, that things had gone too far, for any benefit to be expected from this desperate step. It would probably have rekindled the foreign war, and a civil war; and, though the soldiers might be depended on, their leaders could no longer be so, with the same security. Some, as General Sénéchal, had been stopped at the advanced posts, when going over to the Bourbons. Others had openly declared themselves in favour of Louis. The greater number appeared inflexible: but this difference of opinion had brought on distrust and dissensions; and in political wars all is lost, when there is a divergency of wills and opinions. Besides it would have been necessary, since the committee persisted in rejecting Napoleon, to place at the head of the army some other chief, whose name, sacred to glory, might serve as a stay and rallying point: and on whom could the choice of the committee fall[88]?

Marshal Ney had been the first, to give the alarm, and despair of the safety of the country[89].

Marshal Soult had relinquished his command.

Marshal Massena, worn out by victories, had no longer the bodily strength, that circumstances required.

Marshal Macdonald, deaf to the shout of war raised by his old companions in arms, had suffered his sword, to remain peaceably in its scabbard.

Marshal Jourdan was on the Rhine.

Marshal Mortier had been seized with the gout at Beaumont.

Marshal Suchet had displayed irresolution and repugnance from the beginning.

In fine, Marshals Davoust and Grouchy no longer possessed the confidence of the army.

The committee, therefore, it is grating to the pride of a Frenchman to confess it, would not have known to whose hands the fate of France might be entrusted; and the part it took, that of waiting the issue of events in the capital, if not the most dignified, was at least the wisest and most prudent.

The representatives of the people, on their part, far from showing themselves docile to the advice of Wellington and of Blucher, displayed with more energy than ever the principles and sentiments that animated them. They collected round the tri-coloured flag; and, though the army had laid down its weapons, they were still resolved to contend in defence of liberty, and the independence of the nation.

On the very day when the convention of Paris was notified to them by the government, they exposed, in a new bill of rights, the fundamental principles of a constitution, which alone, in their opinion, could satisfy the wishes of the public: and declared, that the prince called to reign over them should not ascend the throne, till he had given his sanction to this bill and taken an oath to observe it, and cause it to be observed.

Informed almost immediately by sinister rumours, that soon they would be no longer allowed to deliberate, they resolved, on the motion of M. Dupont de l'Eure, solemnly to express their last will in a kind of political testament, drawn up in the following words.

"*Declaration of the Chamber of Representatives.*

"The troops of the allied powers are about to occupy the capital.

"The chamber of representatives will nevertheless continue to sit amid the inhabitants of Paris, to which place the express will of the people has sent its proxies.

"But, under the present serious circumstances, the chamber of representatives owes it to itself, owes it to France and to Europe, to make a declaration of its sentiments and principles.

"It declares, therefore, that it makes a solemn appeal to the fidelity and patriotism of the national guard of Paris, charged with the protection of the national representatives.

"It declares, that it reposes itself with the highest confidence on the moral principles, honour, and magnanimity, of the allied powers, and on their respect for the independence of the nation, positively expressed in their manifestoes.

"It declares, that the government of France, whoever may be its head, ought to unite in its favour the wishes of the nation, legally expressed; and form arrangements with the other governments, in order to become a common bond and guarantee of peace between France and Europe.

"It declares, that a monarch cannot offer any real guarantees, if he do not swear to the observance of a constitution, formed by the deliberations of the national representatives, and accepted by the people. Accordingly any government, that has no other title than the acclamations and will of a party, or is imposed on it by force; any government, that does not adopt the national colours, and does not guarantee,

"The liberties of the citizens;

"Equality of rights, civil and political;

"The liberty of the press;

"Freedom of religious worship;

"The representative system;

"Free assent to levies and taxes;

"The responsibility of ministers;

"The irrevocability of sales of national property, from whatever source originating;

"The inviolability of property;

"The abolition of titles, of the old and new hereditary nobility, and of feudal claims;

"The abolition of all confiscation of property, the complete oblivion of opinions and votes given up to the present day;

"The institution of the legion of honour;

"The recompenses due to the officers and soldiers;

"The succour due to their widows and children;

"The institution of a jury; the indefeasibleness of the office of judge;

"The payment of the public debt;

"Would not ensure the tranquillity of France and of Europe.

"If the fundamental principles, announced in this declaration, should be disregarded or violated, the representatives of the French people, acquitting themselves this day of a sacred duty, enter their protest beforehand, in the face of the whole world, against violence and usurpation. They entrust they maintenance of the arrangements, which they now proclaim, to all good Frenchmen, to all generous hearts, to all enlightened minds, to all men jealous of liberty, and, in fine, to future generations."

This sublime protest was considered by the assembly as a funeral monument, erected to patriotism and fidelity. All the members arose, and adopted it spontaneously, with shouts a thousand times repeated of "Long live the nation! Liberty for ever!" It was resolved, that it should be sent immediately to the chamber of peers: "It must be made known," said M. Dupin, "that the whole of the national representation shares the noble sentiments expressed in this declaration. It must be made known to all worthy and reasonable men, the friends of judicious liberty, that their wishes have found interpreters here, and that force itself cannot prevent us from uttering them."

At the same moment M. Bedoch announced, that our plenipotentiaries were returned; and that one of them, M. Pontécoulant, had affirmed, that "the foreign powers, and particularly the Emperor Alexander, had shown favourable dispositions he had frequently heard it said and repeated, that it was not the intention of the allied sovereigns, to put any constraint on France in the choice of a government; and that the Emperor Alexander would be at Nancy in a few days[90]."

General Sébastiani confirmed these explanations. The chamber, feeling its hopes revive, immediately ordered, that its declaration should be carried to the foreign monarchs by a deputation of its members. "They will understand our language," said M. Dupont de l'Eure, with a noble feeling: "it is worthy of them, and of the great nation we represent."

Thus, at the very moment when the chamber was about to expire, its dying looks were still turned with pleasing confidence toward the foreign kings, whom the inconstancy of fortune had rendered the arbiters of France. It appealed particularly, in all its wishes, to that loyal and magnanimous prince, who had already preserved the French from the calamities of conquest, and who appeared destined to preserve it from evils still more deplorable. His name, uttered with respect, with gratitude, issued from every mouth; it was sufficient, to calm disquietude, allay grief, and revive hope; it seemed to be the pledge of peace, independence, and happiness, to the nation. O Alexander! this high esteem, this tender confidence, of a whole people not thy own, doubt not, will be placed by posterity in the first rank of thy claims to glory.

The committee, however, dissuaded the representatives from applying to the sovereigns. It remonstrated to them, that the foreign powers refused to acknowledge the legal character of the chambers, and this step would expose them to humiliations unworthy the majesty of the nation. The representatives, convinced of their mistake, did not persevere: they tranquilly resumed their labours on the constitution[91], and continued, while the despotic sword of kings hung over their heads, stoically to discuss the imprescriptible rights of the people.

The Duke of Wellington, when the convention was signed, had expressed a desire, to confer with the Duke of Otranto on its execution. The committee did not oppose their interview. It was a certain means of knowing definitively what was to be depended on, with regard to the dispositions of the allies. It was agreed, that the president of the committee should reproduce the arguments of the letter of the 1st of July; that he should endeavour, to keep out the Bourbons, and turn the temporary vacancy of the throne to the advantage of the nation and of freedom.

The Duke of Otranto, on his return, informed the committee, "that Wellington had formally declared in favour of Louis XVIII.; and had said, that this sovereign would make his entrance into Paris on the 8th of July.

"That General Pozzo di Borgo had repeated the same declaration in the name of the Emperor of Russia; and had communicated to him a letter from Prince Metternich, and from Count Nesselrode, expressing the resolution, to acknowledge only Louis XVIII, and to admit no proposal to the contrary." He added, "that the Duke of Wellington had conducted him to the King: that he had gone *for his sake* (*pour son compte*); that he had left him ignorant of nothing with respect to the situation of France, or to the disposition of people's minds against the return of his family. That the King had listened to him with attention, and with approbation that he had manifested an inclination, to add to the charter fresh guarantees, and to remove all idea of reaction. *That, as to the expressions in the proclamations, they would rather furnish opportunities for clemency, than means of severity.*" In fine, he added, "that he had spoken of the tri-coloured cockade, but that all explanation had been refused: that the opposition appeared to him, to proceed less from the King, than from those about him, and from M. de Talleyrand."

After this interview, the Duke of Otranto appeared to act separately from his colleagues; and no longer made his appearance with punctuality at their frequent meetings.

The newspapers soon made public, that he was appointed minister of police to the King. This he had concealed from the committee. The royalists congratulated him on this mark of favour; the patriots loaded him with curses, considering it as the reward of his treachery.

The King's party, which had hitherto kept itself in obscurity, was desirous of making reparation for this long and pusillanimous inactivity by some brilliant act. It plotted the disarming of the posts of the national guard, under favour of night; seizing the Tuileries, dissolving the committee and the chambers, and proclaiming Louis XVIII.

Some precautions taken by the Prince of Essling taught the conspirators, that their designs were known: and they prudently left the execution of them to foreign bayonets. They had not to wait long. On the 7th of July, at five o'clock in the afternoon, several Prussian battalions, in spite of the convention, surrounded the palace, where the government was sitting. An officer of the staff delivered to the committee a demand from Prince Blucher of a contribution of a hundred millions in cash, and a hundred millions in articles for the troops. The committee declared with firmness, that this requisition was contrary to the convention; and that it would never consent, to make itself an accomplice in such exactions. During this debate, the Prussians had forced the gates of the Tuileries, and invaded the courts and avenues of the palace. The committee being no longer free, and not choosing to become an instrument of oppression, ceased its functions.

Its first care was, to record by an authentic protest, *that it had yielded only to force, and that the rights of the nation remained intact*. The Duke of Otranto, the docile composer of the public papers of the government, took up the pen for this purpose: but the committee, fearing the effects this protest might have on the public tranquillity, thought it better, to content itself with sending to the two chambers the following message.

"Mr. President,

"Hitherto we had reason to believe, that the allied sovereigns were not unanimous in their intentions, respecting the choice of a prince to reign over France. Our plenipotentiaries gave us the same assurance on their return. The ministers and generals of the allied powers, however, declared yesterday in the conferences they held with the president of the committee, that all the sovereigns had engaged, to replace Louis XVIII. on the throne; and that this evening, or to-morrow, he would make his entry into the capital.

"The foreign troops are come to occupy the Tuileries, where the government sits. In this state of things, we can do nothing, but put up prayers for our country; and, our deliberations being no longer free, we think it our duty to separate."

This message, the last testimonial of the audacious duplicity of the Duke of Otranto, now become a minister of the King, contained in addition what follows. "Fresh guarantees will be added to the charter; and we have not lost the hope of retaining the colours so dear to the nation:" but this paragraph, of which I give only the substance, was afterwards suppressed.

The chamber of peers, which had received with coldness the bill of rights, and the declaration of the chamber of representatives, separated without a murmur[92].

The chamber of deputies received its sentence of death with heroic tranquillity. When M. Manuel, repeating the memorable words of Mirabeau, exclaimed: "We are here by the will of the people; we will not depart, till compelled by the bayonet: it is our duty, to devote to our country our last moments; and, if necessary, the last drop of our blood:" all the members of the assembly rose, in testimony of their assent; and declared, that they would remain firm at their posts.

But they were not allowed, to fulfil this glorious resolution. The president, M. Lanjuinais, betraying their courage, and despising their will, dissolved the sitting, and retired. "M. President," said General Solignac to him, "the muse of history is here, and will record your conduct."

The next morning, they found the avenues of their palace occupied by foreigners, and the doors of the assembly closed. M. de Cazes, at the head of some royal volunteers, had taken away the keys. This act of violence, against which they protested, at length removed the bandage from their eyes: they perceived the error they had committed, in too hastily removing Napoleon from the throne, and blindly entrusting to other hands the fate of their country[93].

Thus terminated, after a month's existence, that assembly, which the French had chosen, to confirm the imperial dynasty, to secure their liberties and their tranquillity; but which, through precipitancy, want of foresight, and an excess of zeal and patriotism, had given rise to nothing but convulsions and calamities.

The dissolution of the chambers, and of the government, put an end to all illusions.

The tri-coloured flags, that had been retained, disappeared.

The shouts of "Long live the nation!" and "Liberty for ever!" ceased.

M. Fouché went to announce to his new master, that the whole was consummated.

And on the 8th of July Louis XVIII. in triumph took possession of his capital[94], and of his throne.

At the moment when this prince re-entered the Tuileries, Napoleon was busied at Rochefort on the means of quitting France. His presence excited such enthusiasm among the people, the mariners, and the soldiers, that the shore uninterruptedly resounded with shouts of "Long live the Emperor!" and these shouts, repeated from mouth to mouth, could not but teach those, who had flattered themselves with having mastered the will of Napoleon, how easy it would be for him, to shake off his chains, and laugh at their vain precautions. But faithful to his determination, he firmly resisted the impulse of circumstances; and the continual solicitations made him, to put himself at the head of the patriots and the army. "It is too late," he incessantly repeated:

"the evil is now without remedy: it is no longer in my power, to save the country. A civil war now would answer no end, would be of no utility. To myself alone it might prove advantageous, by affording me the means of procuring personally more favourable conditions: but these I must purchase by the inevitable destruction of all that France possesses of most generous and most magnanimous and such a result inspires me with horror[95]."

Up to the 29th of June, the day when the Emperor quitted Malmaison, no English vessel had been seen off the coast of Rochefort, and there is every reason to believe, that Napoleon, if circumstances had allowed him to embark immediately after his abdication, would have reached the United States without obstruction. But when he arrived at the sea-coast, he found every outlet occupied by the enemy, and appeared to retain little hope of escaping.

The 8th of July[96] he went on board the frigate la Saale, prepared to receive him. His suite was embarked on board the Medusa; and the next day, the 9th, the two vessels anchored at the Isle of Aix. Napoleon, always the same, ordered the garrison under arms, examined the fortifications most minutely, and distributed praise or blame, as if he had still been sovereign master of the state.

On the 10th, the wind, hitherto contrary, became fair; but an English fleet of eleven vessels was cruising within sight of the port, and it was impossible to get to sea.

On the 11th, the Emperor, weary of this state of anxiety, sent Count de Las Cases, now become his secretary, to sound the disposition of the English admiral; to inquire, whether he were authorised to allow him liberty, to repair to England, or to the United States.

The admiral answered, that he had no orders: that still he was ready, to receive Napoleon, and convey him to England: but that it was not in his power, to answer whether he would obtain permission to remain there, or to repair to America.

Napoleon, little satisfied with this answer, caused two half-decked vessels to be purchased, with intention, under favour of night, to reach a Danish smack, with which he had contrived to hold intelligence.

This step having failed, some young midshipmen, full of courage and devotion, proposed to him, to go on board the two barks; and swore they would forfeit their lives, if they did not convey him to New York. Napoleon was not deterred by so long a voyage in such slight vessels: but he knew, that they could not avoid stopping on the coasts of Spain and Portugal, to take in water and provision; and he would not expose himself and people, to the danger of falling into the hands of the Portuguese or Spaniards.

Being informed, that an American vessel was at the mouth of the Gironde, he sent off General Lallemand on the spur, to ascertain the existence of the vessel, and the sentiments of the captain. The general returned with all speed, to inform him, that the captain would be happy and proud, to extricate him from the persecutions of his enemies: but Napoleon, yielding, as it is said, to the advice of some persons about him, gave up the idea of attempting this passage, and determined to throw himself on the generosity of the English.

On the 14th he caused the admiral to be informed, that the next day he would repair on board his vessel.

On the 15th in the morning, he went off in the brig l'Épervier, and was received on board the Bellerophon with the honours due to his rank, and to his misfortune. General Beker, who had orders not to quit him, attended him. The moment they came alongside, the Emperor said to him: "Withdraw, general; I would not have it be believed, that a Frenchman is come to deliver me into the hands of my enemies."

On the 16th the Bellerophon set sail for England.

The Emperor had prepared a letter to the Prince Regent, which General Gourgaud was directed, to carry to him immediately. It was as follows.

"Rochefort, July the 13th, 1815.

"Royal Highness,

"Exposed to the factions, that distract my country, and to the enmity of the greatest powers of Europe, I have terminated my political career; and I come, like Themistocles, to seat myself on the hearth of the British people. I put myself under the protection of its laws, which I claim of your Royal Highness, as the most powerful, the most constant, and the most generous of my enemies."

General Gourgaud had orders, to make known to the Prince, if he deigned to admit him to his presence or to his ministers, that it was Napoleon's intention, to retire into any of the counties of England; and to live there peaceable and unknown, under the name of Colonel Duroc.

The Emperor showed no apprehension, no anxiety, on the passage. He relied with security on the noble character of the English.

When he arrived at Plymouth, he was not permitted, to set his foot on shore; and he was soon informed, the allied powers had decided, that he should be considered as a prisoner of war, and confined at St. Helena.

He protested solemnly to the English admiral, and in the face of Heaven and of mankind, against this violation of the most sacred rights; against the violence put upon his person, and upon his liberty.

This protest proving vain, he submitted with calm and majestic resignation to the decree of his enemies. He was removed on board the Northumberland, which immediately set sail for St. Helena.

On passing Cape la Hogue, he descried the coast of France. Immediately he saluted it; and, stretching out his hands toward the shore, exclaimed with a voice of deep emotion: "Adieu, land of the brave! adieu, dear France! a few traitors less, and thou wilt still be the great nation, and mistress of the world."

On the 17th of October the parched rocks were pointed out to him, that were soon to become the walls of his prison. He contemplated them without complaint, without agitation, without fear.

On the 18th he landed; and, after having protested anew against this violence done his person, he repaired to the place of his captivity with a firm and confident step.

Thus terminated the political life of Napoleon.

Some have been astonished, that he chose to survive himself. He might have killed himself; nothing is easier for a man. But was such an end worthy of him? A king, a great king, ought not to die the desperate death of a conspirator, of the head of a party. To use the proper words of the illustrious captive at St. Helena, he ought to be superior to the rudest attacks of adversity.

No! it was worthy of the great Napoleon, to oppose the inflexibility of his mind to the fickleness of fortune; and like the Roman, who was reproached with not having died by his own hand after a great catastrophe, he too made answer: "I have done more, I have lived!"

FOOTNOTE:

Footnote 1: Fragment of a letter from M. Fouché to the Emperor, on the 21st of March.

Footnote 2: I have since been assured, that M. Réal had warned him, by means of Madame Lacuée, his daughter, that the Emperor knew the whole affair.

Footnote 3: The greater part of the deputies were not yet named; but there was no harm in anticipating events.

Footnote 4: When the Duke of Otranto became minister to the King, and was appointed to make out lists of proscription, I was desirous of knowing, what I had to expect from his resentment; and wrote to him, to sound his intentions. He sent for me, received me with much kindness, and assured me of his friendship and protection. "You did your duty," said he to me, "and I did mine. I foresaw, that Bonaparte could not maintain his situation. He was a great man, but had grown mad. It was my duty, to do what I did, and prefer the good of France to every other consideration."

The Duke of Otranto behaved with the same generosity towards most of the persons, of whom he had any reason to complain; and, if he found himself obliged, to include some of them in the number of the proscribed, he had at least the merit of facilitating their escape from death, or the imprisonment intended for them, by assisting them with his advice, with passports, and frequently with the loan of money.

Footnote 5: This preamble, which gave the death-blow to the additional act, was, I believe, the work of M. Benjamin Constant.

Footnote 6: This table, and that mentioned in Art. 33, being of no importance, are not inserted here.

Footnote 7: Notwithstanding the charter, and the laws daily passed, it is found necessary, to recur every day to rules established by the ancient legislation of the senate.

Footnote 8: The well-known words, in which the cortes of Arragon address the kings of Spain at their coronation.

Footnote 9: The Emperor had ordered this proclamation to be burned; but I found it so excellent, that I thought it my duty to preserve it. At the moment when Napoleon set out for the army, I was not in Paris; and one of the principal clerks of the cabinet, M. Rathery, having found it among my papers, had the courage to throw it into the fire.

Footnote 10: I speak generally: I know there were departments, the electoral colleges of which, from various causes, were composed only of a small number of individuals.

Footnote 11: The following anecdote of the young Napoleon I have never seen published. When he came into the world, he was believed to be dead; he was without warmth, without motion, without respiration. M. Dubois (the accoucheur of the Empress) had made reiterated attempts, to recall him to life, when a hundred guns were discharged in succession, to celebrate his birth. The concussion and agitation produced by this firing acted so powerfully on the organs of the royal infant, that his senses were reanimated.

Footnote 12: The Emperor Alexander, at the time of the affair of Fontainebleau, had guaranteed to the Duke of Vicenza, for Napoleon, the possession of the island of Elba. M. de Talleyrand and the foreign ministers remonstrated to him strongly, on the danger of leaving the Emperor on a spot so near to France and Italy; and conjured him, not to oppose their compelling him to choose another place of retreat. Alexander, faithful to his engagements, would not consent to this. When the Emperor returned, Alexander made it a point of honour, to repair the noble fault he had committed; and became, rather from duty than from animosity, the most inveterate enemy of Napoleon and of France.

Footnote 13: He had agents in Germany and in England, who informed him, with perfect accuracy, of every thing going on there. It is true, that these agents made him pay dearly for their services. In London, for instance, he had two persons, who cost him two thousand guineas a month. "If my Germans," said he on this subject, "were so dear, I must give them up."

Footnote 14: A small county in Lower Normandy, the common focus of the rebellion.

Footnote 15: The succours, so pompously announced by the royalist emissaries, amounted only to 2400 muskets, and a few barrels of gunpowder. The chiefs of the insurrection, disappointed in their expectations, bitterly reproached M. de la Roche-jaquelin with having deceived and implicated them by false promises.

Footnote 16: The Emperor had intended this command in chief for the Duke of Rovigo, or General Corbineau: but he foresaw, that it might perhaps be necessary, to proceed to rigorous measures; and he was unwilling, that these should be conducted by an officer attached to his own person.

Footnote 17: The Emperor considered this rigorous measure as a just reprisal for the means employed by the Vendean chiefs, to recruit their army. They are the following:

When the families, that reign in la Vendée, have resolved on war, they send orders to their agents, to travel over the country, preaching up revolt, and indicating to every parish the number of men, that it must furnish. The chiefs of the insurrection in each parish then point out the peasants, who are to go; and enjoin them, to be at such an hour, on such a day, at the place appointed for assembling. If they fail, armed bands are sent in quest of them, generally composed of the men most dreaded in the country: if they resist, they are threatened with being shot, or having their houses burnt; and as this is never an empty threat, the unhappy peasants obey, and set out.

It has been asserted, that the Emperor had given orders, to set a price on the heads of the chiefs of the insurgents. The instructions given to the ministers at war were transcribed by me, and I have not the least recollection of any such order having been given.

Footnote 18: Fourteen millions of francs had been appropriated to the rebuilding of the houses burned down.

Footnote 19: These announced and promised to the Neapolitans the restoration of Ferdinand, their former king, to the throne.

Footnote 20: The departments of the Centre, and of the East, particularly distinguished themselves. A great number of their inhabitants gave considerable sums, and equipped at their own expense companies, battalions, whole regiments, of partisans or national guards.

A single citizen of Paris, Mr. Delorme, proprietor of the fine *passage* of the same name, offered his country a hundred thousand francs.

Another, one day when the national guard was reviewed, caused a roll of paper, tied with a ribbon of the legion of honour, to be delivered to the Emperor. On opening it, it was found to contain twenty-five thousand francs, in notes on the Bank, with these words: "for Napoleon, for my country." The Emperor was desirous of knowing the person, who had made this delicate and mysterious offering; and at length discovered, that it was M. Gevaudan, whose noble sentiments and patriotism had already been proved by several actions of a similar kind.

Footnote 21:

Votes,	Affirmative	1,288,357
	Negative	4,207
Armies,	Affirmative	222,000
	Negative	320
Navy,	Affirmative	22,000
	Negative	275

Eleven departments did not send their registers in time. A great number of soldiers, unable to write their names, did not vote; and the registers of fourteen regiments did not arrive, till the votes had been summed up.

Footnote 22: Montesquieu. Greatness and Decline of the Romans.

Footnote 23: The day on which the Act of Congress appeared.

Footnote 24: At the time of the discussion of the additional act, M. de Bassano, conversing with the Emperor on the chamber of deputies, said to him, that the muteness of the legislative body, was one of the things, that had contributed most to discredit the imperial government. "My mute legislative body," answered Napoleon, with a smile, "was never well understood. It was a grand legislative jury. If it be thought right, that twelve jurymen shall pronounce on the life and honour of their fellow citizens by a simple yes, or no; why deem it strange or tyrannical, that five hundred jurymen, selected from the most eminent men in the nation, should pronounce in a similar manner on the simple interests of society?"

Footnote 25: He had married a Miss Beauharnais, since so celebrated for her generously risking her own life to save his.

Footnote 26: It was the Duke of Vicenza, who first conceived the idea of conferring the peerage on great land-holders, and distinguished merchants. He was not of opinion, that the peerage should be hereditary, and that the choice of peers should be left exclusively to the crown. He would have wished, that men of great landed property, manufacturers, merchants of the first rank, the men of letters, civilians, and lawyers, who had acquired a great name, should be allowed to propose a list of candidates, out of which the Emperor should be at liberty to choose a certain number of peers.

Footnote 27: Lucien Bonaparte had not been acknowledged as a prince of the imperial family by the ancient statutes. Consequently he might be considered, as not making a part of the chamber of peers by right.

Footnote 28: This opinion did not prevent the Emperor from doing justice to the courage and patriotism, which M. Lanjuinais had displayed on some trying occasions.

Footnote 29: A celebrated counsel, who defended Marshal Ney, and the three generous liberators of M. Delavalette, Wilson, Bruce, and Hutchinson.

Footnote 30: Since minister of finance to the king.

Footnote 31: MM. Dupin and Roi, who appeared to him the heads of the party of insurgents.

Footnote 32: She was attacked and taken near the island of Ischia, on the 30th of April.

Footnote 33: This is a remarkable sentence; as it expresses a sound principle: events have shown, how little the French deserve the name of a *great nation*. Tr.

Footnote 34: Ministers without any ostensible office, for their conduct in which they would be responsible. We have had members somewhat similar in our privy council. Tr.

Footnote 35: The members of the French chambers do not speak in their places, but from a pulpit erected for the purpose. Tr.

Footnote 36: These were schools intended for finishing public education.—Tr.

Footnote 37: The Duke of Otranto excelled in the art of bending facts to his own liking. He exaggerated or extenuated them with so much skill, grasped them with so much address, and deduced consequences from them so naturally, that he was often able, to fascinate Napoleon. More securely to deceive and seduce him, he loaded him in his reports with protestations of attachment and fidelity; and he took care to contrive occasions of adding marginal notes with his own hand, in which he adroitly displayed in a distinguished manner his devotion, discernment, and activity. All his reports in general bore the same stamp: with much of cunning, and much of talent, they offered to the eye a rare and valuable assemblage of quickness and judgment, of moderation and firmness: at every word you might discover the able minister, the profound politician, the consummate statesman: in short, M. Fouché would have wanted nothing, to place him in the rank of great ministers, had he been what I shall call an honest statesman (*un ministre honnête homme.*)

Footnote 38: The 5th corps became the army of the Rhine, and the 6th, which at first was only a corps of reserve, took its place, without changing its number.

Footnote 39: Surely the army of the Alps must have been on its right, and that of the Rhine on its left, unless it was stationed with its rear to the enemy.—*Tr.*

Footnote 40: The ascendancy he possessed over the minds and courage of the soldiers was truly incomprehensible. A word, a gesture, was sufficient, to inspire them with enthusiasm, and make them face with joyful blindness the most terrible dangers. If he ordered them mal-à-propos, to rush to such a point, to attack such another, the inconsistency or temerity of the manœuvre at first struck the good sense of the soldiers: but immediately they thought, that their general would not have given such an order, without a motive for it, and would not have exposed them wantonly. "He knows what he is about," they would say, and immediately rush on death, with shouts of "Long live the Emperor!"

Footnote 41: These agents, paid by the king, went and came from Ghent to Paris, and from Paris to Ghent. The Duke of Otranto, who, no doubt, had good reasons for knowing them, offered the Emperor, to procure him news of what passed beyond the frontiers; and it was by their means the Emperor knew in great part the position of the enemies' armies. Thus the Duke of Otranto, if we may credit appearances, with one hand betrayed to the enemy the secrets of France, and with the other to Napoleon the secrets of the Bourbons and the foreign powers.

Footnote 42: The Emperor, before he quitted Paris, had conceived the design of rendering the plains of Fleurus witnesses to new battles. He had sent for Marshal Jourdan, and had obtained from him a great deal of very important strategical information.

Footnote 43: The Duke of Treviso, to whom Napoleon had entrusted the command of the young guard, was attacked at Beaumont with a sciatica, that obliged him to take to his bed.

Footnote 44:

LEFT.

Under Marshal Ney.

1st Corps.

Infantry	16,500
Cavalry	1,500

2d Corps.

Infantry	21,000
Cavalry	1,500
Cavalry of Desnouettes	2,100
Cuirassiers of Kellerman	2,600
	45,200
Artillery, horse and foot	2,400

And 116 pieces of ordnance.

RIGHT.

Under Marshal Grouchy.

3d Corps.

Infantry	13,000
Cavalry	1,500

4th Corps.

Infantry	12,000
Cavalry	1,500
Cavalry of Pajol	2,500
	30,500

Cavalry of Excelmans	2,600
Cuirassiers of Milhaud	2,600
	35,700
Artillery, horse and foot	2,250

And 112 pieces of ordnance.

CENTRE AND RESERVE.

Under the Emperor.

6th Corps.

Infantry	11,000
Old guard	5,000
Middle guard	5,000
Middle guard	5,000
Young guard	4,000
Horse grenadiers	1,200
Dragoons	1,200
	27,400
Artillery, horse and foot	2,700

And 134 pieces of ordnance.

Recapitulation.

Infantry	87,500
Cavalry	20,800
Artillery, horse and foot	7,350
Engineers	2,200
Total	111,850

Pieces of ordnance 362

Footnote 45: General Blucher had not had time to collect the whole of his forces.

Footnote 46: This conjecture was well founded: but Blucher, who had escaped Grouchy, had formed a communication with Wellington through Ohaim, and promised him to make a diversion on our right. Thus Wellington, who had prepared to retreat, was induced to remain.

Footnote 47: I have heard, that the officer, who carried this order, instead of taking the direct road, thought proper to take an immense circuit, in order to avoid the enemy.

Footnote 48:

2d Corps.

Infantry	16,500	18,000
Cavalry	1,500	

1st Corps.

Infantry	12,500	13,700
Cavalry	1,200	

6th Corps.

Infantry	7,000	{4,000 had been joined to Grouchy}	7,000
Division of Domont and Suberwick			2,500
Cuirassiers			4,800
Foot guards	2,500		
Light cavalry	2,100		16,600
Grenadiers and dragoons	2,000		
Artillery			4,500

			67,100

Gérard's division 3000 men.

Footnote 49: This corps had joined the Prussian array since the battle of Ligny.

Footnote 50: The enemy themselves confess, that at this moment they thought the battle lost. "The ranks of the English," says Blucher, "were thrown into disorder; the loss had been considerable; the reserves had been advanced into the line; the situation of the Duke was extremely critical, the fire of musketry continued along the front, the artillery had retired to the second line."

I will add, that still greater disorder prevailed in the rear of the English army: the roads of the forest of Soignes were encumbered with waggons, artillery, and baggage, deserted by the drivers; and numerous bands of fugitives had spread confusion and affright through Brussels and the neighbouring roads.

Had not our successes been interrupted by the march of Bulow; or had Marshal Grouchy, as the Emperor had reason to hope, followed at the heels of the Prussians; never would a more glorious victory have been obtained by the French. Not a single man of the Duke of Wellington's army would have escaped.

Footnote 51: It was afterwards known, that it was General Ziethen, who, on his arrival in line, had taken the troops commanded by the Prince of Saxe Weimar for Frenchmen, and compelled them, after a brisk fire, to abandon a little village, which they were appointed to defend.

Footnote 52: They had at their head Generals Petit and Pelet de Morvan.

Footnote 53:

	Men.
The general loss of the army of the Duke of Wellington, in killed and wounded, was about	25,000
And that of Prince Blucher	35,000

	60,000

That of the French may be estimated as follows:

The 15th and 16th, killed and wounded	11,000
The 18th, killed and wounded	18,000
Prisoners	8,000

	37,000

The loss of the French would have been greater, had it not been for the generous care taken of them by the inhabitants of Belgium. After the victory of Fleurus and of Ligny, they hastened to the field of battle, to console the wounded, and give them every assistance. Nothing could be more affecting, than the sight of a number of women and girls endeavouring to revive, by cordial liquors, the extinguished lives (*la vie éteinte*) of our unfortunate soldiers, while their husbands and brothers supported our wounded in their arms, stanched their blood, and closed their wounds.

The precipitancy of our march had not allowed us, to prepare conveyances and field hospitals, to receive our wounded. The good and feeling inhabitants of Belgium supplied the deficiency with eagerness. They carried our poor Frenchmen from the field of battle, and offered them an asylum, and all the attention necessary.

At the time of our retreat, they lavished on us proofs of their regard not less affecting, and not less valuable. Braving the rage of the ferocious Prussians, they quitted their houses, to show us the paths, that would favour our escape, and guide our course through the enemy's columns. When they parted from us, they still followed us with their eyes, and expressed from a distance how happy they were at having been able to save us.

When they knew, that a great number of Frenchmen remained prisoners with the conqueror, they were eager to offer, and to lavish on them, consolation and assistance. The Prince of Orange himself, as formidable in the heat of battle, as magnanimous after victory, became the protector of a number of brave fellows, who, having learned how to esteem him on the field of battle, had nobly invoked his support.

In fine, completely to acquit the debt of gratitude, at that period so painful to remember, when persecution, exile, death, compelled so many Frenchmen to flee their native land, the inhabitants of Belgium, always tender-hearted, always benevolent, opened their hospitable doors to our unfortunate proscribed countrymen, and more than one brave man, already preserved by them from the vengeance of foreigners, was a second time saved by their generous hands from the fury of enemies still more implacable.

Footnote 54: I say fifty thousand men, for more than ten thousand of the guard took no share in the action.

Footnote 55: This circumstance was told to me, but the following I witnessed myself. A cuirassier, in the heat of the battle, had both his arms disabled with sabre wounds: "I will go and get myself dressed," said he, foaming with rage: "if I cannot use my arms, I'll use my teeth—I'll eat them."

Footnote 56: Among these letters printed was one of mine, written from Bâle to the Emperor on the subject of M. Werner.

Footnote 57: M. de Flahaut saw truly, for it appears certain, that Marshal Grouchy had held parleys with the allies, and that an arrangement on the plan of the Duke of Ragusa was about to be signed, when General Excelmans arrested the Prussian colonel, who was sent to the marshal, to conclude the treaty already agreed upon.

Footnote 58: This information was false.

Footnote 59: This shows how unjustly Napoleon has been reproached with having falsified the truth, and calumniated the army, in that bulletin.

Footnote 60: The general name of that part of the country, which borders the coast.

Footnote 61: This affair, and the death of La Roche-jaquelin, took place on the 11th of June, and were not known at Paris till the 19th.

Footnote 62: These resolutions were sent to the chamber of peers also: but this chamber, knowing, that it had no right, to send for the Ministers, contented itself, *considering the present circumstances,* with giving its approbation to the first three articles.

Footnote 63: In fact, the Duke of Otranto did write to M. Manuel.

Footnote 64: This answer was cut short by the president: I give it here entire.

Footnote 65: The title of Emperor had not been given him in this deliberation. He had been called merely Napoleon Bonaparte.

Footnote 66: The chamber of peers was of course thus annihilated, and excluded from any share in the government.

Footnote 67: Conformably to the orders given him, Marshal Grouchy had confined himself on the 17th, to observing the Prussians: but this he had not done with the ardour and sagacity, that might have been expected of such a consummate general of horse. The timidity, with which he followed them, no doubt inspired them with the idea, that they might fall on the Emperor's rear with impunity.

On the 18th, at nine in the morning only, he quitted his cantonments to march to Wavres: when he reached Walhain, he heard the cannonading at Mont St. Jean. Its continually increasing briskness left no doubt, that it was an extremely serious affair. General Excelmans proposed, to march to the guns by the right bank of the Dyle. "Do you not feel," said he to the marshal, "that the firing makes the ground tremble under our feet? let us march straight to the spot where they are fighting." This advice, had it been followed up, would have saved the army: but it was not. The marshal slowly continued his movements: at two o'clock he arrived before Wavres. The corps of General Vandamme and that of Gérard endeavoured to open a passage, and wasted time and men to no purpose. At seven o'clock he received, according to his own declaration, the order from the major-general, to march to St. Lambert and attack Bulow; which step ought to have been suggested to him before that time by the tremendous cannonading at Waterloo, and by the order *given in the first despatch received in the morning*, to draw near to the grand army, and place himself in a situation to co-operate with it. He did so then. He crossed the Dyle at the bridge of Limale, and made himself master of the heights, without meeting any resistance; but night being come, he halted.

At three in the morning General Thielman attempted, to drive our troops back across the Dyle: but he was victoriously repulsed. The division of Teste, the cavalry of General Pajol, obliged him to evacuate Bielge and Wavres. The whole of the corps of Vandamme crossed the Dyle, took Rosieren, and became master of the road from Wavres to Brussels.

Marshal Grouchy, though the Emperor had recommended to him, to keep open the communications, and to send him frequent accounts of himself, had given himself no concern about what was passing at Mont St. Jean; and was preparing blindly to pursue his own movements, when an aide-de camp of General Gressot came to announce to him (this was at noon) the disasters of the preceding day. The marshal was then sensible, but too late, of the horrible fault he had committed in remaining unconcerned on the right bank of the Dyle. He effected his retreat, in two columns, by Temploux and Namur.

On the 20th in the morning, his rear-guard was attacked, and thrown into disorder. The division of Teste, the cavalry of Excelmans, extricated it from its confusion. The 20th of dragoons, and its worthy colonel, the young Briqueville, retook from the enemy two pieces of artillery, which they had captured. General Clary and his hussars cut down the horse; and the army reached Namur in tranquillity. The indefatigable division of General Teste was appointed to defend this town; and it maintained its post gloriously, till our wounded and baggage had evacuated it, and our troops were in safety on the heights of Dinan and Bouvine.

On the 22d the whole of the army was assembled at Rocroi. On the 24th it formed a junction with the wreck of Mont St, Jean, which the Emperor had ordered, to bend its course towards Rheims. On the 25th it marched for the capital. During its retreat, it was exposed to the exasperated attacks of the Prussians. It repulsed them all with firmness and vigour. The noble desire of repairing the involuntary evil, that it had done us at Mont St. Jean, inflamed the minds of the soldiers with the most spirited ardour; and perhaps this army of brave fellows would have changed the fate of France under the walls of Paris, had not the inspirations of its patriotism, and generous despair, been repressed or betrayed.

Footnote 68: That of forcing Napoleon to abdicate.

Footnote 69: Most of the peers held commands in the army.

Footnote 70: These are the literal terms of General Beker's commission.

Footnote 71:
> With air majestic, and with brow serene,
> As, master of his fire, amid the fray,
> He coolly urges, or restrains the sword.

Footnote 72: I am eager here to pay the general the homage he merits. He knew perfectly well, how to reconcile his duty with the attentions and respect, that were due to Napoleon, and to his misfortune.

Footnote 73: His court, formerly so numerous, was now customarily composed only of the Duke of Bassano, Count Lavalette, General Flahaut, and the persons who were to go with him, as the following orderly officers, General Gourgaud, Counts Montholon and de Lascases, and the Duke of Rovigo. The attachment, that induced the latter to attend Napoleon, was so much the more to his honour, as Napoleon, when he returned from the island of Elba, reproached him very harshly with having neglected him. He passes however in the opinion of the public, though very erroneously, for being one of the contrivers of the 20th of March: but he had always to complain of the public opinion. It imputes to him a number of wicked actions, in which he had really no share, and which he frequently indeed had endeavoured to prevent. The Emperor employed him on all occasions; because he found him possessed of a bold and clear judgment, an acute understanding, and great skill in perceiving the consequences of a thing, and acting with spirit. Unfavourable suspicions have been thrown on the motives, that induced Napoleon, to entrust to him the administrations of the police: but he was called to this important office solely because the Emperor had experience of the infidelity of the Duke of Otranto, who deserted him on all occasions of difficulty; and wished to supply his place by a man of tried attachment, a man who, unconnected with the revolution, and having no party to keep terms with, could serve him alone, and do his duty without tergiversation.

Footnote 74: This epithet was not an insult in the mouth of Napoleon. He even applied it commonly to his ministers, when they showed any irresolution.

Footnote 75: The uneasiness given her by the terrors of 1815 conducted her to the grave. I hope the reader will pardon me these particulars, and this note.

Footnote 76: From accounts communicated to me.

Footnote 77: That is, be marked out the enemy's positions with pins.

Footnote 78: The Emperor, informed of the manœuvres of M. Fouché, said: "He is ever the same; always ready to thrust his foot into every one's slipper."

Footnote 79: These resolutions consisted in sending General Beker to Malmaison, to watch Napoleon.

Footnote 80: On the 2d of July the chamber voted an address to the French.

This address, which perished in the birth, related to the political situation of France with respect to the allies. It appeared to me not very interesting, and I thought I might dispense with a particular account of it. It gave rise, however, to a remarkable incident. M. Manuel, who had the principal hand in drawing it up, had not thought proper, to speak of the Emperor's successor in it; and the chamber decided, to add in the address, that Napoleon II. had been called to the empire.

Footnote 81: The reader will be aware, that I reason here, as well as every where else, on the principles of the mandate given to the committee.

Footnote 82: As these despatches are now uninteresting, I have not inserted them.

Footnote 83: If we may believe the declaration of M. Macirone, confirmed by the testimony of two other secret agents, MM. Maréchal and St. Jul***, the Duke of Otranto wrote to Lord Wellington, by a letter of which M. Macirone was the bearer, and which he concealed in his stockings, that the enthusiasm of the federates and Bonapartists was at the height; and that it would be impossible, to restrain them any longer, if the Duke of Wellington did not hasten, to come and put an end to their fury by the occupation of Paris.

Footnote 84: It was just at this moment, that the Emperor declared to the government, that he was certain of crushing the enemy, if they would entrust him with the command of the army.

Footnote 85: From this passage it appears unquestionable, that Wellington had communicated M. Fouché's letter to Prince Blucher.

Footnote 86: It was the performance of the Duke of Otranto.

Footnote 87: They were published by order of the chamber.

Footnote 88: Events have justified the prudence of the marshals; but I am not judging of events, I am relating them.

Footnote 89: On the 23d of June, M. Carnot, after having delivered to the chamber of peers Napoleon's act of abdication, entered into some details of the state of the army. Marshal Ney rose, and said ... "What you have just heard is false, entirely false; Marshal Grouchy and the Duke of Dalmatia cannot assemble sixty thousand men.... Marshal Grouchy has been unable to rally more than seven or eight thousand; Marshal Soult could not maintain his post at Rocroy; you have no longer *any means* of saving the country, but by negotiations." M. Carnot and General Flahaut immediately refuted this imprudent negation. General Drouot completely refuted the marshal in the following sitting.... "I have heard with regret," said he, "what had been said to diminish the glory of our armies, exaggerate our disasters, or depreciate our resources. I will say what I think, what I fear, and what I hope. On my frankness you may depend. My attachment to the Emperor cannot be doubted: but before all things, and above all things, I love my country." The general then gave a true and authenticated account of the battles of Ligny and Mont St. Jean; and, after having justified the Emperor from the faults, indirectly attempted to be imputed to him, continued: "Such are the particulars of this fatal day. It ought to have crowned the glory of the French army, destroyed all the vain hopes of the enemy, and perhaps soon given a peace to France.... But heaven decided otherwise.... Though our losses are considerable, still our situation is not desperate: the resources yet left us are great, if we will employ them with energy ... such a catastrophe should not discourage a nation great and noble like ours.... After the battle of Cannæ, the Roman senate voted thanks to their vanquished general, because he had not despaired of the safety of the republic; and laboured incessantly, to furnish him with the means of repairing the disasters of which he had been the cause.... On an occasion less critical, would the representatives of the nation suffer themselves to be depressed? Or would they forget the dangers of their country, and waste their hours in ill-timed debates, instead of having recourse to a remedy, that should ensure the safety of France?"

Footnote 90: The plenipotentiaries, who set out from Laon on the 26th of June, arrived on the 1st of July at Hagueneau, the head-quarters of the allied sovereigns.

The sovereigns did not think fit, to give them an audience; and Count Walmoden was appointed on the part of Austria, Count Capo d'Istria on that of Russia, General Knesbeck on that of Prussia, to hear their proposals. The English ambassador, Lord Stewart, having no powers *ad hoc*, was simply invited, to be present at the conferences.

Lord Stewart did not fail, as was foreseen in the instructions given to the plenipotentiaries, to dispute the legality of the existence of the chambers and of the committee; and asked the French deputies, by what right the nation pretended to expel their King, and choose another sovereign. By the same right, answered M. de la Fayette, as Great Britain had to depose James, and crown William.

This answer stopped the mouth of the English minister.

The plenipotentiaries, warned by this question of the disposition of the allies, exerted themselves less for obtaining Napoleon II., than for rejecting Louis XVIII. They declared, I am told, that France had an insuperable aversion to this sovereign and his family; and that there was no prince, it would not consent to adopt, rather than return under their sway. In fine, they hinted, that the nation might agree to take the Duke of Orleans, or the King of Saxony, if it were impossible for it to retain the throne for the son of Maria Louisa.

The foreign ministers, after some insignificant discourse, politely put an end to the conference; and in the evening the French plenipotentiaries received their dismissal by the following note:

Hagueneau, July the 1st.

"According to the stipulation of the treaty of alliance, which says, that none of the contracting parties shall treat of peace or an armistice, but by common consent, the three courts, that find themselves together, Austria, Russia, and Prussia, declare, that they cannot at present enter into any negotiation. The cabinets will assemble together, as soon as possible.

"The three powers consider it as an essential condition of peace, and of real tranquillity, that Napoleon Bonaparte shall be incapable of disturbing the repose of France, and of Europe, for the future: and in consequence of the events, that occurred in the month of March last, *the powers must insist, that Napoleon Bonaparte be placed in their custody.*

   (Signed)   Walmoden.
          Capo d'Istria.
          Knesbeck."

Footnote 91: This constitution, founded on the additional act, differed from it only in abolishing hereditary mobility. M. Manuel, however, who displayed talents of the first order in this discussion, was of opinion, that the order of nobility should not be suppressed, being essentially necessary in a monarchy. Had I to draw up an eulogy of the additional act, or a charge against those who hold it in contempt, I would only refer them to his constitution.

Footnote 92: This chamber, after the abdication of Napoleon, was merely a superfetation. The departure of those peers, who formed part of the army, completed its reduction to an absolute nullity. Without patriotism, without energy, it confined itself to sanctioning with an ill grace the measures adopted by the representatives. M. Thibaudeau, M. de Ségur, M. de Bassano, and a few others, alone raised themselves to a level with the state of affairs. M. Thibaudeau in particular distinguished himself, on the 28th of June and the 2d of July, by two speeches on our political situation; which were considered then, as they long will be, as noble specimens of courage, patriotism, and eloquence.

Footnote 93: I repeat here a preceding observation, that I confine myself to a relation of facts, without deciding upon them.

Footnote 94: On the 8th of July M. de Vitrolles caused the following official article to be inserted in the Moniteur.

"Paris, July the 7th.—The committee of government made known to the King, by the mouth of its president, that it had just dissolved itself."

This article, written with the intention, to make France and Europe believe, that the committee had voluntarily deposited its authority in the hands of the King, called forth strong remonstrances from the Duke of Vicenza. Incapable of paltering with his duty, or with the truth, he went immediately to the King's minister, the Duke of Otranto; reproached him severely with having compromised the committee and declared, that he would not quit his house, till he had obtained a formal disavowal of it. The minister protested, that the article was not written by him; and consented to disavow it.

Count Carnot, Baron Quinette, and General Grenier, having joined the Duke of Vicenza, the latter wrote, in the Duke of Otranto's closet, the letter subjoined; the boldness and firmness of which, I trust, it is unnecessary to remark.

"Monsieur le Duc.—As the committee of government, on its retiring, neither ought nor could charge your excellency with any mission, we desire you, to cause the article inserted in the Moniteur of this day, the 8th of July, to be disavowed; and to procure the insertion of our last message to the two chambers.

(Signed)   Caulincourt.
         Carnot.
         Quinette.
         Grenier."

The Duke of Otranto answered this letter by the following declaration:

"Gentlemen.—The committee of government having dissolved itself on the 7th of July, every act emanating from it posterior to its message to the chambers is null, and ought to be considered as not having taken place.

"Your remonstrance against the article inserted in the Moniteur of the 8th of July is just. I disavow it, as totally unfounded, and published without my authority.

(Signed) The Duke of Otranto."

Footnote 95: The words recorded by M. de Lascases.

Footnote 96: At the same moment Louis XVIII. entered Paris. It was another remarkable singularity, that the King entered the capital the first time on the same day, on which the Emperor went on board the brig, that conveyed him to Porto Ferrajo.